Aspects

of

Development Bank Management

Edited by

William Diamond and V. S. Raghavan

PUBLISHED FOR
THE ECONOMIC DEVELOPMENT INSTITUTE
OF THE WORLD BANK

The Johns Hopkins University Press
BALTIMORE AND LONDON

The Johns Hopkins University Press
Baltimore, Maryland 21218, U.S.A.

The views and interpretations in this book are those
of the authors and should not be attributed to the
World Bank, to its affiliated organizations, or to any
individual acting in their behalf.

Library of Congress Cataloging in Publication Data

Main entry under title:

Aspects of development bank management.

(EDI series in economic development)
1. Development banks—Addresses, essays, lectures.
I. Diamond, William, 1917–   . II. Raghavan,
V. S., 1935–   . III. Economic Development
Institute (Washington, D.C.) IV. Series.
HG3550.A8   332.2   81-48174
ISBN 0-8018-2571-7   AACR2
ISBN 0-8018-2572-5 (pbk.)

Foreword

THE WORLD BANK has been involved since 1950 in supporting the growth of development banking in developing countries. Its objective has been the building of self-reliant institutions that can effectively mobilize resources and allocate them to efficient and productive investments. In this effort the Bank and its affiliates have been conscious of the critical importance of the quality of staff needed to manage the development banks.

Thus training of development bank staff has figured prominently in the curriculum of the Economic Development Institute, the World Bank's staff college for economic administrators in developing countries. Several hundred development bank officials have attended EDI's courses in general development going back to 1956, courses dealing with the evaluation and monitoring of industrial and agricultural projects since 1963, and, since 1973, courses specifically directed toward development bank staff. A distinguishing feature of these last courses is that a majority are sponsored jointly by a group of international and bilateral agencies interested in development bank training, and are conducted in the training centers established by the African Development Bank and by national development banks in India and the Philippines.

EDI courses are generally designed for senior level executives. But the chief executives of development banks perceived a need to exchange views with their peers on the problems that confront them in the task of managing their institutions. To provide a forum for such discussions, EDI conducted two seminars in 1979 and 1980 for chief executives of development banks (and some of their deputies), the first in English and the second in French. This volume brings together most of the papers that served as the basis for discussions at these seminars.

This collection of papers on the management of development banks recalls EDI's very first publication in 1957; the author was William Diamond, who is a joint editor of the present volume. Mr. Diamond, who was one of EDI's original staff members and a senior fellow before his retirement from the World Bank in 1978, headed

v

the Bank's Development Finance Companies Department for many years. V. S. Raghavan, also a joint editor and contributor, has held management positions in development banks for several years in India and Mauritius. He was the member of the EDI staff in 1973–1975 and 1978–1980, mainly concerned with the spread of training courses in development banking. EDI is grateful to the editors for the interest and care devoted to preparing this volume. EDI is also indebted to all the authors for their contributions. I am confident that the development banking community will find these essays useful.

AJIT MOZOOMDAR
Director, Economic Development Institute
The World Bank

Contents

Preface

THIS VOLUME OF ESSAYS is an offshoot of the seminar on Development Bank Management conducted by the Economic Development Institute of the World Bank in February 1979. The object of the seminar was to give a group of top executives of development banks an opportunity to exchange views and experiences, in an organized discussion, on the principal issues they face in managing their institutions.* The officials who attended the seminar, being entirely chief executives of development banks or their deputies, were in a position to speak with authority about the issues on the agenda of the seminar.

To facilitate a systematic discussion, the seminar was divided into sixteen sessions of approximately three hours each. Rather than cover all the activities of a development bank, these sessions were highly selective. The principal criterion for the selection of subjects for the sessions—the linking thread—was the problems the management of developing banks confront and management's role in dealing with them.

Those problems fall into a few broad categories: functions of top management; establishment of long-range corporate objectives and policies; criteria for investment selection; investment monitoring; mobilization of resources; planning and internal controls; personnel development and organization; financial policy; and evaluation of corporate performance. The various sessions in the seminar reflected these concerns, though somewhat imperfectly. Moreover, whichever way the concerns of management were divided for purposes of discussion, some overlapping of subjects and issues was inevitable. This no doubt reflects the fact that, at the level of top management, all issues converge and become interrelated. While the subjects of the sessions, taken together, were far-ranging, they certainly did not deal comprehensively with all the concerns of management.

*An almost identical seminar in French, attended by chief executives of development banks in francophone countries, was given in January 1980.

ix

Each session in the seminar was conducted by a person (generally from the World Bank Group) with considerable experience in a particular field. Considering the experience of the persons attending the seminar, however, what was important was not the ideas put forward by the session's chairman, however qualified he might have been, but the drawing out of the experience of the participants. There were therefore no formal lectures or expositions by the chairman during the seminar. To help stimulate the thinking of the participants, several papers were prepared on the topics chosen for discussion and were circulated in advance of each discussion, as were also some noteworthy papers previously published. It should be added that neither the papers nor the discussion leaders reflected a single viewpoint with respect to development banking. Stimulation of thought rather than direction or even guidance was the objective.

The result was an intense two-week discussion, which was, however, neither conclusive nor complete because, invariably, the three hours allotted for each session proved insufficient to cover all aspects of the issues proposed for discussion. The problems facing each development bank manager are unique to the environment in which he operates; no single "solution" is therefore applicable to the common problems of all development banks.

This volume brings together, for wider circulation among persons involved or interested in development banking, most of the papers circulated in advance of each session of the seminar. All the essays prepared specifically for the seminar have been revised for publication. This revision has included some views reflected in the seminar, but in no sense is an essay intended to be a summary of the discussion in the corresponding session in the seminar. Papers previously published have been lightly edited for inclusion in this volume.

The essays included in this volume have been arranged under eight headings. Each heading has a short introduction by the editors, which highlights the interrelationship of the various issues confronting management and the integral role of management in dealing with them. As with the sessions in the seminar, the content of the individual essays tends to overlap precisely because the issues dealt with are inextricably interrelated. The overlapping seems greater in the essays than it did in the seminar, for each author finds it necessary to define development banking in relation to the subject of his own essay. The volume should be viewed, however, not as a collection of essays on different topics, but as a book on the single subject "development bank management," with each chapter devoted to one of the many interrelated issues on which the chief executive must from time to time focus his attention.

Several points should be made about these essays. First, they do not represent a single viewpoint, certainly not that of the editors. Almost certainly, none of the authors would agree with all the views presented by the others. Second, the object of the essays is not primarily instruction or the passing on of truths, but the focusing of issues and the stimulation of thought. If the reader is led to identify issues and problems he had only vaguely sensed earlier, or is led to view his problems in a new light, or finds useful suggestions for the solution of his problems, the objective of the writers and of the editors will have been accomplished. Development bank managers may (the editors hope) find the essays most useful as the basis for discussion among themselves and with their senior staff. Third, the authors alone bear responsibility for the views they present. (A note on each of the authors appears in the Appendix.) Fourth, it has not been possible to include in this volume essays on such topics as investment monitoring, programming and budgeting, staff selection, use of computers, and performance evaluation, which are important for the management of development banks. The editors hope that a companion volume covering these and other relevant aspects of development banks can be brought out in the not-too-distant future.

WILLIAM DIAMOND
V. S. RAGHAVAN

Acknowledgments

Lillian Ruckman did most of the typing of the manuscript. Christine Houle prepared the manuscript for publication and coordinated production of the book. Nancy Wirtes read and corrected proof, and Raphael Blow prepared the chart. The editors are grateful to all of them.

Aspects

of

Development Bank Management

Part I

Management's Role and Priorities

THE LITERATURE ON MANAGEMENT, which was skimpy until World War II, has since then burgeoned into a substantial and rapidly growing library of books, articles, and specialized periodicals. This literature is fed by the research of schools of business and of management, by the diaries and commentary of managers who have become increasingly self-conscious about their profession, and by the philosophers of management who attempt broad syntheses of its role in, and contribution to, modern society.

While the literature on management is extensive, very little has so far been written about the management of a development bank, and even less on this subject by the manager of a development bank. This may seem odd, given the persistent concern about management among the sponsors (and later, the shareholders, government, and directors) of development banks and among those who support them, especially the external institutions which provide a large part of the finance of many development finance institutions. While the appraisals of the external institutions deal critically with management and often lead to pressure for management changes, they have not led to a systematic treatment of development bank management—as has been the case, for instance, with other matters that concern them: techniques of project selection and appraisal, project supervision and handling of projects that are in trouble, mobilization of financial resources, project promotion, financing small-scale enterprises, and so on. Development bank managers who have written about their own work also usually deal with specific aspects of their activities, such as those mentioned above. What is lacking is an integrated view of their task. Perhaps this is because the profession is still relatively young, and not many managers have been at their jobs long enough to enable them to take a reflective, balanced view of their total experience.

The following papers may help development bank managers focus deliberately on their own functions and on the tasks to which they devote their time. They should lead managers to ask themselves whether their actual day-to-day activities reflect their views of their responsibilities or primarily day-to-day pressures. The first paper, by William Diamond, discusses the principal problems and priorities of managers of development banks as he sees them, that is, as an outside observer. The second paper, by V. V. Bhatt, is a prescriptive view of what the tasks of a development bank's management should be if the institution is to fulfill its social function.

Chapter 1

The Preoccupations and Working Style of Chief Executives of Development Banks

WILLIAM DIAMOND

MOST DISCUSSIONS OF MANAGEMENT deal with the subject in prescriptive terms, analyzing the functions of management and suggesting organizational arrangements that might be helpful to that end. I would like to make some comments on how managers actually behave: that is, what they do and how they spend their time. My reason for dealing with management from this angle is that there are often differences between how a manager (or anyone else, for that matter) ought to act and how he does act. Something can, I believe, be learned from the reality. It is toward the chief executive officer, the one at the top, whatever the specific title, that I want to direct attention.

Qualifications and Performance

In general, bank managers have come from no single background and have had no single type of training. By origin they have been economists, stockbrokers, commercial bankers, central bankers, civil servants, engineers, and soldiers. Their backgrounds are apt to

This article was published in *Focus*, vol. 3 (1977), pp. 6–11. The article was based on an address to participants in the Development Banking Course of the World Bank's Economic Development Institute, May 4, 1977.

be especially diverse in a newly established development bank, in a country that has not had one before. There the profession is new. Later, when development banking experience has begun to grow, it becomes possible to find managers who have come up from the ranks of their own institutions or who have had directly relevant experience in other, similar institutions in the same country. As time progresses, more and more managers have had some sort of professional experience in development banking, so that the newer breed of managers is much more likely to have had development bank experience than the old.[1]

According to my observations, the lack of development banking experience has not in itself been a deterrent to success in managing a development bank. Among the various backgrounds, none seems to have particularly enhanced or detracted from the effectiveness of a development bank manager. Thus, expertise in some particular discipline or line of activity does not seem to have been crucial. What seems to have been far more important is the personality and leadership qualities of the managers, how they conceived of their job, and the objective environment in which they had to work—plus luck.

If this estimate is right, then the emergence of a newer breed of managers, with better professional training and experience, will not necessarily enable them to do a better job than the older chief executives did. Training and experience should enable chief executives to read and understand their environment more effectively, and thus to protect their bank against it, to take advantage of it, and even to influence it. They may help chief executives respond effectively to pressures and thus help the development bank survive despite being buffeted by circumstances. But training and experience may not contribute to personality or leadership qualities and certainly will not affect luck. They will not necessarily help managers make conscious, tactical changes in their bank's course to ensure achievement of its underlying objectives. Nor will they necessarily help anticipate changes in the environment so that managers can adjust the bank's goals before it is forced to move in directions others dictate or sinks into oblivion.

In this light, a training course for chief executives of development banks that focuses on project preparation, appraisal, and supervision can be valuable by sensitizing them to the technologies they should have at their disposal in running their bank. But such a course can be only part of management training, and not necessarily the most important part.

The lack of relevant training and experience in many countries in which the World Bank helped set up development banks led the Bank to recommend the employment of foreign managers who had such experience. Selecting managerial staff is extraordinarily difficult, and it would be surprising if the choice were always successful. If the Bank's recommendations of foreign managers sometimes fell short of expectations, the reason may be essentially the point made above. While some financial knowledge is certainly needed, probably too much emphasis was placed on technical expertise and on directly relevant experience. Perhaps the Bank underestimated the qualities needed to energize in a common cause the many people and groups involved in running a development bank. It almost certainly underestimated the importance of knowing the objective environment, especially the business community, and overestimated the ability of an outsider, no matter how carefully selected, to know and deal with local conditions. There are, of course, situations in which there is no alternative but to seek someone from the outside to lead an institution. In such circumstances, one must not only be careful in choosing; one must also be modest in one's expectations, and must recognize that the outsider's tenure is primarily a period of preparation for local management.

Priorities of Chief Executives

I asked three chief executive officers of development banks associated with the World Bank what they thought were their most important jobs and how they spent most of their time. One manager named as his principal tasks: getting and training staff, protecting his institution's independence, applying his final judgment to pending investment proposals, and considering how to adapt his development bank to changing circumstances in his country. The second gave as his most important and time-consuming task maintaining good relations with the many other institutions which make up the environment in which his development bank works. He named them (in order) as the government, the business community (including both the industrialists who are his clients and bankers who are his partners), other development finance institutions, and management and other training organizations. This second manager said that in day-to-day affairs he relied on team management rather than individual decision. The third gave his principal functions as: long-range planning, anticipating changes in the economic

environment, maintaining good relations with his board of directors and shareholders, and generally supervising the day-to-day
affairs of his company.

The differences in the comments made by these managers were
largely of emphasis, stemming in part from their personalities and
styles and in part from the nature of the companies they manage.
For instance, it became clear that all three managers were concerned about relations with their board members. One company's
shareholders, however, consisted primarily of several well-knit and
collaborative groups of businesses, while the shares of another
company were held primarily by a group of aggressive and competitive businessmen. It was natural that the manager of the latter
should say he had to worry about his board while the former didn't
mention this factor at all.

The third company had been virtually torn apart for some years
by dissension in the board among individuals representing two
powerful business interests. The advent of new, strong management, the resignation of the contentious board members, and the
broadening of representation on the board had resulted in the
virtual elimination of this matter as a subject of active concern.
Obviously, however, a chief executive can ignore this subject only at
his peril—and none of the three did—although only one considered
it an active problem.

Another difference among the managers was that one placed
more emphasis on applying his own final judgment, after reviewing
the technical analyses presented by his staff, in making corporate
decisions. The other two emphasized management-team decision
rather than decision from the apex. Perhaps the difference stemmed
from the fact that the one who emphasized his own final judgment
was the oldest of the three and had spent his life in banking while
the other two, an economist and an engineer, were more techno-
cratic in outlook and behavior. A related difference among the three
men concerned their staffs. The one who spontaneously mentioned
senior staff as a principal concern was also the oldest of the three,
and perhaps the prospect of managerial succession may have
appeared more real to him.

There were other differences among the three managers, but they
should not be overstressed. My questions about their preoccupations and problems were put without warning, and they answered
off the cuff. Moreover, the differences were principally in emphasis
and, under questioning, proved not to be so great as they may have
sounded. In fact, given the differences in the men, the companies,

and the countries, it was striking that the similarities in their responses were so great. The tasks they considered most important and time-consuming were much the same. Moreover, the managers of other development banks who are considered relatively effective and successful would probably have replied in very similar terms. In my talks with these three men over the past decade, and with their counterparts in other institutions, their concerns seemed to be principally the following:

• The economic conditions, government policies, and above all, political and economic prospects in their countries that affected their banks' welfare, survival, and growth.

• New ideas about what their banks might be doing in the next several years. (In this connection, these men have come up with, and have carried out or are carrying out, ideas and plans they had not dreamed of when they took over their present jobs.)

• The development of new sources of finance. (I do not recall many meetings with these men in which they did not speak of visits to, or plans to visit, New York, Tokyo, or European capitals to seek additional finance.)

• Perceived threats from government to independence of action. In earlier years the question of freedom of action generally concerned what was called "government interference." While the question of government force in determining specific policy or investment decisions may sometimes be an issue today, development banks now seem to think that freedom of action depends primarily on mutual understanding—by the development bank of government policies and objectives and by the government of the value of a development bank's experience in devising government policies and in achieving government objectives. Thus dialogue has replaced confrontation as the principal mode of interaction between government and bank.

• Protection against pressures from board and owners (whether private or public). Here, too, with the growing maturity of management and experience of the institution, understanding has replaced confrontation.

• The quality of staff, especially staff of the caliber that might take over management in the future.

Internal, External, Present, and Future Orientations

This recital suggests that the eyes of capable chief executives are primarily on the future rather than on the present and on the external relations rather than the internal affairs of their banks. True, one of the managers referred to the need to develop staff and to his personal concern about applying his own final judgment in making investment decisions, another referred to general supervision of day-to-day affairs, and a third spoke of maintaining contact with technical and managerial training institutions. Obviously staff development and managerial succession were on the minds of all three. But it would not be correct to conclude that personnel was their only significant concern about internal affairs. As became apparent in the discussion that followed, other day-to-day matters do in fact consume much of their time and also that of their counterparts in other institutions. Indeed, some chief executives are unable to emerge from such day-to-day affairs and never find the time to deal adequately with the long-range questions listed above.

The internal affairs that make a heavy claim on chief executives are the protection of the portfolio, the promotion of new activities, and the resolution of staff conflicts.

The protection of the portfolio is a natural concern because it affects the financial integrity of the development bank and its standing, and therefore determines not simply the nature of its future but whether it will survive at all. Individual projects often go bad, and remedial measures are needed to put them back on the track; or companies sometimes fall into serious arrears because of a generalized situation in the country that affects a large number of debtors. Dealing with problem investments or with serious arrears of payments is not a matter which the managers I have known ever fully delegate to others.

Although the promotion of new enterprises and the undertaking of new lines of activity may be initiated by ideas and papers from the staff, and a special unit in the development bank might work on the proposal, the chief executive gives them special and personal attention. This is understandable since promotion is a costly process, a financial commitment is needed sooner or later to back up a promotion, and the development bank has a moral involvement because its commitment brings others into the investment as well.

Conflicts and differences of opinion inevitably occur that staff cannot resolve itself and on which the chief executive is required to make a choice, a compromise, or a synthesis. In a large and diversified development bank, conflicting claims on the institution's administrative budget can be settled only by the chief executive. And personal competition among staff is not unknown and can threaten the stability of the company if not resolved in good time.

The first and third items may be covered by the single word "troubleshooting," but they by no means cover every contingency that arises under that head. The manager is a development bank's principal troubleshooter; and in an area as complex as development and in an institution as innovative as a development bank should be, there is no lack of contingencies which the chief executive will feel compelled to deal with himself.

These, then, appear to be the principal preoccupations of the top managers of development banks. Of course, the mix of these elements changes from time to time. The concerns of the chief executive of a development bank just coming into existence are different from those of the chief executive of a well-established institution. When a development bank is new, a manager is necessarily involved in everything, especially in a small institution in a very underdeveloped country. The principal concerns will necessarily be to find a core staff, to establish the operational disciplines that will govern the staff's work, and to start up operations.

Only when staff is found and trained, operational policies developed, and procedures and practices established and understood can the managers delegate jobs and concentrate their attention on what they consider their most important tasks. Some managers never reach this point: they may not be successful in attracting or developing a staff of the caliber that justifies delegating authority, or they are personally incapable of delegating certain tasks no matter how trivial, and remain so. Even in well-established companies, new managers' use of their time will change after they have been on the job for some time. Finally, circumstances will from time to time arise in the company or in the economy that will force managers to shift time and attention from some matters to others. In general, urgent matters, which must be decided quickly, will almost always have the first claim on their attention. But only at their risk, and their company's, can they for long neglect important subjects in order to deal with urgent ones.

Lines of Communication

The chief executives of development banks develop an effective private intelligence system outside their own institutions. No matter how good a staff's sources of information and analytical capacities, managers draw heavily on their personal contacts in order to keep their fingers on the pulse of the countries, to know what is going on in the business communities and governments, and to maintain contacts with institutions that impinge directly or indirectly on the activity of the development banks. Indeed, chief executives often seem to rely more heavily on their private sources than on their staffs. This seems to be particularly true of information about people and enterprises; such knowledge, privately gathered, looms large in decisionmaking on investments, in promotion, and in keeping tabs on the portfolio. Perhaps this is because directly received intelligence is usually fresh, although it is likely also to be partial and raw, while intelligence coming from the staff is more likely to be old and predigested, bland rather than hot. The staff's reports may have more influence on a manager's view of the situation five to ten years hence, and therefore on his development of long-range strategies, than on his assessment of what will happen tomorrow or in the near future, which is crucial in dealing with current operations and problems. (Incidentally, playing tennis may be good for a manager's health and hence good for his development bank, but playing golf and walking are more likely to be helpful in gathering current intelligence.)

Chief executives tend to hold their cards close to their chests. However much they may believe in open lines of communication with their staffs, they rarely tell all they know. They are likely to prefer to listen and to talk, perhaps because they do not have the time to read or write memos. They sometimes prefer to keep information to themselves and to keep their decisions just slightly mysterious—a device that keeps them at a certain distance from their staff. While such behavior may add to their mystique, it has a cost: unless there is a period of careful preparation, a development bank almost always undergoes a sort of trauma when there is a change of chief executive officer, since neither the institution nor the new manager fully inherits the knowledge of the old manager.

Chief executives spend a great deal of time with government agencies. The more important and complex the operations of a development bank, the greater the amount of time so spent. That so much effort is devoted to relations with government is not only at the managers' initiative, the result of their wish to know what is going on and to clear their lines, also it is likely to be at the government's initiative, the result of its wish to draw on the manager's experience. Managers are likely to find themselves drawn into government or government-sponsored committees as well as consulted on specific issues bearing on government development policy.

Chief executives also develop an intelligence network inside their development banks. They need to know enough, but not too much, about the flow of operations, the condition of the portfolio, the financial situation of the bank, and the staff. There are many mechanisms whereby chief executives can keep in touch and ensure that problems will come to their attention. The method they choose will obviously reflect the size of their companies and the quality of their staffs, as well as their own style of management. For some kinds of issues and problems, especially those affecting staff, their informal contacts with staff are sometimes more valuable than formal reporting.

Finally, chief executives tend to be deeply committed to their jobs. It is not easy to get them far away from the development bank, that is, away from thinking and talking about it. In fact, sometimes they seem to be addicted to it.

Setting Bank Objectives

The activities of the chief executives of development banks reflect both day-to-day imperatives and their conceptions of their job. As noted earlier, their eyes seem primarily on the future rather than on the present. Indeed, the three I talked to did not fully report their activities related to current problems, and it was evident that they felt their jobs (like those of their counterparts I know) were not simply to assist their development banks in overcoming current problems but to guide them toward a useful and effective future. This was the unifying concept underlying and linking their references to keeping abreast of changing circumstances in the country, to maintaining a certain relation with other institutions whose activities impinge on theirs, and to looking for new ideas about what their companies should do in the future. This concept is central to the job of a chief executive. That is, the main task of chief executives is to establish the objectives of the banks they manage, to illuminate these objectives for those who play a part in achieving them, and to keep them under constant review and revision.

It may seem odd to comment on objectives since many people involved in the creation of a development bank or in its operation seem to believe they know precisely what they are doing and why (that is, they know what their objectives are). If the various operational or financial ratios they use to measure progress are satisfactory, they believe all is well and the institution can continue doing the same thing. This is not so, however. Some of the critical activities of a development bank—particularly those relating to innovation, technical assistance, and community education—are not amenable to statistical measurement. Moreover, times change, as do the operational objectives of a development bank or any other institution. Even an enterprise whose objective is explicitly and uniquely the maximization of return on capital must keep abreast of the market, technology, competitors, and government policy. It must plan changes today to meet conditions expected some years hence. Thus it may have to engage in what may in the short run appear to be profitless activity to ensure or establish profitable positions in the future. It may also have to change its product mix, abandoning some old products for new ones. The problems of adjustment are magnified for a development bank.

The illumination of objectives may seem simple. Presumably the sponsors of the company or the government had an objective clearly in mind when the bank was set up; in many cases, they or the first board of directors issued statements of policies that seemed to define the objectives of the bank. But in fact this is not often so. Rather, objectives laid out in charters and policy statements are often sufficiently vague to allow for widely differing interpretations. Charters and policy statements, which typically call for investments in "economically sound projects" or investments that will "promote economic development," are not themselves sufficient to suggest the operational guidelines a development bank needs, nor are they sufficiently precise to provide the criteria on which the management, the board of directors, the stockholders, the government, or the public can assess a development bank's performance. Some vagueness is desirable to permit flexibility in adapting to circumstances without excessive formality. There is, however, another reason for vagueness about objectives. The sponsors of a development bank often have only a hazy idea about the kind of institution they are creating; and that idea may constitute not a single notion but several notions, which are sometimes conflicting. Those notions may vary from reasonably well understood term-lending, whose failure or success may be measured by the returns on the shareholders' capital, at one extreme, to innovative investment promotion, which would call for quite a different type of institution; they may range from an instrument for financing the sponsors' own business ventures to an institution whose purpose is to "contribute to the economy" or "to promote economic development"—concepts that are themselves not very well defined.

It is therefore from the earliest moment of the chief executives' tenure that qualities of leadership and personality are brought into play. From the very first day they are faced with the task of translating vaguely stated general objectives into operational goals that can be understood by those who play a part in achieving the objectives. The determination of a development bank's objectives has a bearing on the directions in which it applies its efforts and on the policies it pursues; it influences the organization of the development bank and it affects the annual budget. Direction of effort, policies, organization, and budget are random and meaningless unless they are explicitly directed toward the achievement of reasonably precise goals.

It should not be thought that a development bank needs to have, or can have, only one objective. Development is not a simple process and it would be surprising, therefore, if the objectives of a development bank were simple or entirely consistent. It is most likely that there will be multiple objectives and that, in the application of those objectives to specific cases, compromises will have to be made rather than simple choices among clear alternatives.

Moreover, establishment of clear, operationally measurable goals is not a once-and-for-all affair. To the contrary, they must be examined critically and revised in the light of changing circumstances. The "promotion of development" may be a ringing phrase which is always applicable to a development bank. But the content of that phrase is likely to change with the passage of time. Many development banks have shifted objectives, or at least emphasis among objectives, over the years, and will shift again to continue addressing themselves to the real development problems of the country. Thus, development banks must periodically reorient or redefine their tasks in the light both of their own experience and of changing national values and objectives.

At a certain level, every development bank learns from its experience; but the experience examined and the lessons learned usually relate primarily to specific investment projects, to conditions in the sectors it finances, and to the financial performance of the bank. Only rarely do chief executives and development banks evaluate performance against their underlying objectives, for which they must rely, not on operational and financial statistics, but on broad judgmental considerations.

Self-evaluation is an important instrument of management. Costs and conformity to objectives are the twin standards by which a manager can evaluate his company's performance. They will certainly be the standards by which creditors, governments, and, in most cases, shareholders will evaluate the performance of the manager and the institution.[2]

Such evaluation is required as an audit of past activities, as an act of responsibility toward sponsor, financier, government, and public. It is also required as a part of the process of reconsidering objectives, policies, and procedures with a view to revising them for the future.

Considerable care needs to be exercised in the reorientation or redefinition of objectives. Sometimes such changes occur under the influence of fashion or of mistaken government policies or in response to the desires of creditors. Obviously a development bank has to take account of the views of those from whom it gets finance; but its objectives should be dictated by its own reading of its experience, of national objectives and of the prospects of the country, and by its views on the role it can play in furthering those prospects.

This process of establishing, monitoring, and revising objectives is essential to keeping a development bank alive.

There is no such thing as a finished, sound, credit worthy, and credible development bank. The sound one, that is, the one living up to its underlying goals, both financial and economic, is a changing one, seeking continually to regenerate itself in the light of changing circumstances. It cannot do so if it relies on automatically and repetitiously satisfying yesterday's standards. . . Continuing rejuvenation requires that a development bank never end the process of reviewing its own work in the light both of its own experience and of society's changing needs; requires that its policies and procedures be changed accordingly; requires that it maintain a mutually effective relationship with the individuals and institutions on whom its effectiveness depends; requires that its staff and its training programs be oriented toward inculcating in everyone, staff and management alike, the concepts of institutional renewal and innovativeness. Leadership in a development bank consists in making sure of all this.[3]

That is the heart of the chief executive's job.

Notes to Chapter 1

1. The development banks referred to here are local development finance companies whether of public, private, or mixed ownership, not international development banks, either regional or worldwide.

2. William Diamond and Ravi Gulhati, "Some Reflections on the World Bank's Experience with Development Finance Companies," Economic Staff Working Paper no. 145 (Washington, D.C.: World Bank, February 1973), p. 23.

3. William Diamond, at inauguration of Regional Course on Development Banking, Bombay, February 26, 1973, published as "Development Banking Perspectives," in *G. L. Mehta Commemorative Volume* (Madras, 1974), pp. 31–32.

Chapter 2

Development Banking:
Top Management Tasks and Structure

V. V. BHATT

DEVELOPMENT BANKS are unique financial institutions in developing countries, specializing in the provision of high-risk, long-term financing for the purpose of industrialization. There were only about a dozen viable development banks before 1946, but after World War II the growth of this type of financial institution has been significant. At present there are about 400 such institutions, of which more than 45 owe their existence and strength to the World Bank.[1]

These banks were expected not only to provide long-term finance but also to play a catalytic promotional role—a development role—in setting in motion a viable, widely diffused process of industrialization. Experience so far indicates, however, that they functioned, with few notable exceptions, as passive conservative bankers,[2] supporting financially well-known and well-entrenched business houses, rather than as *development banks*.[3] Doubtless they have built up specialized skills and techniques in the field of project appraisal and selection. But even in this field their criteria for project selection have been more or less the conventional banker's criteria—financial soundness and repaying ability of the project as well as the promoter. In brief, though they have functioned as sound *bankers*, they have failed as *development bankers*.[4]

The major reason for this failure seems to be the lack of appreciation by their top managements of their specific tasks in the development context. It is the purpose of this paper to indicate the nature

This chapter is reprinted from *World Development*, vol. 4 (1976), pp. 519–27, with permission.

and structure of these tasks if top management is to perform its expected development role. Communication and information systems are vital to the top management task of effective decisionmaking, and this relation is also discussed.

Development Banking: Top Management Tasks

One cannot understand the tasks of management without first analyzing the social function the institution is supposed to perform. Management and the institution managed can be judged only on the basis of their performance with regard to the social need and function from which the institution derives its social classification. Thus the management problem cannot be understood without the perception of the tasks and functions of management in a social context, for without this context no institution can survive.[5] The central focus in any study of management has to be on the tasks of management, since it is from these tasks that objectives, strategy, and structure are derived. It is not possible to discuss meaningfully the problems related to strategy and structure without first understanding the social function and tasks of management.

This social function cannot be defined once and for all: the search for the nature and structure of this function has to be a continuing one in a dynamic and interdependent setting of socioeconomic change. It is the performance of this evolving social function that determines the survival and growth of an institution. If it fails in this endeavor, its fate is sealed even if it is managed efficiently. For business institutions such as development banks, their continuing ability to plough back profits is merely one of the indexes of success; the basic index of their success is the vitality with which they survive and grow.

Neither economists nor management scientists have perceived that the central function and role of top management is essentially a static setting for analysis—a setting in which things change in systematic known ways or in which there is need for mere passive adaptation to exogenous events.[6] The real management problem arises only in a dynamic setting in which decisions have to be made for the future, which is unknowable, and in which information even about the present or the past is, in the nature of things, incomplete and imperfect. If the past, present, and future were known, there would be no management problem.[7]

In the context of development banking, the question therefore arises: What is the emerging social function of a development bank in a given dynamic social setting? As noted earlier, the charter of a development bank cannot define the social function once and for all; it is the task of top management to find out the specific implications of this function in the light of the dynamic, changing socioeconomic reality. The broad purpose and mission can be easily stated: to serve as a catalyst for generating a viable yet widely diffused process of industrial development in a given country. But the precise social function would depend upon the initial stage of development, the development strategy adopted, the available composition of resources, skills, and manpower, the efficiency with which other institutions are performing functions related to development banking, and so on. Top management thus needs to have a precise knowledge of all these elements of the socioeconomic structure in its dynamic setting. Mere knowledge cannot suffice; it has to evolve organic links with the decisionmaking process in the institutions that have an impact on its work, so that its functioning is integrated with that of the related institutions. In this process of interactions, a development bank adapts itself to the other institutions as much as it enforces adaption by the others to its functioning.

To take a concrete case, suppose a development bank is set up in a developing country to provide long-term financial assistance to viable industrial projects. It assumes, to begin with, that project promoters would seek its assistance and that its task is to appraise the soundness of projects and provide such assistance as is really required. The initial task then is to discern by what criteria it should appraise such projects. Should it look merely to the financial viability of the project and its capacity to repay assistance or should it appraise the project from the point of view of its contribution to the development strategy adopted by the country or, more generally, from the point of view of national advantage? Obviously, a development bank has no rationale for its existence unless it looks to national advantage; for its function is not merely banking, but such banking as would promote industrial development. But then the problem is how to develop criteria that reflect national advantage. Obviously, it cannot derive these criteria without reference to the development objectives, strategy, and policies of the country. So it has to have a dialogue with the relevant state agencies for that purpose. But this has to be a real dialogue, not a mere passive adaptation of criteria to what the state agencies may suggest, since a development bank really knows how projects are affected by policies, and it can analyze this concrete evidence to suggest to the relevant agencies how strategy or policies need to be modified in the light of concrete factual evidence. Thus no criteria for project appraisal can be evolved without this interaction with state agencies, and the bank's own criteria have to be modified in the light of the emerging reality.

The application of whatever criteria are devised cannot be a mechanical process. For the criteria might not be appropriate; or the contribution of a particular project to some development objectives might not be sharply brought out by the criteria; or the contribution of a project to one objective might be so overwhelmingly important that its contribution to other objectives needs to be ignored. In other words, the appraisal criteria should be such and should evolve in such a manner that they help in the process of decisionmaking. This implies that they should bring out implications of a project on the basis of which it is possible to make an informed judgment. Criteria, after all, are tools, not substitutes, for decisionmaking.

Decisionmaking is different from decision preparation. The latter is an analytic exercise of processing meaningfully all relevant information. But decisionmaking is not an analytic process. It is based on the perception of the whole problem, not merely on partial fragmentary analysis. This perception, insight, and intelligence relate to the total impact of a project—the quantifiable as well as the unquantifiable.[8] Obviously, it cannot be governed by mechanical formulas, tools, and techniques; if it is so governed, it is the surest index of lack of intelligence and hence lack of ability to make right decisions.[9]

Whatever the decision criteria, if they are not adopted by all financial institutions, a development bank might find that financially viable projects are diverted to other financial institutions, while it is left with only a small number of risky projects. A development bank simply cannot function in a vacuum; it has to have close relations with other financial institutions in selecting criteria to be evolved. This cooperation is also important for mobilizing resources to finance what it considers to be sound projects, but for which it cannot provide adequate assistance.

A development bank is likely to be faced with all or any one of the following problems: (a) its appraisal criteria might be sound but these criteria might not have much significance for the appropriate choice of technology or product mix because most projects are designed by foreign consultants or companies in the light of technology in use in advanced countries; (b) terms and conditions of foreign technical or financial collaboration can be onerous and the negotiating ability of project promoters vis-á-vis their foreign partners might not be adequate; (c) really worthwhile projects are not identified and designed because of lack of entrepreneurial talents in the public sector as well as the private; (d) potential entrepreneurs become frustrated since they do not get the required assistance for giving shape to their project ideas; (e) projects are concentrated in certain geographical areas or certain fields, since infrastructure facilities including technical and financial assistance are not evenly spread across the country or across different industrial fields.

These are some of the problems with which a development bank is likely to be faced at one time or another and, if it is to perform its social function, it has to solve them. This implies that, along with financial assistance, a development bank has to be prepared to provide managerial and technical assistance. Thus, it cannot possibly wait for projects to come to it for assistance; it has to create projects that are consistent with the overall—explicit or implicit—national development strategy. If there are institutions in the field of project identification and formulation, it has to develop personal contact with them for the solution of some of these problems. If there are none, it has to take the initiative in establishing them in cooperation with the relevant institutions, including state agencies.

A development bank cannot perform these different tasks unless it is financially viable. It is inherent in its tasks to experiment with innovative ways of fulfilling its social function; and for this purpose it has to commit key men and resources to new tasks. It cannot do this unless (a) it withdraws resources from less vital and increasingly less important tasks that can well be performed by the other institutions; (b) it shares in the profits of really viable and successful projects by devising appropriate flexibility in its terms and conditions governing assistance; (c) it attracts new resources from institutions that mobilize savings by designing such financial instruments that would appeal to them; (d) it mobilizes resources from state agencies for specific mutually agreed tasks; and (e) it attracts foreign resources from other countries and international agencies.

The following are top management functions: (a) devising selection criteria; (b) interacting with state agencies for modifying development strategy and policies; (c) interacting with other financial institutions in the country as well as abroad for mobilizing resources as well as for performing common tasks; (d) interacting with institutions in the field of project identification and formulation; (e) initiating institutions required to provide technical and managerial assistance to entrepreneurs and establishing organic links with them; (f) devising new ways of mobilizing resources; and (g) attaining financial viability for creating the right setting for survival and growth.

The performance of these tasks requires a top management team that focuses on management tasks rather than on the functions of a hierarchical organization. This team should have a leader and consist of four to five persons with specific responsibility assigned to each, but the members should work as a team in decisionmaking. These tasks are so basic that this team would not have enough time and energy to devote to them if its members were tied up with operational jobs. Nor would they be able to take an overall view of the functioning of a development bank if they tied themselves to specific operational jobs. Anything that pertains to the performances of the institution as a whole and that which others cannot do are their responsibilities.

Nevertheless, the selection of persons for key management jobs has to be their responsibility; for it is this team that has to create the one that can in time replace it. Otherwise, the institution cannot be perpetuated. For this purpose, they have to be in formal and informal contact with potential and actual managers, devise ways and methods of testing and training them, and finally select the really best to succeed them in the top management team. A top management team that considers itself indispensable for the institution has really not performed its top management task; such a team needs to be changed by a well-functioning board, whose only responsibilities are (a) to reinforce top management in its tasks with advice, counseling, and review, (b) to replace the team with a successor team in good time; and (c) to perform the ceremonial duties that can project the right public image about the institution. A board is not a substitute for top management; its role is similar to that of a constitutional monarch in the United Kingdom.[10]

The top management team cannot function without a secretariat that (a) keeps its members informed about each other's activities, (b) identifies and analyzes relevant problems for decisionmaking, (c) processes information about projects—at the appraisal, decisionmaking, and supervision stages—that is relevant to the various tasks of the team, (d) suggests new ways of performing conventional tasks or giving up obsolete tasks, and (e) indicates new objectives in tune with the long-term growth of the institution. This secretariat, or Planning and Policy Cell (PPC), should be manned by a few professional people (maybe four to five) selected from the operating departments for their competence. They should not be kept for more than five years in the PPC, otherwise they would lose touch with reality. After five years, by rotation, they should be sent back to operational departments. The PPC can also perform another function: it can be a testing ground for identifying and selecting the potential members of tomorrow's top management team. It would induce the personnel in the operational departments to take an overall view of the functions of the institution as each one would tend to aspire to become a member of the PPC.

Management theory is silent on the function and structure of top management; but in management practice, this was the very first area tackled systematically—long before Frederick W. Taylor tackled organization design in his functional structure. Top management as a function and as a structure was first developed by George Siemens (1839–1901) in Germany between 1870 and 1880, when he designed and built the Deutsche Bank and made it, within a very few years, into continental Europe's leading and most dynamic financial institution.[11] It was a universal bank, combining commercial banking and development banking functions. These universal banks performed a momentous role in German industrialization.[12]

> In Germany, the various incompetencies of the individual entrepreneurs were offset by the device of splitting the entrepreneurial function: the German investment banks—a powerful invention comparable in economic effect to that of the Steam Engine—were in their capital-supplying functions a substitute for the insufficiency of the previously created wealth willingly placed at the disposal of entrepreneurs. But they were also a substitute for entrepreneurial deficiencies. From their central vantage points of control, the banks participated actively in shaping the major, and sometimes even not so major, decisions of the individual enterprises. It was they who very often mapped out a firm's paths of growth, conceived farsighted plans, decided on major technological and locational innovations, and arranged for mergers and capital increases.[13]

Managerial Communications and Decisionmaking

With all its limitations, there is one fundamental insight underlying management science: an institution or an organization is a system whose parts are human beings with a variety of skills, knowledge, and techniques and who are involved in a joint venture. The main characteristic of such a system is the interdependence of its parts. The primacy attaches to the whole and the parts have to be integrated to form the whole; primary emphasis, thus, has to be on the whole, and the contribution that the parts make to the whole, rather than on the mere technical efficiency of the parts. Technical perfection of a part may sometimes damage the system as a whole. It is a sad irony that in spite of this insight, management science has emphasized the efficiency of the parts—precision of the tools at the expense of the health and performance of the whole.

With this characteristic feature of interdependence, a system cannot function unless the parts move in harmony. This implies communication within the system—each part understanding its relation with the others and with the whole system. Communication does not mean mere provision of information; it has to be meaningful and relevant information that demands action. Information presupposes communication, but there can be communication even without information.[14] Communication as an action-oriented system has to convey signals for action, for decision preparation and decisionmaking. Each part has to act—make a decision or communicate the need for decision to other parts or to the center. These decision signals also function as performance indicators of the part as well as the whole. The test of a good communication system is the economy of information and signals with which it functions.

Communication is an interpersonal phenomenon that depends not on the communicator but on the recipient. Recipients will not act unless they understand precisely the full implications of what is conveyed. This understanding, this perception of the meaning, is not a matter of logic or of information. Rather, it depends on the recipients' range of perception and what they expect to perceive.[15] If the information conveyed is not within the recipients' range of perception or their range of expectation, it has no meaning. Effective communication thus implies communication that the recipient can understand and act upon.

An utterance from the center has no meaning, however clearly spoken or drafted, if the center does not understand the perception capacity or motivation of those who have to act.[16] Commands or orders do not improve the understanding or motivation of the recipients. Communication has to start from the recipients—how they understand their problems, how they intend to act, or how they want the center to act. So the center has to listen to what the recipients want to convey.[17] Communication thus has to be upward, starting with the recipient rather than the emitter—this is what is implied in the concept of listening. But this listening, too, may not be operational unless it is related to what both the recipients and emitters have in common—in other words, to objectives. It is in relation to objectives that the subordinate should communicate upward what his major contribution should be and what he should be held accountable for. The supervisor may disagree and see the reality differently, but he understands what is conveyed and the subordinate understands why he has to act differently. When the perception of both is focused on concrete objectives that are real to both, communication is possible. This is what is meant by management by objectives.

In several development banks there is a plethora of information upward as well as downward—but no meaningful communication. For instance, the appraisal department may furnish a statement of the various projects for which assistance is sought and classify them into their different stages of appraisal. But such a statement has no meaning for top management if it has no decision signals. But suppose the appraisal department has to function within the framework of certain objectives such as: (a) no appraisal should take more than two months and, if a project does require more time, specific problems of that project and their possible solutions should be discussed with top management; (b) a project with complex technology or uncertain demand for its products should be sent for appraisal to a consultant for a thorough examination within fifteen days after the application is received; (c) the specific problems related to a project by a new entrepreneur or in a backward area, as well as the proposed solutions, should be discussed with top management; (d) a viable project requiring more assistance than the institution can provide should be sent to top management with concrete suggestions about the possible ways of raising the required finance; (e) if a project requires modification to be viable, the possible modifications and the related action program should be sent to top management. If such objectives were laid down, the appraisal department would know what is expected of it—the decisions it has to make and the decisions it should suggest to top management. And the information going to top management would also be action-oriented, suggesting the decision problems to be faced. Thus there are a deadline, a firm commitment to action, and precise indicators of performance.

A project supervision department, for instance, does not perform a meaningful function in some development banks. The department collects a mass of information, reports, and impressions based on personal visits, but this information is processed in a form that does not indicate an action program. Such information has no meaning either to the department or to top management. The objectives need to be based on answers to the following questions: (a) What problems are likely to be faced by specific projects, and what aspects of the projects need close supervision? (The answer to this along with a proposed action program should be submitted to top management immediately after assistance is sanctioned.) (b) Have these problems arisen? If so, what is the proposed action? Does it require top management decision? (c) If during the operational phase a project is not working at full capacity, what are the problems and what is the suggested solution? (d) If a project has failed, why has it failed, can life be put into it, and how is this to be done?

In a similar way, there should be clear and precise objectives for the legal section, project promotion and development department, research department, and finance department. For the legal section, the objectives can be: (a) there should be a lag of not more than fifteen days between the sanction of assistance and the completion of legal formalities; (b) if there is likely to be a longer lag, the specific problems, their solutions, and the timing should be indicated; (c) the norm should be that legal formalities be completed at the time assistance is sanctioned.

Project promotion and development department objectives might be defined in terms of the following questions: (a) What are the new project ideas that are consistent with the overall development strategy, and what action is proposed for shaping them into implementable projects? (b) Who is approached for undertaking identified projects? What specific assistance is needed, and what action is required for the provision of such assistance? (c) What are the specific problems of entrusting projects to new entrepreneurs or to entrepreneurs in backward areas? How can these problems be solved and what action is required for the purpose?

Research department objectives can also be framed in terms of questions to be answered: (a) What is the development strategy—explicit or implicit—of the country, and are actual policies in the industries field consistent with this strategy? If not, what modifications in policies are necessary, and what action can be taken? (b) How should appraisal criteria be devised? How do they enlighten, and in what way are they likely to conceal, significant implications of projects? (c) For what projects is it necessary to evaluate the soundness of appraisal procedures and criteria, government policies, and the institution's policies after completion? (d) What new projects can be identified that are related to the projects under implementation or completed and operating projects—new projects that are small and ancillary to large projects or related in any other way? (e) What projects can be identified on the basis of trade statistics as viable import-substituting or export-promoting projects?

Similarly, finance department objectives may be defined by answers to the following questions: (a) What is the resource picture in light of actual and potential commitments? (b) How should the resource gap be met? What are the new, specific ways of raising resources, and what policy changes do they indicate? (c) If there is a resource surplus, in what manner should it be deployed to further the interest and objectives of the institution—the overriding objective being the generation of a viable and widely diffused process of industrialization?

Few development banks have a separate finance department; it is generally merged with the accounting department. As Drucker says, "The justification has been that both deal with money. But, of course, accounting does not deal with money; it deals with figures. The consequence of the traditional approach has been the slighting of financial management," because the accountant approach inhibits the exploration of innovative ways of raising resources.[18]

With such key objectives, the communication system can become meaningful and relevant for decisionmaking. Mere perfection of the information system can never be the objective of an action-oriented system. While the pursuit of knowledge is essential for decisionmaking, it should be understood that decisions can never be perfect because of uncertainty, and that however superior the information, knowledge, skills, tools, and techniques, they are no substitute for a clear perception of reality, which is complex and constantly changing. Action in the present should never be guided only by the past— that is, simply according to skills, knowledge, and techniques. But perception of the living reality is not a matter of logic, it is a matter of intelligence—keen sensitivity to men and things, in their measurable and nonmeasurable aspects, as they interact in the present. Perception, judgment, and intelligence differ among different persons and that is why there is good management and bad, in spite of the common inheritance of skills, knowledge, techniques, and so on.[19]

Good and effective major decisions require a clear understanding of the problem, its possible solutions, and the required action by the relevant group of people in the institution. Quite often top management may misunderstand the problem, and its decision, however quick and apparently sound, might be an answer to an irrelevant problem. A decision might not be the correct one if the possible alternative courses of action have not been explored; nor will the decision be immediately effective if those who must take action do not understand the problem, its solution, and the proposed action.

For major policy decisions—involving innovative departures from conventional approaches—it might be worthwhile to pose the problem to all relevant departments of the bank. The advantages would be (a) a clear understanding of the problem or the non-problem by top management as well as other managerial cadres, (b) exploration of alternative solutions and action programs, (c) commitment by the relevant departments to action with all its implications—commitment of key personnel, assignment of responsibilities, performance expectation and its systematic feedback to top management. With all this preparation for a decision, whatever top management decides is likely to be appropriate and, more important, effective.

Selection of appraisal criteria, new promotional activities, new ways of raising resources, shortening of administrative and other procedural lags, and new and more effective ways of project supervision are some of the problems that can be tackled in this way. This method ensures good communication and the performance of the system as a whole, since it motivates the entire institution to consider its problems, possible solutions, and the action programs required. This is the Japanese method of decisionmaking by consensus—not consensus in terms of the lowest common denominator, but as an art of making effective decisions. What is important in a Japanese business enterprise is not an answer to a question but the question itself. Consequently, much time is spent defining the question by all managerial and other cadres involved. This results in the problem being fully understood and the alternative solutions and action programs being explored and examined. Once this is done, the decision becomes almost obvious, as does the action program, to the relevant personnel. In this way, making a decision and acting on it become two simultaneous processes rather than two distinct stages. Normally, a decision is made and then has to be "sold" to the people who must act on it. Hence, the time taken in effective decisionmaking is longer than in Japan. Further, in Japan conflicts are ironed out at the stage of decisionmaking, and the entire institution identifies itself with the problem and its solution. This promotes harmony, a sense of participation, and hence a sense of identification with the interests and performance of the entire institution.

Notes to Chapter 2

1. J. D. Nyhart and Edmond F. Janssens, *A Global Directory of Development Finance Institutions in Developing Countries* (Paris: Development Centre of the Organisation for Economic Co-operation and Development, 1967).

2. V. V. Bhatt, "Aspects of Functions and Working of Some Development Finance Companies" (Washington, D.C.: Economic Development Institute, World Bank, 1974; processed). See also V. V. Bhatt, "On Technology Policy and Its Institutional Frame," *World Development*, vol. 3, no. 9 (September 1975).

3. William Diamond and Ravi Gulhati, "Some Reflections on the World Bank's Experience with Development Finance Companies," Economic Staff Working Paper no. 145 (Washington, D.C.: World Bank, February 1973), p. 23.

4. Ibid.

5. Peter F. Drucker, *Management: Tasks, Responsibilities, Practices* (New York: Harper and Row, 1973), chap. 4 and pp. 508–10.

6. Joseph A. Schumpeter, *Business Cycles*, vol. 1 (New York: McGraw-Hill, 1939), pp. 98–99. Schumpeter writes, "The assumption that business behavior is ideally rational and prompt, and also that in principle it is the same with all firms, works tolerably well only within the precincts of tried experience and familiar motive. It breaks down as soon as we leave those precincts and allow the business community under study to be faced by—not simply new situations, which also occur as soon as external factors unexpectedly intrude but by—new possibilities of business action which are as yet untried and about which the most complex command of routine teaches nothing. Those differences in the behavior of different people, which within those precincts account for secondary phenomena only, become essential in the sense that they now account for the outstanding features of reality and that a picture drawn on the Walras-Marshallian lines ceases to be true—even in the qualified sense in which it is true of stationary and growing processes: it misses those features, and becomes wrong in the endeavor to account by means of its own analysis for phenomena which the assumptions of that analysis exclude ... Those differences belong, as a special case, to the class of facts usually dealt with under the heading of Leadership." Used with the permission of McGraw-Hill Book Company.

7. Kenneth J. Arrow, "Limited Knowledge and Economic Analysis," *American Economic Review*, vol. 64, no. 1 (March 1974). Arrow writes, "The uncertainties about economics are rooted in our need for a better understanding of the economics of uncertainty. Even as a graduate student, I was somewhat surprised at the emphasis on static allocative efficiency by market socialists, when the nonexistence of markets for future goods under capitalism seemed to me a much more obvious target ... But he cannot know the future. Hence, unless he deludes himself he must know that both

sets of expectations may be wrong. In short, the absence of the market implies that the optimizer faces a world of uncertainty . . . In fact, of course, the basic economic factors are changing, partly endogenously because of capital accumulation in its most general sense, partly exogenously with predictable and unpredictable changes in technology and tastes; equally if not more important, though, is the fact that the dispersion of information which is so economical implies that different economic agents do not have access to the same observations. Hence, it is reasonable to infer that they will never come into agreement as to probabilities of future prices . . . A further implication is that the past influences the future . . . The past is relevant because it contains information which changes the image of the future: the probabilities which govern future actions are modified by observations on the past. It follows that present decisions with implications for the future are functions of the past values of variables as well as present values . . . What still needs to be exploited more, however, is that the inference to the future is necessarily uncertain . . . A truncated theory of temporary equilibrium in which markets for future goods are replaced by some form of expectations, themselves functions of current prices and quantities, has indeed been developed, though its empirical content is necessarily meagre if the formation of expectation is left unanalysed."

See also, "Kenneth Arrow on Capitalism and Society," *Business and Society Review*, no. 10 (Summer 1974). Arrow writes, "I've stressed earlier the information element—that links in the chain of communication are in part human. They have to be human because human transducers are incredibly efficient in certain ways, though very inefficient in others. They are relatively poor in arithmetic, but they are very good in integrating disparate pieces of information. There is no likelihood that they will be replaced. So long as they exist, the qualities that make human beings differ from each other and that impede or enhance communication among them will be important . . . It's also true that when there's flexibility in decision-making, there's power, as well as information transfer. The ability to wield power and the efficiency with which it's harnessed for profitable aims make the difference between successful and unsuccessful firms. They may also determine whether the economy as a whole is more or less efficient."

8. Joseph A. Schumpeter, *History of Economic Analysis* (London: Oxford University Press, 1954), pp. 788–89. Schumpeter writes, "Theorists—especially of the planning type—often indulge in the deplorable practice of deriving "practical" results from a few functional relations between a few economic aggregates in utter disregard of the fact that such analytic set-ups are congenitally incapable of taking account of deeper things, the more subtle relations that cannot be weighed and measured but may be more important to a nation's cultural life than things that can."

9. On the distinction between thought (which is inevitably based on the past—knowledge, skills, techniques, tools) and intelligence (or perception or insight), see J. Krishnamurti, *The Awakening of Intelligence* (New York: Harper & Row, 1973), pp. 509–38. See also Arthur Koestler, *The Act of Creation* (New York: A Laurel Edition, 1967), chap. 7, p. 177. Koestler writes, "Language can become a screen which stands between the thinkers and reality. This is the reason why true creativity often starts when language ends." On decisionmaking, see also John Maynard Keynes, *The General Theory of Employment, Interest and Money* (New York: Harcourt, Brace, Jovanovich, Inc., 1965) pp. 161–63. Keynes writes, "The characteristic of human nature is that a large proportion of our positive activities depend on spontaneous optimism rather than on a mathematical expectation, whether moral or hedonistic

or economic. Most, probably, of our decision to do something positive, the full consequences of which will be driven out over many days to come, can only be taken as a result of animal spirits—of a spontaneous urge to action rather than inaction, and not as the outcome of a weighted average of quantitative benefits multiplied by quantitative probabilities . . . Thus if the animal spirits are dimmed and the spontaneous optimism falters, leaving us to depend on nothing but a mathematical expectation, enterprise will fade and die; though fears of loss may have a basis no more reasonable than hopes of profit had before . . . We are merely reminding ourselves that human decisions affecting the future, whether personal or political or economic, cannot depend on strict mathematical expectation, since the basis for making such calculations does not exist; and that it is our innate urge to activity which makes the wheels go round, our rational selves choosing between the alternatives as best as we are able, calculating where we can, but often falling back on our motive of whim or sentiment or chance."

10. See Drucker, *Management: Tasks, Responsibilities, Practices*, chap. 52.

11. Ibid., chap. 49.

12. Alexander Gerschenkron, *Economic Backwardness in Historical Perspective* (Cambridge, Mass.: Harvard University Press, 1962), p. 12.

13. Alexander Gerschenkron, *Continuity in History and Other Essays* (Cambridge, Mass.: Harvard University Press, 1968), p. 137.

14. Edward J. Hall, *Silent Language* (Garden City, N.Y.: Doubleday, 1959).

15. Robert Buckout, "Eyewitness Testimony," *Scientific American*, vol. 231, no. 6 (December 1974).

16. Drucker, *Management: Tasks, Responsibilities, Practices*, chap. 38.

17. Elton Mays, *The Social Problems of an Industrial Civilization* (Boston: Harvard Business School, 1945).

18. Drucker, *Management: Tasks, Responsibilities, Practices*, p. 539.

19. See notes 7, 8, and 9.

Part II

Establishing Goals and Strategies

THE ACCEPTANCE OF RESPONSIBILITY for furthering the nation's development policies is the special factor that makes a bank a development bank. Whatever its name, that responsibility makes a conventional financial institution a development finance institution. Any kind of financial institution can be so transformed—a commercial bank, a mortgage bank, an investment company. What is the effect of accepting that responsibility?

A development bank's goals are generally assumed to be stated in the documents that created it and in the statements and declarations of its sponsors. More often than not, its purpose was expressed as the provision of medium- and long-term finance for a sector or sectors of the economy thought to be inadequately served by existing institutions; its policies largely involved the development bank's activity as an allocator, rather than as a mobilizer, of resources. This simple formulation of purpose and then of policies to achieve it is too vague to provide the development bank with operational objectives capable of providing guidelines to all those involved in the operation of the institution. Translating vague purposes into objectives that are fairly precise and capable of measurement is a principal task of management.

The establishment of operationally clear objectives and policies is not done once and for all; they need continuous revision and adaptation in the light of the institution's growing experience and maturity, of the economic progress of the country and especially of the financial structure, and of changing perceptions of the development process. The chief executive's role is to manage the adaptation of the development bank to these changing circumstances. This means looking and planning ahead, rather than reacting in an ad hoc fashion to the pressures of events or of governments.

The following paper by William Diamond discusses the meaning of the "developmental" function of a development bank and describes how some development banks have revised their policies and strategies in the light of changing circumstances. The paper also raises the unconventional question whether, as the economy and the development bank mature, it is not more important to influence all the institutions in a country's financial system to assume a developmental role than to focus attention on a particular category of institutions called "development banks."

Chapter 3

Notes on Purposes and Strategies

WILLIAM DIAMOND

IT IS CUSTOMARY to say that a development bank's business is development, or that accepting responsibility for furthering the nation's development policies is the special factor that makes a bank a development bank, or that a development bank's activities must contribute to the national interest. It is often said that its basic aim is to make a demonstrable contribution to the development of the economy in which it operates. Such statements are often tautologies. They are always vague. The word "development" usually lacks specific content. This should not be surprising, for it has different meanings to different people, in different places, and at different times.

What Is a Development Bank's Business?

It might be assumed that a development bank's business has been worked out in the discussions among its founders and expressed in the documents (legislative or corporate) that created the bank. This is not generally so. The charter is usually broadly and vaguely phrased, in part because there may not have been a clear understanding among all parties involved as to precisely what the development bank's business should be, but also in order to give the institution maximum flexibility to adapt to future circumstances.

The sponsors or boards of many development banks have prepared statements of operational policies, which have laid out in somewhat more detail the specifics of the institutions' corporate purposes. Such statements usually consist in part of a declaration of principles of risk diversification and other aspects of financial prudence which, important though they are, do not go far toward defining the development bank's business. For the rest, statements of operational policy provide fairly general indications of the sectors or areas in which the development bank intends to operate. They try to forge at least a rhetorical link with national development objectives or government economic priorities. Some policy statements seem to reflect a defensive outlook rather than an aggressive one which identifies potential markets and expresses the determination to exploit them.

In recent years some development banks have prepared periodic "strategy statements," often in response to the demand of their financiers. Such statements have included fairly precise formulations of short-range objectives: targets for a year or two ahead. These short-term plans help focus the efforts of a development bank and provide a gauge against which to measure progress over the period. The strategy statements thus come close to laying out the short-term objectives which must underpin the annual work program (budget) of the development bank.

One is often left with the impression, however, that there is an unfilled gap between the corporate goal of promoting development and the fairly precise short-term program and targets, a gap that is not adequately bridged by the traditional "statement of operational policies." What appears to be missing is a reasonably clear definition of the development bank's business, that is, what lines of action it proposes to achieve its corporate purpose, the activities to which over the long run it intends to commit its resources and its efforts. The term "strategy" is generally used in this regard—not in the sense of short-term objectives referred to earlier, but in the sense of defining the broad lines of corporate effort.

The question may be asked whether a long-range strategy need be defined. There is one reason above all for doing so. Many individuals and entities are involved in achieving the institution's corporate purpose: government, providers of finance, shareholders, boards of directors, and, above all, staff. Their every effort needs to be consciously directed toward that basic goal. A new board member or staff member needs something more precise than "the diversification of industry" and something more general than "opening two new branch offices and increasing loan volume by 15 percent next year." Providers of finance, too, generally want something more pointed than the former and more far ranging than the latter to justify their financing.

It is a primary task of the management of a new development

bank to give practical meaning as early as possible to the vaguely expressed developmental purpose for which the institution was created. This is likely to be necessary even if sponsors have agreed on a statement of policy, and it is rarely an easy matter. Management has not always been clear (not any clearer than sponsors or governments) in defining what the business of the institution should be. And when management has formulated a clear strategy or set of activities, it has the further and difficult task of orienting the other parties needed to put it into effect.

It should be acknowledged at this point that the absence of an explicit statement of operational policy or strategy does not mean that a development bank does not have a long-range strategy. It may well exist in the chief executive's mind and may provide the framework for all his decisions and actions. But the main point of such a strategy is lost if it is his secret—that is, if it is not known to, and explicitly designed to orient, the entire board and staff, to say nothing of outsiders. The importance of that alignment of effort becomes greater as the institution grows larger and as responsibilities are divided (as inevitably they will be) among an increasing number of individuals. An explicit course must guide their decisions and actions, as well as the manager's. It needs to be reflected in the development bank's operational programs, short-term objectives, and budgets.

By and large the principal activity of development banks has been providing medium- and long-term financing for productive investment and reaching decisions with respect to such investments, not on the basis of the security that can be offered by the client, but rather on the basis of the long-range economic viability of the enterprise being financed. This hard-core activity derived from the general perception of the sponsors of development banks that there existed an important gap in the institutional arrangements for creating and financing productive projects—a gap that a new specialist institution was needed to fill. While other factors might also be perceived to be missing (such as management and entrepreneurship), term capital was seen as the crucial one, and providing it was considered necessary to attract and give effect to the others. This function was the justification for the support given such institutions by their governments and by bilateral and multilateral agencies.

With the focus thus placed on the provision of capital, the task of the development bank seemed to be fairly simple. The appraisal of investment proposals and the monitoring of investments after they are made became the core of the development bank's work—the subject of the principal decisions required of management, the process around which the development bank was organized and administered, and the principal purpose of staff training and development.

Two issues stem from this view of the activity of a development bank. For one thing, the seemingly simple task of investment appraisal and follow-up began, before long, to take on quite different practical forms in different environments. It became apparent that appraisal involves ideas and concepts on which there might be very different viewpoints. One of the most important of these concepts, for instance, is whether a particular investment proposal is economically sound. This is not by any means a theoretical matter. It is in the institution's interest no less than in the general public's interest to determine the economic soundness of a project. It affects the quality of the portfolio of a bank as much as does the efficiency of the borrower's management and is therefore as necessary as financial analysis in determining the risks in an investment.

A second, closely related issue concerns the objects of the development bank's investment. Not all parties involved in a development bank have been content simply to provide capital not available from other sources, nor have they been content with growth measured only by the provision of more capital to a larger number of clients. Governments and external financiers expected not only sound loans and equity investments in growing volume, but investments that helped accomplish certain broad economic goals (such as decentralization of industry, assistance to new entrepreneurs, promotion of certain types of enterprises, diversification of industry, and expansion of exports). Some private shareholders might have been satisfied with the purely financial function, especially if it yielded a dividend. But many were not content because their interest in the development banks as an investment had never been great. And the management and staff of a development bank, who sooner or later become the main forces driving it onward, were generally motivated by something more than the need to establish and maintain a financially viable institution. To one degree or another, virtually all the involved parties have wanted justification for their relations with the development bank that went beyond the provision of term capital. One might suggest that the maintenance of financial viability (profitability) itself was rarely the goal of the development bank. It was rather the measure of success in carrying out its purpose and the basis on which it could hope to acquire the additional capital required for growth.

Defining the development bank's long-range strategy, that is, laying out a long-range operational plan for achieving the institution's underlying purpose (in effect, defining its business), must obviously vary from one company to the next and from one country to another. The response of a development bank in a country in which entrepreneurship is conspicuously absent will be different from that of an institution in a country where entrepreneurial wheeling and dealing is widespread; different in a small country with very limited natural resources, including trained manpower, from what it might be in a larger one with a good supply of resources. Again, the establishment of corporate goals for a private development bank involves issues quite different from those in a government-owned one. But the job cannot be avoided.

Changing Corporate Business

Whatever the strategies decided upon in the early days of a development bank, circumstances sooner or later change and suggest or require significant changes in, or redirection of, the activities of the development bank. For instance:

• Government policies change and—by the use of force or incentives—direct financing efforts to particular sectors or particular target groups. Such changes may result from any number of circumstances: for instance, a new perception of the crucial problems of development (say, the renewed stress on poverty), a new political party in power (that might decide industry needs to be export-oriented), or persistent inflation.

• The economy expands, and as a result the structure of industry undergoes change. Both the size and the nature of the financial requirements of industry might change drastically.

• Economic change brings about significant developments in the financial sector. New institutions emerge to provide specialized services, some of which might be in direct competition with the development bank. Perhaps because of new government regulations, the sharp lines that once existed between different types of financial institutions (say, between commercial and term-lending banks) might become blurred.

• The development bank senses new opportunities for business, some the result of economic change (such as the expanding demand for export credits), and others the result of innovative efforts by the development bank itself (such as the deliberate promotion of new, potentially profitable enterprises).

• The development bank's search for new financial resources might call for new activities (for instance, a shift into mobilizing short-term deposits, some of which can be used for term-lending).

• As the development bank grows and acquires experience, it takes on imperatives of its own, as do all institutions. Among those imperatives is a need to continue to grow. Indeed, expansion may in some circumstances be an essential condition for survival; and it may require not simply doing more of what has been done, but doing new things. Another imperative is to provide an increasing number of career opportunities for the young staff the institution has helped develop.

Any of these circumstances (and others) can bring about significant changes in a development bank's business. Some specific cases of reorientation or change, already brought about or in progress, are described in the following paragraphs.

The Case of the Korea Development Finance Corporation

The Korea Development Finance Corporation (KDFC), a private development bank, was established in 1967. Its 1977 annual report announced:

> The nation's economy has experienced a great change since the Corporation was established. In order to adapt itself to such a change, it is believed that the time has come for the Corporation to review [the] current financial environment under which the Corporation pursues its corporate purposes and to study its future role as a financial institution in the rapidly developing industrial society. With a view to providing more diversified financial services to private enterprises, as well as securing a stable basis for mobilization of adequate financial resources, the Corporation has undertaken a special study to seek suitable ways for continuous self-development under the new environment with the favorable support of the government and the World Bank.

Behind this brief statement lay the following. There had been general approval of KDFC's ten-year record. Its performance had been satisfactory to shareholders from a financial point of view, and the company had had a demonstrably significant development impact. Nevertheless, looking ahead to the future, it saw prospects of eventual decline in its position in the economy. The general economic environment in which it operated had changed beyond recognition since KDFC was established. Exports had grown from about $250 million to more than $10 billion.[1] The composition of these exports had changed radically, as the structure of industry deepened and broadened. The nature and volume of industry's demand for capital and financial services changed correspondingly. Demand for domestic funds increased with the expanded availability of locally produced capital goods. Gross national product (GNP) rose from about $150 to $700 per capita. The spectacular growth of exports and the other economic changes which exports fueled had transformed Korea's economic and financial relations with the rest of the world.

At the same time, the financial sector of which KDFC was a part became more complex and more competitive. Once there had been five city banks, some ten provincial banks, and several special government banks (including two development banks). Now there were in addition twenty-one branches of foreign banks in Seoul with almost seventy branches or offices around the country, eleven short-term financial institutions, five merchant banks, several securities investment companies, three leasing companies, and various other capital market institutions. Some of these institutions were competing directly with KDFC. The relending of foreign exchange borrowed abroad was the major part (about 90 percent) of its business. Foreign exchange, however, had ceased to be a scarce commodity in Korea; it was readily available from other domestic and foreign financial institutions. Although KDFC had a competitive edge in the longer term it offered, the conditions related to its lending made other sources of finance more attractive to some clients. Moreover, the spread on KDFC's foreign exchange relending was dropping to the point where profitability was being affected. Unlike other types of financial institutions, KDFC was unable to mobilize domestic currency resources. Deposits were forbidden by law, and debentures were severely limited by legal restrictions, by the ceiling on KDFC's debt/equity ratio, and by their cost in current Korean conditions.

This assessment of its position and prospects led KDFC to conclude that, unless it could develop new sources of domestic finance and could compete with other institutions in providing the financial and other services required by Korean industry, its future would be quite limited. This prospect was not lost on its staff, whose ablest members could look to Korea's dynamic industrial and commercial enterprises for more remuneration, higher status, and better career prospects. In these circumstances, KDFC commenced the special study of its role referred to in its 1977 annual report.

A consensus was quick to emerge that an overall shift in KDFC's orientation was necessary. It had to transform itself as quickly as possible from an institution concentrated primarily on foreign exchange lending into a diversified multifaceted industrial bank, capable of offering the full spectrum of financial services and facilities to Korean industry, providing counsel as well as loan and risk capital, and flexible enough to adapt itself quickly to changing market conditions, both to the needs of industry and to the competitive situation.

A consensus is one thing, action is another. Studies were made and action was taken on a variety of aspects: the legal framework within which KDFC operates, to identify the need for changes; financial policies the government should adopt to encourage capital mobilization in the financial sector generally; the types of financial instruments KDFC would need to mobilize domestic resources; the corporation's charter, corporate activities, and policies with a view to laying a base for expansion and diversification; the equity base appropriate for a company so oriented; the internal organization and staffing required to enable KDFC to handle efficiently both new activities and a larger volume of activity, including the kind of staff called for by merchant banking.

KDFC's own conclusions were not sufficient to achieve the transformation that it sought. Prior decisions and actions were required by the government on many matters: to review and revise policies and laws affecting the mobilization of savings, their channeling into bank and nonbank financial institutions, and the structure of financial institutions required for efficient intermediation. KDFC therefore found it necessary to develop its views in close consultation with government. Other financial institutions also had an interest in the matter and were brought into the discussion. The underlying motivation was that the changes contemplated in law, in government policy, and in KDFC activities were essential to the country's continued economic development. Studies, discussions, and government consideration reached a climax in December 1979 when the National Assembly passed the Long-Term Credit Bank Act, which provided a new framework for KDFC activity. And in June

1980 KDFC was formally transformed into the Korea Long-Term Credit Bank.

The Case of the Industrial and Mining Development Bank of Iran

The Industrial and Mining Development Bank of Iran (IMDBI), a private institution, started up in the late 1950s, just as the Iranian government was beginning to accelerate its drive toward industrialization. It took a few years for IMDBI to get into full gear. By 1963 it was expanding aggressively, together with the Iranian economy generally. Its former managing director once called attention to IMDBI's luck in being on the spot and ready at the right time.

IMDBI was a key factor in the industrial expansion and diversification of Iran. Its contribution came, not simply through the provision of finance, but more important, through its promotional activities. In an environment with little entrepreneurial and managerial experience, IMDBI took the lead in defining new investment projects, bringing to the attention of the government the conditions needed to make financially attractive projects which seemed economically desirable, finding the partners and other elements needed to bring the new enterprises into existence, and sometimes taking the responsibility for their execution and operation, at least through an initial period. The companies in which it had an active organizational involvement numbered well over 100. In the process of this elaboration of its activity, IMDBI also became involved in the establishment of consultant services, other institutions related to the development of the capital market, educational facilities related to business, and a variety of peripheral activities required in a rapidly growing economy.

Such activities required an aggressive management and resourceful staff. But they depended on two other factors as well: one was a close and continuing dialogue with government, the second was adequate financial resources. IMDBI was able to call on the government for the resources it required and could obtain from the government special funds as an agent to provide an underpinning in particularly risky cases.

In due course, IMDBI perceived that many of its clients, and Iranian industry more generally, were finding it difficult to obtain short- and medium-term finance. Accordingly, IMDBI acquired a commercial bank, first to facilitate its own customers' access to working capital and then to serve a broader clientele. The expectation was that the functions of the two institutions would "efficiently complement one another and provide better service to the community and our clients." IMDBI's activities took it abroad as well, involving it in the creation of a joint Misr-Iran Development Bank in Cairo and a new consortium bank in London, whose main function was to syndicate loans for the Iranian government and for public and private Iranian corporations, including IMDBI itself.

From term finance to industrial promotion and management to diversified domestic banking to foreign banking to international banking—that was IMDBI's course over fifteen years. This course led the managing director, Abol Gasem Kheradjou, to pose a question in an address he made in New Delhi in 1975, a question not simply about his own institution but about development banks generally.

> Looking to the more distant future, it is perhaps a moot point when the developmental function of a financial institution might take a less dominant place as against its investment and merchant banking functions. We have to be ready for the day when this happens, as it happened perhaps to the Industrial Bank of Japan or some of the French banks. We feel that in the long run we should be working towards a fully integrated banking function, providing a full range of services with a number of closely affiliated banking institutions.

He referred to the acquisition of a commercial bank as a step toward the moment "when you cannot claim you are a development bank any more because you are providing a fully integrated banking [service], short-term, long-term, everything; then you become like *banques d'affaires* doing other business."

IMDBI rode the crest of the Iranian economic wave of the 1960s and the 1970s; indeed, it reinforced that wave, adding to its amplitude and force. Obviously, the story is not over; it remains to be seen how IMDBI will be transformed by the new circumstances in Iran, what old activities it will shed, and what new activities it will take on.

The Case of the Development Bank of Singapore

The Development Bank of Singapore (DBS) was established in July 1968 to take over the financing functions of the government's Economic Development Board. It came into existence as part of the institutional restructuring of government agencies deemed appropriate to the new strategy for Singapore's economic development. Government ownership amounted to just under half the share capital, and the government interest was clearly dominant. In the context of Singapore, however, although DBS was the chosen instrument for pursuing certain governmental objectives, it operated in direct competition with other institutions active in similar fields; indeed, its successes stimulated competition. In effect, it operated like a private enterprise.

DBS's charter was broadly framed, allowing it to go into term-financing, guarantees, equities, real estate, and commercial banking. But it was originally intended to focus on term-lending and equities in industry. As a matter of policy, it limited its commercial banking operations to its clients for development finance and even then provided it only when adequate facilities were not available from other sources. Within a year, however, it became engaged in commercial banking and real estate. By 1972 its policy restrictions on commercial banking were entirely removed. It was ready to make available all the services and facilities provided by other commercial banks and securities dealers operating in Singapore, subject to the same banking act and securities regulations that governed the others.

DBS was thus fully launched on the road to becoming a financial conglomerate. As DBS put it in a prospectus in March 1976, "the Bank has diversified its activities in order to complement and enhance its development financing activities and now has a substantial commercial banking business, conducts real property development activities, and offers insurance services, merchant banking, and related financial services both directly and through its subsidiaries and affiliates." It became deeply involved in underwriting, often as managing underwriter, especially in the field of Asian dollar bonds, in which it was a pioneer. Real estate operations included the building and management of office space and shopping centers, condominium housing, and downtown redevelopment. It offered clients "a wide range of technical and managerial consulting services," including advice and assistance at all stages in the planning and execution of investment projects, assistance in joint-venture and shareholder negotiations, and in the negotiation of purchasing and marketing agreements. It became, in effect, a "universal bank."

The basis of this rapid transformation of DBS is to be found primarily in a shift in government policy just as DBS started up operation. DBS was conceived as part of the development strategy of the government of Singapore in the late 1960s, following the separation of that city-state from Malaysia and the decision to transform

Singapore into an export-based manufacturing center. The government provided aggressive leadership and overall direction, while permitting a relatively freely operating economy. DBS was to be a principal stimulator for the expansion of industrial activities, but by the time it had fully opened its doors, the outlines of a new development strategy were beginning to be drawn and by 1971–72 had taken shape. The new emphasis was to be not primarily on export-oriented, labor-intensive manufacturing, although efforts in that direction were to continue. The drive was to be toward making Singapore a "regional center" for "brain services and brain service industries" (in the words of the finance minister). The development of Singapore as a financial center for the entire region assumed a priority even higher than that enjoyed by export competitiveness. So also did the construction of the urban physical and institutional infrastructure that the development of such a center required.

DBS became a flexible institution acting as leader and example for other financial institutions, both domestic and foreign, in responding to the new orientation of government development policy. Although DBS received important support from the government, particularly in the form of financial resources, it was required to work competitively with other financial institutions, providing them with a model of what could be done in the development of new services, without special privileges from the government.

DBS's transformation was not a simple adaptation to environmental changes or to government policy. DBS took its general marching orders from the government, which held almost half its shares. What is notable in the case of DBS, however, is that it was required to march together with any competing institutions that emerged under the same policy impetus.

The Case of the Industrial Development Bank of India

The Refinance Corporation for Industry, Ltd. was created in the mid-1950s by the Reserve Bank of India. Its function was to encourage the commercial banks to make medium- and long-term loans to industry. In 1964 the Industrial Development Bank of India (IDBI) was created as a wholly owned subsidiary of the Reserve Bank. It took over the operations of the Refinance Corporation. It was also given the responsibility for financing, promoting, and developing industry generally and for providing finance to, and coordinating the working of, other industrial financing institutions in the country. It thus became an "apex development bank." In 1976 ownership of IDBI was transferred from the Reserve Bank to the central government, without, however, changing its mandate in any significant respect.

In its initial years, IDBI's main activity was the provision of direct assistance to large industrial projects promoted by private entrepreneurs and support to other financial institutions through refinance facilities and subscription to their share capital and bond issues. But it soon expanded the scope of its operations well beyond these limits. In 1965–66, when domestic machinery manufacturers started to experience marketing difficulties because of recession, IDBI introduced rediscounting facilities for sales of machinery on deferred payment terms. This allowed indigenous machinery manufacturers to offer credit terms similar to those offered by foreign suppliers. In 1969 IDBI decided to meet the needs of term finance for expansion projects undertaken by industrial concerns in the public sector, which did not seek support from the government's budget for their financial requirements, except for share capital increases.

IDBI also went into the field of export financing. Initially, it refinanced medium-term export credits granted by commercial banks. Direct loans for large contracts for the export of capital goods were introduced around 1970. Subsequently, IDBI started granting direct credits to overseas buyers and financial institutions to enable them to import Indian capital goods.

About the same time, IDBI expanded into a new promotional activity—technoeconomic surveys of backward regions and the preparation of feasibility reports on project proposals identified by these surveys. These tasks were generally undertaken in conjunction with other financial institutions, with the leadership of the group varying from one area to another. In 1972 IDBI began to establish regional consultancy organizations (there are now nine), taking a 51 percent interest, while the rest was divided among other financial entities. When a substantial number of industrial enterprises fell into difficulty in 1970–71 because of labor and other problems, IDBI took the initiative of forming the Industrial Reconstruction Corporation (as its subsidiary) for the resurrection of such enterprises.

Although IDBI is a statutory corporation, whose board and chief executive are appointed by the government, its rapid expansion of old functions and assumption of new activities have been largely the result of its own initiative: the effect, not of specific directives from government, but of a firmly aggressive pursuit of its broad mandate under the law.

Three African Cases

Three African development banks confronted the question of expansion into commercial banking and reacted in quite different ways.

The Banque Ivoirienne de Développement Industriel (BIDI) was created in 1964 to provide medium- and long-term finance to industry. Loans were supposed to be for periods of more than one year, but with stress on loans for five years and longer. BIDI could take limited deposits from its long-term clients but did not do so to any significant extent.

In 1975 the Central Bank of the West African States (which serves the six member countries of the West African Monetary Union) introduced certain banking reforms to increase credit to priority sectors by providing incentives to commercial banks to increase the volume and extend the terms of their lending. In particular, the Central Bank increased to ten years the period for which it would rediscount loans for all banks. At the same time, development banks were allowed to accept deposits, lend on short term, open checking accounts, and provide a full range of commercial facilities. The effect of this reform was to establish an incentive for commercial banks to extend significantly the duration of their lending and to put development banks and commercial banks in direct competition with each other. True, commercial banks would have to develop some medium- and long-term resources so that they would not have to rely entirely on rediscount facilities, and would have to develop staffs capable of assessing medium- and long-term investments. But the pressures were such that commercial banks were expected to move in this direction.

The potential effect of these reforms was not lost on BIDI. It was clear that BIDI might well lose some of its long-term lending business, an event that could affect its profitability. It could compensate for this possibility by increasing its short-term lending and other commercial banking activities and by developing the deposit base such activity required. BIDI faced this prospect with some trepidation, however. Taking deposits and providing the full range of commercial facilities would involve radically new activities for which its management felt BIDI lacked adequate expertise, and which would call for changes in its charter and policies. However reluctantly, BIDI's management began to move in this direction, seeking to expand and prepare its staff to undertake the new activity within its existing corporate structure.

The National Investment Bank of Ghana (NIB) was established in 1963 as a statutory corporation. Its business was the conventional development banking business of identifying investment opportunities, encouraging participation of internal and external capital in Ghanaian enterprise, and providing medium- and long-term capital. Its operations remained largely limited to such activities until 1975.

Under the impetus of a new chief executive, NIB commenced commercial banking operations in April 1975 as a service to its term-loan clients. It required that all customers receiving term loans open a commercial account in NIB, an arrangement that was designed to assure its clients ready access to working capital, to improve its knowledge of its customers' operations, and to facilitate the recovery of arrears. Both deposits and short-term credit grew rapidly in the next few years. By 1977 NIB's commercial activities yielded more than a third of gross profit and about two-thirds of profit after appropriation, even though the commercial portfolio was only one-fourth as large as the term portfolio. In 1978 NIB began extending its commercial operations to its regional offices; it also began to extend commercial credits to new clients in the hope of developing term-lending business subsequently. In this case, the addition of a new function resulted from a wish to serve normal clients, a search for new business, and an aggressive desire for profit.

The government of Mauritius and the Development Bank of Mauritius (DBM), which was wholly owned by the government, jointly promoted the State Commercial Bank (SCB) in 1973. This action was taken because the sponsors believed that small-scale entrepreneurs did not have adequate access to working capital and a new institution was required to fill the gap. DBM's shareholding in SCB, originally 10 percent, was raised in early 1978 to 25 percent. Even this increased share in ownership does not adequately reflect the extremely close working relation that has developed between the two institutions. For small and medium-size enterprises, SCB provides working capital and DBM takes care of term needs. SCB also participates in term loans granted by DBM for large projects. There is close cooperation between the two institutions in liquidity management. For practical purposes, these are two close affiliates, working in harness, though they are legally separate entities.

Unlike the development banks in the Ivory Coast and Ghana, DBM decided to set up its commercial banking operation in a separate entity, because it felt that the mixture of the two functions in the same institution would divert attention from DBM's more fundamental task of term-lending.

Preparations for Change

Obviously, development banks, like other enterprises and institutions, reorient and redefine their tasks. The shifts in strategy and activity in the cases cited resulted from management aggressiveness in pursuit of new business or furtherance of a "development mandate," changed circumstances in the economy, evaluation of the development bank's own experience, or some combination of these factors. Another source of reorientation, not illustrated here, is direct pressure from government to pursue certain lines of activity; few development banks have not experienced such pressure.

Nothing need be said about the first element, management aggressiveness. No single factor is so important to producing an innovative and dynamic bank as an aggressive and dynamic chief executive; the two generally go together. It behooves a group of shareholders or a government to choose a chief executive carefully—and a chief executive, to give particular care to the selection (and, if possible, the preparation) of his successor. A chief executive does not usually have control over the choice of his successor and generally has little direct influence over him. But to the extent that he can groom a successor, and let that successor emerge as a personality in his own right, he can have an influence on his institution's future far beyond his own tenure.

As for the other principal factors, a development bank needs to establish for itself appropriate mechanisms for keeping its own experience and the economic environment under continuing review. This may seem obvious and simple, but it is neither. For one thing, it is possible for a development bank, like any other institution, to forgo the difficult process of self-analysis and self-criticism, knowing that sooner or later the results of external criticism and of changes in the external situation will be brought to its attention. But to await external pressures before modifying its directions and strategy is risky: it might then be too late; it might have lost its support or find itself unable to meet the competition, which will inevitably emerge, and be unprepared to cope with the new tasks forced upon it. Prudence suggests that a development bank explore the lessons of its own experience early and continuously and that it try to anticipate changes in the economy and in government policy. To do this requires a deliberate, self-conscious effort.

As for learning from its own experience, in a sense, a development bank does this every day. A project runs into difficulty, or several of them in the same industrial sector experience a similar problem. The development bank probes the reasons, feeds the results back to those responsible for appraisal, and tries both to correct the existing situation and to guard against its recurrence. Follow-up of specific investments and the uses of the results thereof have been objects of the attention of development banks from their earliest days. But what has not been so common is a critical review of the results of the development bank's overall activity against the background of its own basic purpose and its strategy for accomplishing that purpose. Such a comparison is vital.

It has already been noted that some shareholders and some creditors may be content with a sound portfolio and a financially satisfactory record of operation; but other shareholders and other creditors will not and are likely also to ask: Is the broad corporate goal being accomplished? If not, why not? What needs to be done to further it? The government may be concerned only with achievement of certain policy objectives. The board, management, and staff of a development bank are likely to be concerned with the development bank's prospects for continued growth as an autonomous decisionmaking entity, which in turn are related not only to its financial viability, but also to its demonstrated contribution to underlying corporate goals. The viewpoints of government, shareholders, board, creditors, management, and staff are all somewhat different but overlapping—not exactly the same, but reconcilable.

A principal job of management is to produce that reconciliation. Each chief executive will do so in his fashion. But he can do so only if his judgment is informed by responses to such questions as:

- Do the overall effects of the individual projects financed by the development bank further the basic purpose of the bank?
- What noninvestment activities have contributed to achievement of its purpose?
- What internal or external factors have limited that achievement? How can they be overcome?

- Are the development bank's policies and procedures effective in promoting their achievement? Does experience suggest any change in them or in the institution's activities?

Outsiders will continually ask these questions, especially if they have a direct stake in the success of the development bank. They will also ask: Are the resources made available being used effectively? Is the development bank doing a "good" job? Prudent management will be no less concerned with such questions and will not wish to rely on occasional ad hoc reviews; and it will try to develop a mechanism for continuing appraisal, not only of the overall financial results of the development bank's operations, but also of the total effect of the institution. Where to locate such a mechanism administratively, whom to make responsible for it, and how to ensure that its results receive adequate attention are questions with which management must deal.

Self-evaluation may be a painful process, for it carries connotations of praise or blame. Keeping a finger on the pulse of the country—scanning the economic environment, so to speak—will be less painful. It, too, calls for continuing effort. Intelligence gathering at the association of manufacturers or even from friends in the Ministry of Planning will perhaps be useful for day-to-day decisionmaking on detailed issues, but it is likely to be casual and discontinuous, and therefore inadequate for the substantial and intensive assessment of prospective economic conditions. This does not necessarily mean that every development bank needs an economic staff. It does mean, however, that the manager should have ready access to reliable persons who can take responsibility for systematically keeping him informed of economic developments and changes in government policy, which are likely to have a long-range effect on the development bank's activities.

Devising alternative economic scenarios for a year or two ahead is an essential part of the budget process. But long-range forecasting of economic prospects is no less essential for reviewing corporate strategies and reorienting its activities. As already suggested, slowness in visualizing the trend of events is likely to result in the emergence of more dynamic institutions better suited to the new circumstances, and thus in the decline of the development bank.

Some Implications of Changing Activities

One observation that emerges from the previous discussion is that, as the economy in which it operates grows, a development bank is likely to become only one of a group of financial institutions providing specialized services. This should not be surprising. With the growing size and complexity of an economy, especially if it grows rapidly, there is demand not simply for a large volume of capital but for new kinds of services as well. The demand stimulates efforts to provide such services, sometimes by existing institutions diversifying their activity, sometimes by new entities created to serve the new needs. In such an environment, a development bank finds itself forced to diversify.

One question that confronts a manager who contemplates moving into new lines of activity is whether new functions should be carried on within the framework of the existing corporate structure or established in separate corporate entities. For instance, in the Industrial Credit and Investment Corporation of India, a merchant banking operation has been set up as a department within the institution itself; by contrast, the Korean Development Bank has joined with other institutions to establish a separate merchant banking company. The Development Bank of Singapore is deeply involved in the full range of commercial banking services and, indeed, sometimes rejects the characterization of development bank even though those words appear in its name, while the Industrial Mining and Development Bank of Iran, when it decided its clients needed readier access to working capital, chose to acquire an existing commercial bank. Nevertheless, both DBS and IMDBI became, in effect, financial conglomerates. Most development banks, plagued with enterprises in trouble of one kind or another, build up intensive care units within the framework of their normal follow-up activity. The Industrial Development Bank of India chose to establish a subsidiary for this purpose because of its concern that the seriously "sick" cases would not receive adequate attention in the regular organization. The National Investment Bank of Ghana went into commercial banking because of its wish to develop new business and to enhance its profitability and did so within the existing corporate structure; but the Development Bank of Mauritius, seeing the unfilled needs of its small-scale clients for working capital, preferred to share in creating a new commercial bank.

Obviously, many factors will determine the framework within which a development bank will carry out new activities. Among them are: the effect of taxation, especially in the case of a privately owned development bank; the availability of adequately trained staff for the new functions and the likelihood that they will receive the attention they need in the light of the staff's other preoccupations; and management itself—not all chief executives will be comfortable in accepting responsibility for radically new lines of activity with which they are not personally familiar. Obviously, the organizational, managerial, and staff implications of both expansion and diversification need to be explored with care before explicit decisions regarding them are made.

Where Does a Development Bank Fit in a More Complex Economy? A Speculation

Attention is drawn again to the comment of IMDBI's managing director that the diversification of his institution might well approach the point at which it could no longer reasonably be called a development bank. His comment, as well as the evidence of the cases cited, suggests the possibility that, at a certain moment in the economic growth of a country, development banking in the sense in which it is generally used may cease to have any special significance. At some point, the financial sector may offer a variety of institutions, each of them serving a useful purpose. Among them are savings banks, commercial banks, long-term credit institutions, venture capital companies, institutions providing advisory financial services, others dealing with the needs of specific target groups, institutions dealing with various other aspects of the capital market—all of them involved in mobilizing resources from some individuals and entities and transferring them to others. Each has its special functions. In that context, a development bank may cease to have the importance it now enjoys; it will be one useful institution among many. Indeed, it is likely to have had to adopt new strategies which may lead it, on the one hand, in the direction of "universal banking," or, on the other hand, to spinning off independent or affiliated specialized financial institutions. In such a context, a development bank manager will see his institution taking on a new identity. His institution's function is determined, after all, not simply by the will of the owners, but by the total environment in which it operates. If the latter changes, the former will too.

In such a situation interest will focus, not on one institution that provides a particular service (term capital), but on the ways in which the many financial institutions can be influenced to provide the diverse services needed for economic growth and social development. What will be important is that the financial institutions provide efficiently the services the community requires. Governments and central banks are in a position to encourage and to influence those activities toward socially useful purposes.

Some institutions that provide financing for development banks recognize the diversity of services a growing financial sector demands and are willing to provide financing for various institutions. The World Bank Group, for instance, and the International Finance Corporation in particular, have for a decade provided assistance to development banks engaged in mixed banking and in financing several sectors or several different target groups. More important, however, the group has become active in financing specialized institutions. It has promoted and financed short-term credit institutions, securities investment companies, venture capital companies, leasing companies, investment management companies, and mortgage banks; and insurance companies are on its early agenda. This is a far cry from the development banks on which the group concentrated until a decade ago.

In the context of a financial sector that is becoming more diversified and complex, providing capital and services for development calls for promoting the establishment of *all* varieties of financial institutions a developing country requires and encouraging and assisting them to provide the services required of them. It may be of greater interest, then, to focus attention, not on development banks, but on developmental finance.

Note to Chapter 3

1. Here, $1 billion equals $1,000 million.

Part III

Economic and Social Evaluation of Projects

FINANCING INVESTMENT PROJECTS is central to the activity of a development bank. The criteria it uses for making its investment decisions are therefore critical to the achievement of its objectives. The criteria of a conventional financial institution are oriented toward the health of the enterprise being financed, the profit of its equity holders, and the protection of its creditors. The techniques of appraising projects using these criteria involve no mysteries, and the older and more experienced banks have become quite skilled in doing so. But these criteria do not necessarily further the development objectives of a nation, which are also the objectives of a development bank, hence, the search for methods of economic evaluation, by which to measure the economic return of the project to the nation as opposed to its financial return to the project's owners. In more recent years this search has resulted in the emphasis on social evaluation to measure the social equity of the investment. Unfortunately, the methodology of economic and social evaluation is not universally agreed. Indeed, various methodologies are used, which are the subject of continuing debate. Moreover, there is no universal acceptance of the rationale for, the need for, or the desirability of, economic and social evaluation of investment projects. Such evaluation is often considered excessively complicated because of the lack of the data required to adjust a project's financial returns to reflect its effect on the economy or on income distribution. In addition, many people consider it the responsibility of government to provide the policy framework for sound industrial development and, if government has done so, a development bank need not go beyond conventional financial analysis.

Despite these criticisms, an increasing number of development banks are trying to apply economic analysis to their investment proposals. Under pressure from national governments and from international creditor institutions, they go beyond the traditional economic appraisal, which consisted of a pro forma reference to a government priority and an estimate of the number of jobs to be created or of the foreign exchange to be saved or earned. Instead, they are attempting a more sophisticated economic analysis, which permits a comparison of the costs and benefits expected of a project and lays a basis, therefore, for deciding what is acceptable from a national viewpoint and what is not.

The following papers deal with both issues referred to above—the methodology and the rationale. The first, by V. V. Bhatt, concerns economic evaluation. The second, by F. Leslie C. H. Helmers, starts from economic analysis but proceeds to social analysis to determine the effects on income distribution. Both these papers relate economic and social evaluation to the development bank's underlying function of helping to further the nation's development objectives. The third paper, also by Helmers, deals with the kind of concrete problem that might face any development bank in its daily business. In the case he discusses, cost-benefit analysis is used in appraising a proposal to establish rice-processing and handling facilities in Indonesia, to choose which among several different technologies would best serve both economic efficiency and social justice.

Three points are worth stressing. The first concerns the distinction often drawn between national welfare, which economic analysis is designed to measure, and the welfare of the firm, which financial analysis conventionally measures. These tend to be considered quite different, if not in outright conflict. In fact, the line is not quite so sharp. For instance, quite aside from development objectives, both the client and the financier have much to gain from economic evaluation. Strictly as a financial institution, a development bank seeks to build up a balanced portfolio that avoids excessive risk. Economic analysis illuminates the link between the financial viability of a project and such government policies (always subject to change) as import restrictions, exchange rates, and tax or other privileges. Explicit knowledge of the dependence of the project on specific government policy instruments is also vitally important to the enterprise and to its owners. Both the owner and the creditor must be prepared to react to various possible scenarios in which, for one reason or another, the government decides to abandon or to change the instruments on which viability depends.

The second point is that economic evaluation may indeed indicate which projects are acceptable from a national viewpoint. Its principal use, however, is not to screen but rather to improve the design of projects. As the following papers make clear, economic evaluation can point the way to changes in the project, in capacity or factor proportions or technology, which would increase the project's (or the enterprise's) efficiency. Or it may point to inefficiencies resulting from government policies, and when these are discovered it may be possible to persuade the government to make such changes in policy or in its administration as will justify appropriate changes in the project itself.

Third, both economic and social objectives are complex, and benefit-cost analysis cannot capture all the indirect benefits of a project. Thus, taking account of the differential effects of a project on the income of various social classes does not tell the whole story. A development bank's decisions may have other beneficial social effects. The bank might focus particular attention on bringing new persons into the entrepreneurial class; it might seek to alleviate regional disparities; it might wish to promote small-scale enterprises, or provide special assistance to small industrialists so that they can rise in the social hierarchy. Such activities provide social benefits; but they are not necessarily fully reflected, or even reflected at all, in a benefit-cost ratio.

If the full potential of economic and social analysis is understood, the government, the entrepreneur, and the development bank will all stand to gain. That potential rests not in using it to separate "good" from "bad" projects. It consists primarily in using it to make bad projects good and good ones better and to evaluate economic policies by showing how they actually affect enterprises. If economic evaluation is to be effective in project design, it needs to be brought to bear at a very early stage of project preparation. If it is to be effective in influencing government, a development bank must establish a relationship of mutual respect with those who plan and administer economic policy.

Chapter 4

On a Development Bank's Selection Criteria for Industrial Projects

V. V. BHATT

IT IS DIFFICULT to make any choice without a clear understanding of the criteria and of the various alternatives from which a choice is to be made. This implies a meaningful and clear presentation of the alternatives. The choice criteria depend on the objectives one seeks, and the alternatives depend on the implications of various feasible courses of action. If the objectives are clearly perceived and can be quantified and combined into a single quantitative measure, and if the information relating to all the feasible courses of action is perfect and can also be expressed quantitatively, and hence in terms of the choice criteria, the choice would be simple, and the selection process mechanical; there would be no managerial problem.

Reality is different, however. The objectives might not be clear, and some might not be quantifiable or measurable. Further, the relative significance of the various objectives changes with time and circumstances, and the objectives may not be independent of the information about alternative courses of action. This information can never be perfect because not only is the future uncertain and unknowable, but also information relating to the present as well as the past is always incomplete.[1] Thus the decisionmaking process becomes complex, and the appropriateness of a specific decision depends on the ability of decisionmaking organs to respond creatively to the challenge for action (see chapter 2).

It is not possible to rely merely on mechanical rules or criteria, techniques or tools, formulas or standards, all of which are related

This article was reprinted from *Economic Development and Cultural Change*, vol. 25, no. 4 (July 1977), pp. 639–55, by permission of The University of Chicago Press.

to the past—of which there is no complete understanding—since decisionmaking relates to the present and the unknowable future. Instead, to make a correct decision—as it appears at the time, for no decision can be perfect—requires both analysis of data and perception of the total process of change in the data and its direction.

In this chapter, the problem of selection criteria for industrial projects, as it relates to development banks, is posed and discussed. First, the social objectives that need to be incorporated in the choice criteria are indicated. Second, the techniques of devising and applying choice criteria of different degrees of refinement are described. Third, the choice criteria that seem to be relevant for a large number of industrial projects likely to be supported by a development bank are indicated. Fourth, the type of economic analysis that is essential even before attempting the task of economic evaluation is discussed, and fifth, the primary purpose of economic evaluation—providing a development perspective and orientation to development banks—is indicated.

Development Objectives and Choice Criteria

The choice criteria of a development bank must indeed have a direct relation with the development objectives of a country. A development bank cannot act like a normal commercial bank; it has no raison d'être unless it seeks to promote industrial development consistent with the country's development objectives. Hence, it cannot judge the soundness of a project merely on the basis of its ability to service its debt to the development bank. Doubtless a project should be financially sound in this sense, for unless it can service its debt the development bank itself would not remain a viable institution. But at the same time, a project should be consistent with development objectives, otherwise a development bank would not be able to contribute to the development process of the country. If projects that are sound from *both* these points of view are not available, it is the function of a development bank to take the initiative, in cooperation with other related agencies. Institutional and other policies need to be changed to make projects that are economically sound (supporting development objectives) also financially viable and to facilitate the identification and formulation of such projects.

But then the question arises of how to define the economic soundness of a project. Obviously it must be related to development objectives; but this poses another question: What are the development objectives, and which of these objectives are relevant for a development bank? In the first instance, it is necessary to pinpoint the development objectives of a country. Are they the objectives indicated by the government in its development plans or other documents? This question is important because some objectives perform, to use Bagehot's expression, a "ceremonial" function, while some others perform the "efficient" function. Quite often the declared objectives have merely a ceremonial function, while the efficient objectives are seldom announced and have to be inferred from the development strategy and policies that are actually—explicitly or implicitly—formulated by the government. In such a case, the task of a development bank becomes difficult. If the ceremonial and efficient objectives are different, a development bank can and should point out the difference and indicate, on the basis of concrete evidence at its disposal—the implication of actual industrial projects that are completed or under implementation—the strategy and policies that need to be pursued to attain the declared objectives. But if in spite of this evidence the government consciously maintains this difference, a development bank has no alternative but to conduct its operations according to efficient objectives while at the same time continuing to perform the educative function of pinpointing the implications of the actual departure from the ceremonial objectives. Thus, in operation what is relevant for a development bank is the development strategy of the government as expressed in concrete policies and action programs.

To discuss in more concrete terms the implications of this divergence between ceremonial and efficient objectives, one might take the case of the objective of social justice. The only effective way of promoting this objective is through productive employment of the available labor force. Since a greater part of this labor force is already "employed" in the traditional sectors—agriculture, rural industries, rural transport, and other related occupations—it is essential to improve progressively the technological base of these traditional sectors in such a manner as to raise labor productivity as well as real incomes of the potentially employable labor force. The development of the "modern" sectors, in this case, has to be consistent with this strategy and actually subserve its objectives. There must be an organic relation between the growth of the traditional and modern sectors for ensuring full employment at rising levels of productivity and real incomes.[2]

In a case like this, it is the development strategy and the related policies themselves that seek to promote social justice, and the choice criteria of industrial projects must ensure the most efficient way of increasing the supply of scarce resources. The scarcest resources are capital (saving), foreign exchange, and labor with skills of various kinds. But if no attempt is made to improve the technological base of the traditional sectors through an active and relevant technology policy—and this cannot be done by mere imitation of foreign technology—the objective of social justice loses its significance, and any attempt to incorporate it in the choice criteria for industrial projects by assigning different weights to the incomes of different socioeconomic groups would merely result in the inefficient allocation of scarce resources that would make them even scarcer. Social justice, of course, would not be attained, and other development objectives would also remain unfulfilled.

Similarly, the objective of increasing employment and thus improving income distribution by incorporating shadow wages in the choice criteria of industrial projects implies a certain technology policy as an integral part of a development strategy. But to increase employment through this device, there should be various technological choices available. If technology is imported, it should be adapted and modified, if possible, to suit the resource structure of the country. This requires the ability to ask meaningful questions of foreign consultants about various technological choices, which is not possible without a degree of indigenous technological competence in the fields of engineering as well as technological research. Without such competence, the actual choices at the project design stage would be made merely on the basis of technology in use in developed countries, and these choices by and large would be unaffected by the magnitude of shadow wage rates selected for deriving the choice criteria. On this subject, the observations of Little and Mirrlees are very relevant:

> A large number of economic choices will have been made already, either at the level of the initiating department, commission, or other decentralized public authority, or by the designing engineers . . . Now industrial engineers—good ones, anyway—are economists, but they are not usually the kind of economists who are trained to look at matters from the point of view of the economy as a whole. They will, or should, have profitability very much in mind. But they will, of course, assess profitability in the light of actual prices.
>
> The value of . . . choosing from a list of projects according to a criterion using accounting prices, supposed to reflect real scarcities and benefits better than actual prices, is clearly reduced if

each such project has in effect been chosen from a long list of variants by a criterion (profitability) which uses actual prices. For instance, if it is desirable to put stress on employment by using a low accounting price for labour, then clearly this stress should take effect at the level of project design and not merely at the level of final project selection. Indeed, it may be at the former level that a low accounting price for labour would have its main effect . . .

Of course, the sheer unfamiliarity will make for difficulty at first . . . Where outside, especially foreign, firms of consultant engineers are involved, the difficulties may be greater. First, their psychological objection to accounting prices may be stronger as a result of private enterprise laissez-faire training, which does not sufficiently admit the possible divergence of social and private interest. Secondly, they generally have something to sell, which has usually been evolved in the light of actual prices. Designs are not all made afresh, from the bottom up, for the project in hand . . .

Only very few western firms appear to have made any effort to adapt their designs to the different scarcities prevailing in developing countries . . . Sometimes, indeed, the plant which western engineers design for a developing country is more "modern," i.e., capital intensive potentially labour saving—than anything that exists in their own country. There are two obstacles to overcoming the problem. The first, and possibly most important, is often the lack of an informed and critical client, determined to get a plant which will be very profitable . . .

For the reasons given, it may not be easy to get foreign engineers to adapt . . . However, it must be admitted, when everything in favour of accounting prices has been said, that communication between . . . departments, etc.; between departmental administrators and engineers and scientists; and between the local client and the foreign firms is easier in terms of (predicted) actual prices.

For this reason, it is always better to try to make actual prices realistic, whether it be by refraining from malign governmental interference with the price mechanism, or whether it be by benign governmental "doctoring" of the price mechanism. Although this may not always be possible, it is certainly best to keep the use of accounting prices as limited as possible.[3]

What then should one say about such refinement of choice criteria, which might make little or no sense to the decisionmaker on the one hand and to the project designer on the other?

Again, it is not merely a question of the project designer's using accounting prices for making technological choices. Even if he does use them, the range of choice is usually limited to alternatives already in use in the developed countries, especially with regard to the core processes and products: the choice is wider for processes related to materials handling and other auxiliary operations.[4] Of course this does not mean that there are no additional alternative core processes and products even within the range of modern technology.[5] These alternatives, however, can be known only as a result of active search through an appropriate method of language that is "intentionally more general than the ones used in engineers' process flow sheets; it is rather similar to the language used in the laboratory stage."[6]

Identification of alternatives open for choice and possibilities for adaptations would not go very far unless given packages of technology could be broken down into various components or modules; and in so doing, one ought to go beyond those best-practiced technologies on the shelf, giving open-minded reconsideration to discarded laboratory results, as well as to technologies now considered obsolete by today's major industrial concerns. Quite a few exercises exist showing that there are in fact hundreds of alternative process design possibilities for a given product line, even in industries with relatively continuous processes. An information-intensive and brain-intensive "unpacking" effort could thus rediscover nearly continuous stretches of the neo-classical economist's isoquant. It appears that the concept of "modules," which facilitates such unpacking and innovative adaptation of industrial technology, deserves further exploration for the benefit of R and D planning and related information service policy on LDCs.[7]

Thus the use of accounting prices would not, indeed cannot, produce the results desired, without an active technology policy to upgrade traditional technology and adapt modern technology to the resource structure and stage of development of the developing countries. Thus the first priority in any development strategy should be the development of relevant technological competence and not mere refinement of appraisal criteria for industrial projects; the latter is irrelevant and meaningless without the former.[8]

The use of accounting prices, again, cannot remove "distortions" caused by institutional rigidities. In a backward area, one might take a low shadow wage rate for unskilled labor to try to improve income distribution; but if the required labor is not available be-

cause appropriate changes have not been in agricultural organization or because institutional factors keep labor immobile, the low
shadow wage has no meaning since it would not result in increased
employment. Similarly, the use of accounting prices would not
produce the desired results if the financial structure were biased
toward urban and metropolitan areas and modern industries.[9]
Again, without an appropriate development of the infrastructure—
transport and marketing, education and health, technical and managerial assistance, credit institutions, and the like—the choices
indicated and desired by the use of accounting prices would prove
infructuous.[10]

Choice Criteria Based on International Prices: Analytic Basis and Techniques

A development bank thus needs to evolve choice criteria consistent with overall development strategy and policies. Since social
justice or an income-distribution objective can only be attained
through an appropriate development strategy, as indicated earlier,
the major emphasis of a development bank must be on the efficient
use of scarce resources. For many countries, the scarcest resources
are saving, foreign exchange, skilled manpower, and entrepreneurial and managerial talents. From an economy's point of view, it is
thus essential to concentrate on initiating a process of efficient
allocation and on creating these scarce resources.[11]

In the case of countries where the major scarce resources are
skilled manpower and entrepreneurial and managerial talents, it is
quite likely that a conflict may arise between the requirements of
efficient resource allocation and efficient resource creation. Import
controls and high tariff rates are in essence a reflection of this
conflict, and since resource creation in these fields is of paramount
significance for generating a self-sustaining process of development, and since it depends critically on on-the-job learning and
experience, these external economies of projects need to be taken
into account in devising choice criteria. These benefits are real and
substantial, even though they may not be quantifiable. Nevertheless, since a greater part of these benefits are broadly common to all
industrial projects, it may not be necessary to take them into
account while judging the worthwhileness of a specific project. But
there may be particular cases of projects in backward areas or
relating to new fields—in terms of technology, product, or manage-

ment—where these benefits may be specific to individual projects, and in such cases they need to be taken into account—of course on the basis of well-informed, sound judgment and not mere wishful thinking and prejudice.

Quantifiable costs and benefits are external to the project but arise as a result of the project and need to be explicitly taken into account. Generally the most effective way is to treat vitally inter-related projects as a single project complex. A development bank is usually faced with a single project or project complex. It does not have a large number of projects at a time from which it can choose on the basis of its selection criteria. Hence, it has to devise criteria for accepting or rejecting a single project. This implies that it should have well-formulated cutoff points on which acceptance or rejection can be based.

In the industrial field, the real choice is between domestic production and imports. If a product can be imported at a cost lower than that of domestic production, then prima facie it may not be worth producing at home. The question then is how to compare domestic costs with import costs, particularly when domestic prices are out of line with international prices because of certain economic policies. In this case, the simplest procedure is to express all domestic costs in terms of international prices; since the comparison is in terms of an identical measure, or yardstick, it is valid.[12]

Domestic cost can be split into cost of tradable goods (and services) and cost of nontradable goods (and services). For tradable goods, it should be possible in principle to obtain the import c.i.f. prices. For inputs that are imported, there is no problem; for inputs domestically purchased but tradable, it might not be difficult to obtain import c.i.f. prices, particularly if a country imports these inputs even to some extent. For nontradable inputs such as construction, power, transport, and trade, their cost structure can in principle be broken down in terms of cost of tradable inputs and cost of nontradable inputs such as unskilled labor. In principle, the only nontradable inputs would be unskilled labor and raw land; the wage rate for unskilled labor would consist largely of what workers consume (mainly tradable goods) and hence can be expressed in international prices. Raw land will have alternative uses, and this opportunity cost of raw land can be translated into international prices through the use of a shadow exchange rate. For these non-tradable inputs, the valuation procedure can be simplified by using appropriate conversion factors; that is, domestic prices can be multiplied by a conversion factor (multiplier) that expresses a general relation between international prices and domestic costs and is based on a sample study of sectors such as construction, power, and transport. The use of such conversion factors, if available, would simplify the valuation problem. In cases for which even this is not possible, a shadow exchange rate can be used for the purpose—this in fact reflects a general economy-wide relation between international and domestic prices.

It may be emphasized that the unit of account can be either local currency or any foreign currency. It would be easier and simpler to use local currency as a unit of account since this would allow all international prices to be expressed in local currency at the official exchange rate. This exchange rate has no other significance, and any exchange rate (even other than the official one) is good enough for the purpose, as long as it is consistently used.

Once the cost and benefit streams are derived in international prices over time—for a period inclusive of the gestation lag and project life, normally twenty to twenty-five years—the yield of a project can be expressed by its internal rate of return. This internal rate of return, usually called the economic rate of return, can then be compared with the cutoff rate of return, which for many countries would be within the range of 15 to 20 percent a year. The cutoff rate can be determined on the basis of the actual experience of industrial projects—a rough average of the rate of return realized in the case of existing viable industrial projects. It can also be derived on the basis of the growth target for industrial output and certain assumptions with regard to saving (plowing back) in relation to gross benefits. If the target rate for the growth of industrial output is 10 percent a year and industrial investment constitutes 50 percent of the gross return (that is, 50 percent of the gross return is used for consumption), the rate of return on industrial projects should be 20 percent.

Let industrial output be expressed as Y, gross returns as P, total capital as K, the proportion of gross returns plowed back into investment as s, investment as I, and rate of growth of industrial output as g. Then $\Delta Y = I \cdot Y/K$, where Y/K is the inverse of the capital coefficient. This can be expressed as:

$$\Delta Y = sP \cdot \frac{Y}{K},$$

therefore

$$\Delta \frac{Y}{Y} = s \cdot \frac{P}{Y} \cdot \frac{Y}{K}, \text{ and}$$

$$g = sr,$$

where r is the rate of return, P/K. If $s = 0.5$ and $g = 0.10$, $r = 0.10/0.50$ or 20 percent.

For calculation of this economic rate of return, all taxes and subsidies are ignored, being merely transfer payments, and the financing pattern is also of no significance from the economy's point of view. But if foreign capital is involved (for financing imports) and is specific to the project (if it is not specific, it should be treated as a cost item, since, in principle, it is also available for other projects), imports financed by foreign capital should be treated as benefits and the debt-servicing obligations as costs.[13]

Feasible and Relevant Choice Criteria

This consistent use of international prices for deriving choice criteria might not be desirable for several reasons:

• Resource allocation and creation might not turn out to be efficient if the various agencies related to the project—project designer, project promoter, government agencies in charge of various licenses such as industrial and import licenses, taxes and subsidies, and other financial institutions—do not use the same set of prices. As argued by Little and Mirrlees, the communication so essential among these various agencies is easier if actual market prices (predicted) are used. That really implies that, if government agencies did use accounting prices, they would, as a matter of development strategy and actual policies, "doctor" the actual prices to be consistent with accounting prices; if they do not do so, a development bank cannot improve the efficiency of the process of resource allocation and creation by using accounting prices.[14] Of course this does not mean that some sample studies of completed and operating projects by a development bank on these lines would not be useful. In fact, it is one of the functions of a development bank to undertake studies that bring out the implications of actual government strategy and policies and thus persuade and induce the government to modify its strategy and policies to suit its broad development objectives.

• Use of international prices involves not only the availability of the required data but also considerable analytic ability and judgment in processing, interpreting, and using them. These skills are scarce, and the appraisal department of a bank may not have enough personnel with the required ability. Even if such personnel were available, it is questionable whether they could be used to better purpose. Further, the margin of error in project evaluation may turn out to be considerable if sophisticated techniques are used unintelligently and on the basis of fragmentary data.

• If a simpler technique can serve the same purpose of enabling top management to make good decisions, there is no case for perfection of technique as an end in itself. Choice criteria are tools for decisionmaking and not products in themselves to be perfected.

What, then, are the conditions any choice criteria should satisfy? Above all, they should communicate meaningful information to enable the decisionmaker to make a decision. For instance, top management should know the financial soundness of a project; its economic rate of return at market prices, which determines the actual outcome with regard to generation of government income, saving, and consumption; and the efficiency with which the product is to be produced. Top management should also know such concrete implications of the project so that it can suggest specific changes in government policies; it is easier to persuade the government to make specific changes on the basis of concrete evidence than to persuade it to make radical changes on general considerations that policymakers may not understand.

For the purpose of indicating the financial soundness of a project, the after-tax rate of return—the financial rate of return—at market prices would be adequate. But this is not the rate of return to the economy as a whole; hence there is a need for calculating the economic rate of return on the basis of market prices. To judge the efficiency of the project, it would suffice to calculate its "exchange rate," that is, the domestic-resource cost per unit of foreign exchange earned or saved for the year in which capacity output is likely to be realized.

In principle, the time streams of both domestic costs and net foreign exchange earnings can be discounted to the present, and thus the ratio can be calculated on the basis of present values; but for industrial projects with more or less equal gestation lags and project life, this computation does not seem necessary.

Domestic costs for the purpose would comprise interest cost (at the cutoff rate of return) on the capital expenditure on inputs domestically bought, depreciation on this capital cost, cost of domestically purchased current inputs, and cost of both skilled and unskilled labor. These domestic costs should be divided by net foreign exchange earning or saving (in terms of foreign currency); that is, the value of the product or products domestically sold at import c.i.f. prices plus exports valued at export f.o.b. prices minus all the foreign exchange cost items (interest cost on capital expenditure on imported inputs, depreciation on this capital cost, and value of imported current inputs at import c.i.f. prices, including import of skilled labor). All these items should be valued net of taxes and subsidies. This ratio would indicate the exchange rate of the product or the domestic cost incurred for earning or saving one unit of foreign exchange. The cutoff rate should be the shadow exchange rate, which implies that all projects with an exchange rate equal to or lower than the cutoff rate should be selected.[15]

These three pieces of information—financial rate of return, economic rate of return, and exchange rate—are indeed very meaningful for top management. The first relates to financial soundness, the second to economic soundness on the basis of generation of saving, and the third again to economic soundness, based on competitive efficiency.

If a project satisfies the economic criteria but is not financially sound, top management has a good specific case to induce the government to modify its tax subsidy policies to make the project financially sound. If it is financially sound but does not meet both economic criteria, it needs to be examined further or even rejected. If it is financially sound and also meets the criteria for the economic rate of return but does not satisfy the efficiency test, the reasons should be determined. If it is found that the cost of a domestic input is higher than its import c.i.f. price, top management has good reason to suggest to the government that it relax import control on this input. If, consequently, the government permits even a partial import of this input (not necessarily for this project), it should be valued at import c.i.f. prices and should be treated as a foreign exchange cost.

Thus these three criteria help top management not only in its own decisionmaking but also in persuading the government to make specific changes in policies in terms the policymakers are likely to understand: financial rate of return, economic rate of return, and exchange rate.

The shadow exchange rate should be based on actual data of viable industrial projects in operation and such changes in government policies as are relevant for this purpose. Of course the shadow exchange rate needs to be changed in the light of the emerging situation and context. Such calculations of the shadow exchange rate would also help government policymakers modify their exchange rate policies and trade policies concerning import control, tariffs, and subsidies.

The project studies of some development banks indicate that these three criteria provide tests in most cases as good as the economic rate of return based on international prices.[16] Thus a refined analysis might be necessary only in the case of very large and complicated projects, which in any case should be subjected to much deeper analysis than that implied in these three tests, at the project stage as well as the final project appraisal stage.

So far the wage rate is taken at its actual market value. Is there a case for a shadow wage rate? Again, the available evidence indicates that this might not make much difference in the case of a large number of projects.[17] This evidence relates only to "modern" projects, however, and development banks by and large have not financed projects for "traditional" industries such as handlooms or processing agricultural products and food. Nor are they financing small to medium-size industries in rural areas that supply local markets with traditional inputs to agriculture or traditional consumption goods.

If the technological base of the traditional industries is to be upgraded, technical and financial assistance is required from development banks.[18] For such enterprises, it is logical to treat shadow wage as zero, since the labor force is already available, either employed or likely to be employed. For such enterprises, both economic criteria—economic soundness based on generation of saving and competitive efficiency—should be derived on the basis of a zero wage rate. This is likely to be consistent with the development strategy and objectives of social justice.

For modern industries in rural areas and serving local markets, the shadow wage rate should be taken as the rate at which labor is likely to be willing to be employed, irrespective of whether the actual wage rate is higher because of trade-union activity or government legislation. This also accords with development objectives related to employment and income distribution.

Industrial projects that serve national or international markets are likely to be located in urban metropolitan or port areas. In their case, the social cost of employing labor is often higher than actual wage costs, for the public authorities would have to provide water supply, drainage, transport, and housing to enable the projects to function. Further, the crowding and congestion in metropolitan or port areas have a nonquantifiable but real social cost in potential tensions and conflicts. For these reasons, it does not seem appropriate to assume a shadow wage lower than the actual wage. In any case, a shadow wage for these areas has no meaning for the efficient allocation and creation of resources unless the government provides a subsidy equal to the difference between actual and shadow wage costs—which is unlikely since the government would have considerable expenditure in providing public utilities.

This system of shadow wage rates introduces the necessary bias in favor of traditional and rural industries and at the same time tends to make the modern urban industries internationally competitive without burdening the government with a system of subsidies. In a dualistic economy, the price structure also needs to be dualistic to be in accord with a development strategy that emphasizes both growth and social justice.

Economic Analysis Prior to Economic Appraisal

The economic appraisal section (EAS) of the appraisal department of a development bank must necessarily base its appraisal on the detailed analysis of the project—its organization, management, and technical and financial soundness—made by the financial appraisal section (FAS). But EAS should not accept the FAS analysis without cross-checking it first, since quite often those who are preoccupied with details miss the overall picture. Key areas in which general cross-checks are necessary are demand estimation, gestation lags, capital and input structure, and the structure of returns. The actual demand estimates should be checked on the basis of the past relation between the demand for the product and national income, or agricultural output, or industrial output (whichever is relevant); this overall measure would at least indicate the prima facie plausibility of the actual demand estimates. If the actual demand estimates do not tally with such a relation, and a valid explanation is not available, the demand estimates may need to be worked out afresh.

For a preliminary economic analysis of a project, the project data obtained from FAS should be processed and presented in a form amenable to economic analysis. Statements A, B, and C in the appendix to this chapter illustrate one form; this information should then be converted in terms of ratios indicated in Statement D.

The purpose of Statement D is to compare significant economic relations of the project with such relations in similar projects already implemented or being implemented (or in similar projects in other countries, preferably countries at a similar stage of development). Such a comparison would show whether the FAS appraisal appears to be sound; if, however, there is significant divergence for which FAS has no valid explanation, the appraisal might have to be done again by FAS.

The gestation lag and capital cost of projects are generally under-estimated in developing countries.[19] The type of economic analysis indicated here would pinpoint such underestimation and thus in-duce FAS to be more "realistic" in its appraisal work. Such economic analysis implies that the research department of a development bank should appraise projects already implemented and collect data on similar projects in operation in other countries (preferably developing countries at similar stages of development). Such stud-ies are extremely useful for devising valid criteria and procedures for appraisal work as well as for improving such criteria and proce-dures on a continuing basis.

This comparative analysis would provide significant information for economic evaluation of the project and hence for decision-making. For many small to medium-size projects, such economic analysis should suffice for the purpose of economic evaluation and final decisionmaking. The return structure (see appendix, item D.3) would enable the decisionmaker to judge the financial as well as economic soundness of a project.

Development Perspective

Economic evaluation of a project is significant in itself, but it is much more significant as a reflection of the development orienta-tion of a development bank. The perspective of a development bank differs from that of an ordinary financial institution since a develop-ment institution seeks to promote industrial development consis-tent with the overall national development strategy. Economic evaluation of current or future projects as well as completed proj-ects enables it to discuss with government and other related agencies the adequacy and relevance of various policies related to industrial development. This dialogue benefits all parties; govern-ment and other agencies can formulate and modify their policies on the basis of specific and concrete evidence, while a development bank can perform its special function in a much more meaningful way than would be possible without such a dialogue. For what is the rationale of a development bank without this development perspective?

Appendix: Format for Economic Analysis

Statement A: Structure of Costs (Current Inputs) and Returns

	Year 1	Year 2 . . . Year 20
	D I E	*D I E*

1. Output value
   a. Quantity
   b. Price per unit
   c. Capacity output
   d. *a* as a proportion of *c*
2. Change in inventory of finished goods
3. Sales (1 − 2)
4. Current inputs (net of indirect taxes)
   a. Material inputs
   b. Power
   c. Steam, fuel, and water
   d. Transport
   e. Others
5. Gross value added (1 − 4)
6. Wages and salaries
   a. Number of wage earners
   b. Average wage rate
   c. Total wages
   d. Number of salary earners
   e. Average salary rate
   f. Total salary
7. Gross profits or surplus (5 − 6)
8. Depreciation
9. Net value added (5 − 8)
10. Taxes
    a. Direct
    b. Indirect
11. Net profits (7 − 8 − 10)
12. Interest charges
    a. On short-term borrowing
    b. On long-term borrowing

Note: D = domestic market (sales or purchases); *I* = imports; *E* = exports.

13. Dividend on equity
14. Retained profits $(11 - 12 - 13)$
15. Profits to equity holders $(13 + 14)$

Statement B: Capital Structure

	Year 1	Year 2 ... Year 20
	D I E	*D I E*

1. Capital expenditures (net of indirect taxes)
   a. Land
   b. Building and construction
   c. Machinery and equipment
   d. Others
2. Inventory (net of indirect taxes)
   a. Stock of materials
   b. Work in progress
   c. Others
3. Total capital expenditures (net of indirect taxes) $(1 + 2)$
4. Indirect taxes
5. Total capital expenditure (inclusive of indirect taxes $(3 + 4)$

Statement C: Cash Flow

	Year 1	Year 2 ... Year 20
	D I E	*D I E*

1. Social cash flow $(A.7 - B.3)$
2. Private cash flow $(A.7 - B.5 - A.10)$
3. Borrowing
   a. Short-term
   b. Long-term
4. Repayment
   a. Short-term loans
   b. Long-term loans

Statement D: Structure of Capital, Inputs, Returns,
and Financing at Capacity Output

	I	II
	Project under Appraisal	Similar Projects Implemented or under Implementation

1. Capital structure
   a. Capital-capacity output ratio $(B.3/A.1.c)$

    b. Capital-gross value added ratio (B.3/A.5)
    c. Inventory-capacity output ratio (B.2/A.1.c)
2. Input structure
    a. Wages-output ratio (A.6.c/A.1.c)
    b. Salaries-output ratio (A.6.f/A.1.c)
    c. Materials-output ratio (A.4.a/A.1.c)
    d. Power-output ratio (A.4.b/A.1.c)
    e. Other services-output ratio (A.4.c + d + e/A.1.c)
3. Return structure
    a. Gross profits to capital (A.7/B.3)
    b. Net profits to capital (A.11/B.5)
    c. Profits to equity holders to equity (A.15/[B.5 − C.3])
    d. Interest-borrowing ratio (A.12/C.3)
    e. Ratio of exports + domestic sales − imported current imports to imported plant and equipment (all in terms of foreign exchange at import c.i.f. or export f.o.b. prices, whichever are relevant)
4. Financial structure
    a. Debt service coverage (C.2/[C.4 + A.12])
    b. Debt-equity ratio (C.3/[B.5 − C.3])
5. Gestation lag
    a. Lag between start of construction and commercial production
    b. Lag between start of construction and capacity output

Notes to Chapter 4

    1. Kenneth J. Arrow, "Limited Knowledge and Economic Analysis," *American Economic Review*, vol. 64, no. 1 (1974), pp. 1–10.
    2. V. V. Bhatt, "On Technology Policy and Its Institutional Frame" (Washington, D.C.: Economic Development Institute, World Bank, December 1974), processed.
    3. Ian M. D. Little and James A. Mirrlees, *Manual of Industrial Project Analysis in Developing Countries*, vol. 2 (Paris: Development Centre of the Organisation for Economic Co-operation and Development, 1968), pp. 64–66.
    4. See V. V. Bhatt, "Capital Intensity of Industries," *Bulletin of the Oxford University*, vol. 18, no. 2 (1956), pp. 184, 191–92: "The substitution of capital by labour, though not very common in the basic technical processes, is fairly common in certain auxiliary operations . . . The most important of these operations seems to be materials handlings . . . The underdeveloped economies, it seems, have not been able to develop a new technology suited to their own economic conditions . . . The industries of the underdeveloped economies import not only the technology but also the capital goods necessary for that purpose from the developed economies. From the input combinations of the handicraft technology to the input combinations of the modern

technology . . . constitutes a big jump and because of the lack of development of any intermediate technology, the industries of the underdeveloped economies face a sharply discontinuous production function, which is continuous only within the ranges permitted by the handicraft technology on the one hand, and the technology of the developed economies on the other . . . taking all the factors into consideration, the capital coefficients would be on average about the same in both developed and underdeveloped economies." See also Bhatt, *Employment and Capital Formation in Underdeveloped Economies* (Bombay: Orient Longmans, 1960); David Morawetz, "Employment Implications of Industrialization in Developing Countries: A Survey," *Economic Journal*, vol. 84, no. 335 (1974), pp. 491–542; and S. N. Acharya, "Fiscal-Financial Intervention, Factor Prices, and Factor Proportions: A Review of Issues," (Washington, D.C., Development Economics Department, World Bank, 1974); processed.

5. Bhatt, *Employment and Capital Formation.*

6. Development Centre of the Organisation for Economic Co-operation and Development, *Choice and Adaptation of Technology in Developing Countries* (Paris, 1974), p. 81.

7. Ibid., p. 17.

8. See Janos Kornai, *Rush versus Harmonic Growth* (London: North-Holland Publishing Co., 1962), pp. 35 and 46–48. Kornai writes, "Theory gets entangled . . . in the tactical problems of consumption, while the 'Strategy,' the Study of fundamental complimentary phenomena gets lost . . . Far be it for me to deny the possibility of substitution among inputs or that prior signals really exert an effort on those controlling production, save, that the actual role of these phenomena is much more modest and limited than that suggested by traditional production theory . . . Using the terminology introduced in connection with consumption: the new classical production theory got one-sidedly absorbed with the 'tactical' problems of input combinations. For long-term planning, a theoretical foundation is needed that can be used in formulating the 'strategy' of technical development . . . The development of production technologies, as well as the improvement in the quality of production or, using another term, both process and production innovation is promoted by research in natural and technical sciences. It is particularly development that is of general importance for every country. Research results may be perhaps taken over from abroad, but 'development' is a non-competitive activity that must be organized by every country itself."

9. V. V. Bhatt, *Structure of Financial Institutions* (Bombay: Vora and Co., 1972).

10. V. V. Bhatt, "Sterility of Equilibrium Economics: An Aspect of Sociology of Science," Economic Development Institute Seminar Paper no. 9 (Washington, D.C.: World Bank, 1974), processed.

11. Kaldor writes, "The difficulty with a new start is to pinpoint the critical areas when economic theory went astray. In my own view, it happened when the theory of value took on the centre of the stage—which meant focussing attention on the *allocative* functions of markets to the exclusion of these *creative* functions—as an instrument for transmitting impulses to economic change." See Nicholas Kaldor, "The Irrelevance of Equilibrium Economics," *Economic Journal*, vol. 82, no. 328 (1972), p. 1240.

12. See Little and Mirrlees, *Manual of Industrial Project Analysis*, chaps. 11 and 13.

13. Foreign and Commonwealth Office, Overseas Development Administration, *A Guide to Project Appraisal in Developing Countries* (London: Her Majesty's Stationery Office, 1972).

14. Amartya K. Sen, "Control Areas and Accounting Prices: An Approach to Economic Evaluation," *Economic Journal*, vol. 82, no. 3255, suppl. (1972), pp. 486–501. United Nations, *Guidelines for Project Evaluation*, pt. 4 (New York, 1972).

15. Bhatt, *Structure of Financial Institutions*, chaps. 11 and 13. See also Michael Bruno's report, "The Optimal Selection of Export-promoting and Import-substituting Projects," in United Nations, *Planning the External Sector: Techniques, Problems and Policies* (New York, 1967); and "Domestic Resource Costs and Effective Protection: Clarification and Synthesis," *Journal of Political Economy*, vol. 80, no. 1 (1972), pp. 16–33; and I. M. D. Little and J. A. Mirrlees, *Project Appraisal and Planning for Developing Countries* (London: Heinemann, 1974), chap. 18.

16. Industrial Credit and Investment Corporation, "ICICI's Development Impact," vol. 1, part 3 (Bombay, March 1973), processed; see also, Industrial Development Bank of India, *Annual Report, 1972–73* (Bombay, 1973).

17. "ICICI's Development Impact."

18. Bhatt, *Development Banks*. See also, OECD, *Choice and Adaptation of Technology*, p. 126.

19. Industrial Development Bank of India, *Annual Report, 1971–72* (Bombay, 1972).

Chapter 5

Industrial Development Banks and Social Benefit-Cost Analysis

F. Leslie C. H. Helmers

THE FUNCTION of an industrial development bank is to assist its government's structural industrialization objective by providing technical assistance and long-term capital. This definition applies to industrial development banks in the developed as well as the developing countries. In the former, governments began to set up development banks after World War I to cope with special problems stemming from depression, wartime destruction, regional imbalance, and the like. Immediately after World War II, with the accent on postwar industrial reconstruction, this process of setting up specialized institutions accelerated. At present, some of these banks are also very much involved in industrial restructuring activities. For instance, the Industrial and Commercial Finance Corporation in the United Kingdom, the Kreditanstalt für Wiederaufbau in Germany, the A. B. Industrie Kredit in Sweden, and the Herstelbank in the Netherlands are assisting their governments in reallocating resources from the labor-intensive industries in these countries, which have proven to be economically not competitive with those in the developing world, to the more viable capital-intensive industries in which the developed world at present has a comparative advantage.

In the developing world, too, in the second quarter of the century, governments began to establish special financial institutions to promote economic growth. But the major increase in the number of such institutions, both public and private, took place in the years following World War II because of the belief that industrialization was the key to economic progress. The argument of the economic literature, during the war and immediate postwar periods, that industrialization was essential to achieve national income growth, and the belief that the terms of trade for raw materials would turn against the developing countries, created a general trend in the developing countries in the 1950s and 1960s to industrialize. Since there were shortages of equity and loan capital, which could not be satisfied by the commercial banks (even nowadays it is almost impossible to obtain a syndicated loan from the international banks with a maturity longer than seven to eight years), as well as shortages of entrepreneurial talent and technical know-how, it made much sense to establish industrial development banks to fill these gaps. There are, at present, several hundred industrial development banks in the developing world.

Development Bank Objectives

Clearly, industrial development banks are important in the promotion or restructuring of the industrial sectors in their respective countries. In view of this, one would have thought that every industrial development bank would apply developmental criteria in making its investment decisions. This is far from true, especially in the developing world. Only a fraction of the total number of industrial development banks in the developing world—the institutions with which this paper will be mainly concerned—go beyond purely financial criteria in that they apply some form of economic evaluation in the selection of their projects. The others remain content to employ only financial analysis (as do financial institutions in economically advanced countries).

At first sight it may appear that there is something to be said in favor of not using economic and social criteria in an investment bank's decisionmaking. After all, governments can influence the primary, secondary, and tertiary income distribution in their countries and thereby create economic environments conducive to industrialization. While the secondary redistribution—the direct transfer of income from one party to another—is not very feasible in the developing world, primary and tertiary activities have played a very important role in the postwar period. Tertiary activities in the form of government expenditures for infrastructure in the industrial sector have without doubt stimulated the industrial expansion many developing countries have experienced. Similarly, governments have taken measures to influence primary income distribution, that is, the incomes accruing to the factors of production, in order to promote industrialization. In fact, most of the developing countries have established high protective barriers and sometimes applied quantitative restrictions to increase entrepreneurial incomes and to foster import substitution in the industrial sector. Since the role of an industrial development bank in such a climate can be seen as that of a purely financial intermediary, it is not surprising that many development banks have been willing to approve investments on the basis of the traditional profitability tests without further consideration of the economic or social priority of these investments.

Such an approach to the development process has, however, been unfortunate because it has often exacerbated the problems of developing countries, or at least missed the opportunity to alleviate them. First, in many countries the lending of the industrial development banks has been mainly to the large-scale, capital-intensive manufacturing sector, thereby contributing relatively little employment creation. Second, such lending has increased import dependence since many new industries have to import their raw materials and equipment. Third, in many countries the bulk of the lending has been for import substitution, which has hampered exports. Fourth, as a result of this emphasis on import-substitution industries, the terms of trade have often turned against the agricultural sector and hence worsened income distribution. Fifth, it was often not percieved that the period of import substitution soon comes to an end so that many of the developing economies found themselves stuck with financially very profitable but economically inefficient industries.

The point is not that import-substitution policies as such are wrong. To the contrary, there is much to be said for import substitution as a strategy for industrialization if the established industries can eventually operate efficiently. But to determine this, one needs to go beyond a purely financial analysis. The point is, therefore, that many of the excesses could have been prevented if a sound economic and social evaluation of the industrial investments had been made. Since most planning organizations are not familiar with the details of various industrial activities at the micro level, it is in this respect that industrial development banks have a fundamental function to fulfill. They are the only institutions that do have detailed information about the industrial development process, and they are therefore the only institutions that can determine whether the industrialization process is on the right track. To do so, they must investigate not only the "bankability" of their projects, but also whether the proposed investments make sense economically and socially. Such evaluations will often be extremely useful to industrial entrepreneurs. It may help them obtain the subsidy or tax incentive necessary to make an economically and socially sound project viable from a financial point of view as well; it may also help them modify a project if, as originally proposed, it is not in the national interest, so that they can still proceed. The task of an industrial development bank is thus not an easy one. It has an advisory role in relation to the government and the industrial entrepreneur, as well as an implementation task. To do all this, it must understand the government's industrialization strategy and be well versed in the financial, economic, and social benefit-cost analysis of projects, so that its development lending will be able to meet the national objectives.

If it is accepted that an industrial development bank has a developmental task to fulfill and that, in order to do so, it needs to employ developmental criteria in its lending operations, then the question arises of what these criteria should be. Since they are to be derived from the national development goals, it will be useful to review what is now generally perceived to be the objective of development. Immediately after World War II, this was not seen as a difficult issue: the objective was to maximize national income. Toward the end of the 1960s and in the early 1970s, however, it became apparent that this development strategy had not helped the poorest income classes. Notwithstanding the very high rates of income growth—historically at unprecedented high levels[1]—almost no trickle-down of growth occurred, and at present some 600 million people in the noncommunist developing countries, or about 20 percent of the total population, appear to live close to the margin of subsistence. In many developing countries, the maximization of national income has, therefore, been replaced as an explicit development objective by the concept that growth not only of total national income, but also of the incomes of the poorest income classes, should be pursued, or, in other words, that the objective of development should be equitable social growth.

Two strategies have evolved to meet this objective of social growth. On the one hand, there is the so-called incomes approach, which recognizes that a dollar of income accruing to the poorest income classes has a higher social value than a dollar of income accruing to the community at large, so that projects that raise the incomes of the poor have high social priority. On the other hand, there is the so-called basic needs approach, which is much less exactly defined by its proponents and appears to have several meanings.[2] To the extent that the emphasis in a developmental strategy is intended to raise the incomes of the poor to some minimal target level, this approach is completely equivalent to the incomes approach. To some, however, the basic needs approach means something else. For instance, one writer explicitly rejects the incomes approach because the use of distributional weights always leads to some inefficiencies and calls for the direct provision of goods and services to the poor to meet a certain minimum standard of food, clothing, shelter, medical care, and education.[3] To the extent that the poor are destitute in the sense of having incomes below the minimal subsistence level, there should be no quarrel with this approach. If people are starving, then the direct provision of goods and services is, of course, essential for survival. But what about the persons who find themselves in situations of secondary poverty, that is, living on incomes above subsistence level but lower than a socially accepted minimum income? A Chinese proverb aptly describes the policy to be followed: "Do not give me a fish, but teach me how to fish." If the poor are to have a productive, good, full life, then charity is not the answer, and a reorientation of investments toward increasing the incomes of the poor through the creation of good, productive employment becomes a mandatory element of any development strategy.

Often the objectives of a national development plan are expressed in terms other than those of social growth. Many national development plans, for instance, set as their targets the attainment of full employment, improvement of the balance of payments, achievement of price stability, and self-sufficiency in the production of certain goods. The first three policies, however, are fully consistent with the objectives of growth and equity: measures to create full employment, to improve the balance of payments, and to achieve price stability are part of the kit of tools with which the fundamental objective of social growth can be achieved. The self-sufficiency target does not belong to this category, but sometimes it might well be a valid national objective for reasons related to the international division of power. When a government has decided to pursue the objective of self-sufficiency in a certain good, and is willing to accept the inefficiencies that often result from such a policy, economic and social considerations, of course, recede. In general, however, this approach is the exception to the basic policy of achieving social growth.

Economic Analysis

A few comments about the economic analysis of projects are in order because this type of analysis remains important in the social approach to benefit-cost analysis. About a decade ago, a new methodology—the so-called Little-Mirrlees method—appeared to challenge the traditional approach to the economic evaluation of projects and has thereby given rise to much confusion.[4] It will be useful to see how this approach differs from the traditional one.

A good description of the traditional economic analysis of projects can be found in the UNIDO *Guidelines*.[5] Basically, the traditional economic analysis of projects consists in a simple extension of financial analysis in that inputs and outputs are not valued at their market prices but at their real scarcity values. In the classic analysis, these scarcity values are found for international tradables, that is, exports, imports, exports that are to be diverted to the home market, or domestic goods that are to substitute for imports, by multiplying their border prices in foreign exchange with the opportunity cost of foreign exchange, and for nontradables by estimating directly the domestic scarcity prices. By contrast, under the Little-Mirrlees method, all goods, tradables as well as nontradables, are valued in border prices. For the tradables this is done directly; for the nontradables, the procedure is to break down the goods, with the help of input-output tables, into their constituent inputs. Successive rounds of this procedure, so that intermediate products will also have been broken down, result in goods that can be immediately evaluated at border prices and labor. Labor, too, is then converted into border prices by estimating the basket of goods that the workers in question consume and then valuing this basket in border prices. Thus, for every type of good, a conversion factor is found that converts the domestic price into a border price. Little and Mirrlees agree that it is sometimes difficult to arrive at a detailed breakdown for a particular good or service and suggest that a standard conversion factor (SCE) be used. This factor should be representative of a wide range of goods and is in practice calculated as the reciprocal of the opportunity cost of foreign exchange.

The Little-Mirrlees methodology as originally proposed gives the strong impression that the efficiency of a project should be determined only on the basis of its international competitiveness, hence

Table 5-1. *Equivalence of the Traditional and Little-Mirrlees Methods of Project Analysis*
(millions of rupees)

Item	Traditional method		Little-Mirrlees method			
	Cost at official exchange rate	Foreign exchange component	Economic cost	Cost at official exchange rate	Conversion factors	Cost at border prices
Imported equipment	20	20	25	20	1.00	20
Civil works	80	20	85	80	0.85	68
Total cost	100	40	110	100	—	88
Exchange premium	—	10 (25%)	—	—	—	—
Total	100	—	110	100	—	88

the border prices, and that the relative prices in a country are not important. This is, of course, wrong. Governments do influence the primary income distribution patterns in their countries by interfering with the price mechanism, and domestic prices are therefore sometimes quite relevant. For instance, if steel as an intermediate product is valued at its border price rather than at its higher domestic scarcity value, then projects using steel may appear efficient whereas in reality they may lead to additional economic losses. Little and Mirrlees had to concede this point to their critics,[6] and in their second study they mention explicitly that in such cases the conversion to border prices should be based on the shadow rate of foreign exchange. With this concession, the Little-Mirrlees methodology becomes completely equivalent to the traditional one, the only difference being the choice of the numeraire, that is, border prices under the Little-Mirrlees approach and domestic prices under the traditional approach.[7]

The equivalence of the two methods may be demonstrated by a simple example, illustrated in table 5-1, which shows the different evaluation of, say, the cost of a factory, under the two methods. The facilities are assumed to cost Rs100 million, with a foreign exchange component of 40 percent. Under the traditional method the economic cost of the facilities would be Rs110 million, if the shadow foreign exchange rate is 125 percent of the official rate. But, under the Little-Mirrlees method, the economic cost in border prices is estimated at Rs20 million for imported equipment and at Rs68 million for civil works (Rs20 million of foreign exchange and Rs60 million of local costs, converted at an scf of 0.8), for a total of Rs88 million.

Although imported equipment and civil works each have their own conversion factor, it does not make any difference whether domestic prices or border prices are used as the numeraire. Total costs are estimated at Rs88 million in border prices and at Rs110 million in domestic prices. With a shadow foreign exchange rate of 1.25, the two are equal as shown in table 5-1.

Although theoretically the two approaches lead to the same result, there are, nevertheless, several practical problems with the Little-Mirrlees methodology. First, most project evaluators prefer the valuation in domestic rather than in border prices since the border prices for nontradables are hypothetical without any economic value. It is difficult to relate these border prices to prices in the real world. Second, the Little-Mirrlees procedure gives the impression of being very precise; but in practice serious errors may occur. For instance, although Little-Mirrlees suggest that as many conversion factors as possible be calculated, they also mention that, when there is insufficient information for certain types of activities, such as construction, general conversion factors for these activities should be used. Since there are many ways in which, for instance, a building can be constructed, it is rather spurious to base a cost estimate on some standard technique rather than on the technique actually employed. Third, the Little-Mirrlees method leads to numerous calculations when it is expected that the opportunity cost of foreign exchange will change during the life of the project under consideration, because all the conversion factors need to be recalculated. Under the traditional method, no undue problems arise since it is easy to adjust the shadow foreign exchange rate. All these practical problems have not made the Little-Mirrlees methodology very popular in the developing world, and most development banks that have experimented with the method have reverted to the traditional economic project analysis.

Appraising Income-Distribution Effects

Income distribution is often given important consideration in the design of a project,[8] and it has an intertemporal as well as interpersonal dimension. In fact, much of the recent literature on income distribution has paid more attention to improving the distribution of national income over time than to improving the distribution of national income between persons. How should one proceed in the intertemporal analysis? Basically, the procedure is to attach a premium to investments; that is, to evaluate investments at a shadow price and then to accept only those projects from which, in addition to the investment, the premium will be recovered over the life of the project. Since, under this method, short-life projects will need to have much higher economic rates of return than long-life projects to be accepted (otherwise the premium will not be recovered over their lifetimes), the proponents of the intertemporal approach to benefit-cost analysis will indeed favor long-life projects and thereby deepen the capital structure of a country.

Several comments are in order. First, all this assumes that the government in question is constrained in its use of other possible instruments that could help increase the level of investments in a country; but this assumption is often not correct. Governments can and do use fiscal and monetary policies to increase investments and future incomes to desired levels, and there is then no need to employ the shadow price of investment approach to benefit-cost analysis. Second, even if a government is originally constrained by the body politic, it is still dubious whether the body politic would be willing to accept the approach. For, in fact, the method is very discriminatory. It not only favors the next generation to the detriment of the present generation but also increases income disparities in the present as well as in the future. Very probably, therefore, the body politic will reject the approach as soon as it becomes aware of what it entails. Third, in practice the shadow price of investment approach can lead to substantial inefficiencies. For instance, the Nehru-initiated, capital-deepening policies in India—which, by the way, were probably largely responsible for the shadow price of investment theory—have led to serious efficiency problems. Steel mills prematurely established some fifteen to twenty years ago operated for a long time with economic losses and are only now beginning to work efficiently. When the above considerations are taken into account, the inescapable conclusion is that usually the shadow price of investment approach should be rejected and that only in very special cases is something to be said for it.

Then there is the approach to benefit-cost analysis that considers the distribution of income between persons. Theoretically, this type of analysis is based on the fact that an additional unit of income at a low-income level has socially a higher value than an additional unit of income at a higher-income level. In classic economic theory this fact is well accepted, but it was not thought necessary to introduce social weighting of incomes into the benefit-cost analysis of projects because it was believed that an appropriate distribution of incomes could always be achieved through transfers, that is, by taxing high-income persons and transferring income to low-income persons. In many developed countries, tax cum transfer mechanisms have indeed become important instruments of poverty alleviation. In the developing world, however, direct transfers are less socially acceptable. Furthermore, the incomes of the poorest classes often cannot be sufficiently increased by means of transfers because of the extremely large amounts that would be necessary.

In the developing world, projects have therefore become increasingly more important instruments for raising the incomes of the poorest classes. In the agricultural sector, for instance, many countries have land settlement programs, although economically smallholder land is not as efficient as plantation development. Feeder roads are often constructed to help the farmers market their produce, but the rate of return of such roads may be lower than those of highways. Also, in irrigation projects, water is often supplied to more small holdings than would maximize output. Such tradeoffs between economic efficiency and income increases must also often be considered in the industrial sector. For instance, it might well be more efficient to mass produce cups out of plastic than to make them by hand out of sheet metal, but opening a factory to make plastic cups would destroy the informal labor-intensive sector that is producing metal ones. A capital-intensive shoe factory might have high financial and economic rates of return, but, again, the informal labor-intensive sector that produces shoes by hand must be considered. A plywood plant can be set up to operate capital intensively or labor intensively; again the choice might well depend on income distribution considerations. An industrial development bank should, therefore, not only be aware of the social policies its government intends to pursue, but also employ techniques that enable it to make investment and lending decisions in line with these policies.

The social benefit-cost approach based on interpersonal income consists in principle of a simple extension of the economic analysis of projects: the parties who gain and those who lose because of the project should be identified, and appropriate income distribution weights should be attached to the gains and the losses. But how can these weights be calculated? A very specific function, which was originally suggested by Bernoulli in 1738 and recently strongly recommended by Tinbergen and Chenery,[9] assumes that geometric increases in income produce arithmetic increases in utility, as in the formula $\Delta U = b\Delta Y/Y$, where U is utility, Y is income, and b is the base income against which utility and income increases are to be measured. This function may also be written as $\Delta U/\Delta Y = b/Y$. Hence, the utility increase from an additional unit of income, and therewith the income distribution weight to be attached to this additional unit, can be determined from the base income and the original income level and is inversely proportional to the latter. For instance, if $b = \$1,000$ a year and a laborer receives an additional dollar to his annual income of \$500, the weight on this additional dollar would be 2.0 since $b/Y = \$1,000/\$500$. Of course, other functions can be used to determine income distribution weights. The Bernoulli function, however, has the advantage of being simple and seems to be in line with empirical investigations. A project analyst might therefore use the Bernoulli function as a starting point and apply sensitivity tests with other weights to confirm whether the results are plausible.

Two pitfalls are inherent in this social analysis. First, the use of income distribution weights based on a diminishing marginal utility of income schedule over the whole range of incomes in a country leads inevitably to the conclusion that the optimal income distribution situation is one in which all incomes are equal. At the point of income equality all persons would have the same marginal utility of income, and it would therefore no longer be necessary to transfer a dollar of income from a rich person whose marginal dollar has a low utility to a poorer person whose marginal dollar has a higher utility. Since a society rarely tries to achieve equality of incomes, the notion that all incomes should be weighted must, therefore, be rejected. Although societies are usually concerned about the very low and the very high incomes, they are indifferent to the actual distribution of incomes in the middle ranges. In the social analysis of projects, therefore, a dollar should be counted as a dollar in the wide range of middle incomes, and income distribution weights should be attached only to the incomes of the poorest and of the richest income classes. It is worth repeating here that high incomes should be weighted only when they cannot be adequately taxed and low incomes only when income transfers to the poor are not feasible, which is the case in much of the developing world.

The weighting system proposed here has important consequences. While it is sometimes recommended in economic literature that average income should be taken as the base, the socially more acceptable method would be to work with two base levels: one for the very low and the other for the very high incomes. The base for the poorest income classes can then be defined as the minimum target income the poorest classes should have—and in most cases this can be defined as the minimum wage, as set by government, of a fully employed, unskilled laborer. Similarly, the incomes of highly trained professionals such as physicians, cabinet members, and managers may be taken as the base level against which higher incomes are to be valued. The difference between the two methods is shown in the following example. If the average family income in a country is $3,000 while minimum wage income is $1,000 a year (as in the previous example), then the income weight on an additional dollar accruing to a person with an annual income of $500 would be 6.0 under the average income method and 2.0 under the target income.[10] That the minimum target income method leads to more acceptable weights needs, after this example, no further elaboration.

The second possible error in the application of the social benefit-cost approach to projects is that one would be willing to accept all projects with a social rate of return higher than the opportunity cost of capital. Since projects with a low or even negative economic rate of return might well have high social rates of return because of the premiums to be attached to the income increases of the hired laborers, this can lead to the acceptance of many economically unsound projects. When there is no other way to increase incomes of the poor, such an inefficient project might well be justified; but such cases are exceptional. Usually, there are many other possibilities of raising the incomes of the poor—for example, other projects, price subsidies, price support programs, or transfers in kind—and thus as a general rule, one should not be willing to negate efficiency considerations. In principle, therefore, social benefit-cost analysis of projects should be applied only to those projects that have satisfactory economic rates of return. The employment of social analysis would then ensure that, in the range of efficient projects, only those with a socially high priority would be implemented.

If an industrial development bank were to analyze the financial, economic, and social aspects of its projects, and if it were willing to reject all projects that do not have a satisfactory financial, economic, and social rate of return, would there be a substantial difference in its lending and investment operations? The answer is definitely affirmative. To return to the examples, if a social benefit-cost analysis had been applied, then the plastic drinking ware, the shoe, and the capital-intensive plywood plants would in all probability not be established. Of course, if an industrial development bank is to fulfill its function adequately, it should not limit itself to the scrutiny of feasibility studies for the proposed investments. Projects do not fall from heaven like manna; they must be prepared. Since in many cases the banks are aware that a project will eventually be submitted to them for loan or equity financing, they are in an excellent position to reshape projects to conform to the country's industrialization objectives. As mentioned above, if after preliminary investigation the financial rate of return appears too low to provide the entrepreneur with sufficient incentives, then development banks can and should try to save the project by using their influence to obtain appropriate tax incentives and subsidies. Similarly, a project can be modified to make it economically and socially attractive while maintaining its financial profitability. For instance, rather than a plastic drinking ware plant, it might be just as profitable to construct a plant producing plastic irrigation hoses. With suitable financial incentives, a shoe factory can be made attractive to operate in a labor-intensive manner, thereby also increasing its economic and social rates of return in comparison with that of a capital-intensive plant, and so on.

Often consultants retained to design a project, especially those from or trained in the Western world, have a bias toward the establishment of capital-intensive facilities. This might be because they hope eventually to be involved in the construction of the plant; often it is because they believe that only large-scale plants will help modernize a developing economy.[11] As a result, many feasibility studies do not examine alternative technological possibilities, and it is often overlooked that less capital-intensive facilities might well have higher financial as well as economic and social rates of return than the recommended large-scale plants. If consultants are aware that the eventual financier will insist on a comparative analysis of alternative technologies, then the likelihood of a bias toward the capital-intensive end of the spectrum of processing possibilities will be considerably reduced.

Many industrial development banks are now lending only for capital-intensive operations, thereby exacerbating the poverty problems with which many of the developing countries have to cope. Economic and social analysis of projects would lead to more lending by such banks to the small-scale, labor-intensive industrial sector, thus mitigating the problems of poverty.

One after another, developing countries are now experiencing political and social turmoil, and there is no doubt that social stability can be ensured only if policies are geared not only toward growth of total national income, but also toward growth of the incomes of the poorest classes. By employing social benefit-cost analysis in the evaluation of their prospective investments, industrial development banks can make an important contribution toward the achievement of social stability.

Notes to Chapter 5

1. See David Morawetz, *Twenty-five Years of Economic Development, 1950 to 1975* (Baltimore, Md.: Johns Hopkins University Press, 1977).

2. For a general discussion of the basic needs strategy, see International Labour Office, *Employment, Growth and Basic Needs: A One World Problem*, Report of the Director General (Geneva, 1976).

3. Arnold C. Harberger, "On the Use of Distributional Weights in Social Cost-Benefit Analysis," *Journal of Political Economy*, vol. 86, pt. 2 (April 1978), pp. S87–S1200.

4. I. M. D. Little and J. A. Mirrlees, *Manual of Industrial Project Analysis for Developing Countries*, vol. 2: *Social Cost-Benefit Analysis* (Paris: Development Centre of the Organisation for Economic Co-operation and Development, 1968); and I. M. D. Little and J. A. Mirrlees, *Project Appraisal and Planning for Developing Countries* (New York: Basic Books, 1974).

5. Partha Dasgupta, Amartya Sen, and Stephen Margolin, *Guidelines for Project Evaluation*, United Nations Industrial Development Organization Project Formulation and Evaluation Series, no. 23 (New York: UNIDO, 1972).

6. For the criticisms voiced during a symposium on the Little-Mirrlees *Manual* by, for instance, Partha Dasgupta, Frances Stewart, and Paul Streeten, see *Bulletin of the Oxford University Institute of Economics and Statistics* (February 1972).

7. For a detailed review of the equivalence of the two methods under various assumptions as to trade policies, see Bela Balassa, "Estimating the Shadow Price of Foreign Exchange in Project Appraisal," *Oxford Economic Papers*, N.S., vol. 26 (July 1974), pp. 147–68.

8. For a detailed study on the economic and social analysis of projects, see F. Leslie C. H. Helmers, *Project Planning and Income Distribution*, Series Development and Planning Erasmus University, Rotterdam, vol. 9, 2d ed. (Boston, The Hague, and London: Martinus Nijhoff, 1979).

9. Jan Tinbergen, *Some Features of the Optimum Regime in Optimum Social Welfare and Productivity* (New York: New York University Press, 1972); and Hollis Chenery and others, *Redistribution with Growth* (London: Oxford University Press, 1974).

10. For the derivation of income weights in the case of nonmarginal changes in income, see Helmers, *Project Planning and Income Distribution*.

11. For the review of a case in which the bias was obvious, see Peter C. Timmer, "The Choice of Technique in Indonesia," in Peter C. Timmer, John W. Thomas, Lewis T. Wells, and David Morawetz, *The Choice of Technology in Developing Countries: Some Cautionary Tales*, Harvard Studies in International Affairs, no. 32 (Cambridge, Mass.: Harvard University Center for International Affairs, 1975). A discussion of Timmer's analysis appears in chapter 6, below.

Chapter 6

Choice of Technology:
The Case of the Indonesian Rice Mills

F. LESLIE C. H. HELMERS

SELF-SUFFICIENCY in rice production has been for a long time an important objective in Indonesia's development strategy, and the prevention of losses in the processing and storage of rice is, of course, of major importance in reaching this goal. Following a request by the government of Indonesia, the consultant firm of Weitz-Hettelsater Engineers was retained in 1970 by the U.S. Agency for International Development (USAID) to undertake a study of rice storage, handling, and marketing in Indonesia. The firm had considerable experience in this field since it had also undertaken USAID-financed studies in Brazil, the Philippines, and Bangladesh. All these studies recommended building large storage and processing facilities, and USAID officials had agreed in principle to finance such facilities.

An advance draft of the Indonesian rice storage, handling, and marketing study was presented in December 1971 to the Indonesian government and USAID. As in its three previous studies, the consultants recommended an investment package that put heavy emphasis on the construction of bulk storage and processing facilities. Table 6-1 recapitulates the recommended facilities. The recommendations of the advance draft report were, however, rejected by the Indonesian government, and the consultants were instructed to revise their study. In the end, they produced a report that did not

A Dutch translation of this article has appeared under the title "Over de optimale techniek voor het pellen van rijst in Indonesie," in *Samenleving en Onderzoek*, edited by J. J. Klant, W. Driehuis, H. J. Bierens, and A. J. Butter (Leiden and Antwerp: Stenfert Kroese Publishers, 1979).

Table 6-1. *Rice Mills Recommended by Consultants for Indonesia*

Number of units	Facility Code	Facility Type	Investment cost (millions of U.S. dollars)
9	K-1	15,000 metric tons bulk terminal	22.6
59	H-1	4,500 metric tons bulk satellite	26.7
122	G	Japanese type of integrated rice mill	11.0
420	C	Husker-polisher mill	3.9
Total			64.2

make any recommendations but that estimated the benefits and costs of the various alternatives.

What went wrong with the advance draft? Timmer—a member of the Harvard Advisory Group/Bappenas Research Project in Indonesia at the time the report was produced—has recently reviewed the draft in detail.[1] As he pointed out, there may have been a bias on the part of the consultants toward facilities they might have some role in building at a later date. But, in addition to this, the consultants must have had a deeply felt bias that only the most capital-intensive facilities could help modernize the Indonesian rice-processing sector. In reading through the advance draft, one cannot help but conclude that economic considerations played only a secondary role and that from the start the consultants wanted to justify the construction of the large-capacity facilities. Ironically, Timmer's review, which tries to introduce the correct factor-pricing into the analysis, is also deficient in several respects and ends up with a bias toward the labor-intensive end of the spectrum of possible technologies.

This paper will comment on and amend the consultants' and Timmer's approaches to how the economically optimal rice-processing facility should be determined and will then discuss whether the recommended facility is also socially optimal. Since the consultants' data were to some extent revised by Timmer and it is no longer possible to judge the accuracy of the original estimates, Timmer's data will be used. Furthermore, Timmer's contention will be accepted that in Indonesia the market prices of capital and foreign exchange reflect their real opportunity costs. With respect to labor, Timmer believes that the market wage rate is in order, but he also works with an opportunity cost of labor equal to half the

market rate. This last assumption will be adopted here as being a
likely minimum value. In view of the uncertainty of the data, this
review consists more of a methodological analysis than of an accurate calculation of the benefits and costs of the different facilities.

In fact, the consultants had little justification for their proposal to
construct large-scale facilities. Although they reviewed many possible technologies and collected a wealth of data, the methodology
followed must be severely criticized since it consisted of a mere
comparison of paddy savings with investments. The relevant data
for each of the recommended facilities are reproduced in table 6-2.
The consultants projected initially that the Japanese type of mill
(the G facility) would operate on a two-shift basis and the bulk mills
on a three-shift basis. But, as Timmer has pointed out, this is
actively discouraged in Indonesia, thus table 6-2 presents milling
capacities on a one-shift basis.

The husker-polisher type of mill (the C facility) has the lowest
capacity and investments (cost of buildings, equipment, and in-
stallation). In contrast to the other types of mills, it has no storage
facilities. Whereas the C mill can be manufactured in Indonesia, the

Table 6-2. *Economic Evaluation of the Indonesian Rice Mills
According to the Consultants*

Per plant	Husker-polisher (C)	Japanese integrated rice mill (G)	Bulk satellite (H–1)	Bulk terminal (K–1)
Milling capacity				
Tons of paddy per year[a]	1,000	2,500	7,200	21,600
Tons of rice per year[a]	590	1,575	4,680	14,472
Investment costs (U.S. dollars)	8,049	90,511	453,283	2,605,926
Paddy use if the paddy were hand-pounded (tons)[b]	1,035	2,762	8,209	25,384
Annual savings of paddy				
Tons	35	262	1,009	3,784
Percent	3.5	10.5	14	17.5
U.S. dollars[c]	1,658	12,411	47,796	179,248
Assumed lifetime of facilities (years)	15	20	25	25
Benefit-cost ratios at 12 percent	1.4	1.0	0.8	0.5

a. The facility is assumed to operate eight hours a day and 300 days a year.
b. With hand-pounding, 1,754 tons of paddy are used to produce 1,000 tons of rice.
c. At the rate of Rs18 per kilogram, which is equivalent to US$47.37 per ton at the
exchange rate of Rs380 = US$100.

other mills have substantial import components. The next larger capacity mill (the G type) is a so-called integrated Japanese rice mill. It has a storage capacity of 756 tons of paddy and a milling capacity of 2,500 tons of paddy a year, that is, two and a half times that of the C type mill, but its investments are about eleven times larger than those of the C mill. The bulk satellite (the H-1 mill) increases capacity by a factor of three, but its investments increase by a factor of five. It has a storage capacity of 4,500 tons of paddy. The bulk terminal (the K-1 type) represents a similar jump in capacity and investments and must be considered one of the most capital-intensive rice mills in the developing world. Its storage capacity is 15,000 tons of paddy.

As may be seen in table 6-2, all the milling operations result in substantial paddy savings in relation to the hand-pounding operation. When these savings are evaluated at the price for village dry paddy at the mill of Rs18 per kilogram (US$47.37 per ton), the annual benefits vary from US$1,658 to US$179,248, depending on the type of mill. Discounting the benefits over the lifetime of the investments at a rate of 12 percent (the highest rate used by the consultants, but substantially below the opportunity cost of capital if Timmer's data are accepted), the benefit-cost ratios appear to vary from 1.4 to 0.5. Although in table 6-2 the milling data of Timmer rather than those of the consultants have been used, the benefit-cost ratios are well in line with those of the consultants under their assumptions of a 7 percent paddy savings and multiple-shift operations. The consultants believed, however, that the 7 percent saving was a minimum and arrived at the considered judgment that the largest facility would have a benefit-cost ratio of 1, and the smaller facilities benefit-cost ratios substantially higher.

It is not the intention here to challenge the assumptions underlying the calculations of the benefit-cost ratios in table 6-2. But the calculations are methodologically wrong and the benefit-cost ratios are used in a rather naive manner. It is obvious that the paddy savings calculated by the consultants do not present the real benefits of the different types of facilities. (A correct calculation of these benefits will be presented below.) Furthermore, the consultants give the impression that it is the benefit-cost ratio of the entire package that counts. In their opinion, the benefit-cost ratio for the entire program is from 2 to 2.5, and they consider the recommended package therefore worthwhile from the standpoint of the nation as a whole. This is, of course, not correct. Even though the entire program may have a satisfactory benefit-cost ratio, there may be inefficient elements of the program that substantially reduce the overall benefit-cost ratio below what it could be. Although a correct way of calculating the optimal technology will also be discussed later in this note, it will be useful first to review the Timmer analysis.

Table 6-3 presents the details of the Timmer approach. Very rightly, he points out that the larger facilities produce a better quality rice that fetches a higher price so that the consultants' procedure of calculating the benefit of each facility on the basis of only the paddy savings must be rejected. The correct approach, according to Timmer, is to calculate the value added of each facility by subtracting the cost of the rough rice input from the value of the milled rice. His next step is to calculate what the investment costs and labor requirements are if the same value added is to be produced in each facility. After these data are found, an iso–value added curve is constructed or, equivalently, the rate of substitution between capital and labor is calculated. I have not reproduced Timmer's iso–quant in value added, but show the rates of substitution in table 6-3. As may be seen there, the investments required to substitute for one laborer in order to produce the same value added vary considerably. For the husker-polisher type of mill, the required investments are only about US$300; for the largest mill, about US$23,000. Timmer reasons that the present value of an unskilled worker's wage over his working life of fifty years represents the investments society as a whole would be willing to incur if a laborer is to be substituted by capital. For instance, if one assumes that a laborer would earn $80 a year (the market wage rate) during fifty years, and that the discount rate is 24 percent (the assumed opportunity cost of capital), then the present value of these earnings would be US$333. Hence, according to Timmer, no facilities should be constructed if the investments per laborer displaced are larger than US$333. Over a wide range of discount rates, it appears that the husker-polisher mill (the C type) is the optimal one and that the G, H-1, and K-1 type of facilities cannot be justified. It is interesting to note that, in the Timmer analysis, hand-pounding is the preferred method of processing if the opportunity cost of labor is US$40 a year instead of US$80 a year. In that case the present value, at a discount rate of 24 percent, of the earnings of a laborer over his working life is US$167 instead of US$333. Since the investment per laborer displaced in the C facility is US$296, it is not economic to move from hand-pounding to the C type of operation.

Unfortunately, Timmer's analysis is deficient in several respects. First, his calculation of value added is incorrect since, as shown below, there are many material inputs in addition to rough paddy.

Table 6-3. *Economic Evaluation of the Indonesian Rice Mills According to Timmer*

Item	Hand-pounding (Z)	Husker-polisher (C)	Japanese integrated rice mill (G)	Bulk satellite (H-1)	Bulk terminal (K-1)
Per 1,000 tons of paddy input					
Investment cost (U.S. dollars)	0	8,049	36,204	62,956	120,645
Operative laborers (number per year)	22.00	12.00	6.40	3.75	1.81
Milled rice output (tons per year)	570	590	630	650	670
Market price (U.S. dollars per ton)	105.26	118.42	126.31	130.26	131.57
Value of output per year (U.S. dollars)	59,998	69,868	79,575	84,669	88,152
Value of paddy input per year (US$47.37 per ton)	47,370	47,370	47,370	47,370	47,370
Value added per year (U.S. dollars)	12,628	22,498	32,205	37,299	40,782
Per $25,000 value added per year[a]					
Investment cost (U.S. dollars)	0	8,944	28,104	42,197	73,957
Operative laborers (number)	43.55	13.33	4.97	2.51	1.11
Rate of substitution along iso–value added curve					
Incremental investment costs (U.S. dollars)	—	8,944	19,160	14,093	31,760
Laborers displaced (number)	—	30.22	8.36	2.46	1.40
Investment costs per laborer displaced (U.S. dollars)	—	296	2,292	5,729	22,686

— Not applicable.

a. Timmer works with a constant value added amount of Rs10 million, but of course any amount can be taken for the construction of the iso–value added curve.

Timmer's value added estimate is thus an overestimation. Second, his contention that value added represents the benefits of the facilities is also methodologically incorrect. Value added is a correct benefit concept if the opportunity cost of labor is zero, but Timmer states definitely that that is not the case. Also, it is doubtful that the working life of a laborer in Indonesia is as much as fifty years. The most important criticism, however, concerns Timmer's iso–value added analysis. Timmer is quite right in that it is not possible to construct an iso–quant in gross value of milled rice. Although economic textbooks often show such iso–product curves, they are constructed under the assumption that either capital and labor are the only factors of production or that all other production costs remain the same when capital and labor are substituted for each other. That these conditions are never fulfilled in real life needs no elaboration, and Timmer is thus right in rejecting the iso–product analysis. But his iso–value added analysis is just as wrong. While in any economic analysis the value of a good must be determined by its scarcity value, this is not the case, as indicated in table 6-4, in the Timmer analysis. Because the value added per ton of rice in the case of hand-pounding is only slightly more than one-third of that in the case of the largest processing facility, the plant output necessary to produce the same total amount of value added a year is three times larger in the case of hand-pounding than in the case of the largest facility. In other words, in Timmer's analysis, a ton of rice produced by hand-pounding is considered almost three times more valuable than a ton of rice produced in the largest facility. The Timmer analysis has thus a strong built-in bias toward labor-intensive methods of production.

If the consultants' and Timmer's methodologies must be rejected, what is the correct analysis? Before proceeding further, it is essential to get the data at least conceptually correct. From the consultants' advance draft report, which contains all the relevant data, albeit spread throughout the report, the benefits and costs of the different processing techniques are reproduced in table 6-5. A few comments are in order. First, the operating costs in table 6-5 include the opportunity cost of working capital. Normally, in a discounted cash flow analysis, when the opportunity cost of capital is not precisely known, working capital is treated as an investment that will be recovered at the end of the useful life of the facilities. In this case, it is assumed for ease of exposition (see below for a further discussion) that the opportunity cost of capital is exactly 24 percent, so that the cost of working capital can be precisely calcu-

Table 6-4. *Value Added and Plant Output Data in Timmer's Iso–Value Added Analysis*

Item	Hand-pounding (Z)	Husker-polisher (C)	Japanese integrated rice mill (G)	Bulk satellite (H-1)	Bulk terminal (K-1)
Value added per ton of output (U.S. dollars)[a]	22.15	38.13	51.12	57.38	60.87
Plant output required to produce US$25,000 of value added per year (tons of milled rice)	1,129	656	489	436	411

a. Data from table 6-3.

lated. Second, it is assumed that the opportunity cost of unskilled labor is US$40 a year, that is, half the going market wage rate. Third, the analysis has not taken into account that the more capital-intensive facilities could reduce the nutritional value of the milled rice. The cost of the additives to restore the nutritional value is, however, not high so that the error in the benefit calculation can be neglected. Fourth, the assumption that the facilities have an average lifetime of fifteen years is contrary to the consultants' estimates of much longer lifetimes given in table 6-2, but well in line with the actual data presented in the advance draft report, which showed that the weighted average lifetimes of the facilities vary from thirteen to seventeen years. Since it is not the intention to bias this analysis toward the capital-intensive processing techniques, a fifteen-year lifetime has been adopted. Table 6-5 shows that under the above assumptions, the benefit-cost ratios of the different facilities vary from 10.3 to 1.2. The consultants' estimates of the benefits of the different facilities as presented in table 6-2 are thus much too low. For instance, the paddy savings of the K-1 bulk terminal are only about US$180,000 in the consultants' analysis (table 6-2), whereas the real benefits are almost US$800,000 (table 6-5), resulting in a benefit-cost ratio of 1.2 rather than 0.5.

Does this mean, as the consultants contend, that the large bulk terminal facilities are justified? Far from it. What the analysis should determine is the most advantageous manner in which rice can be milled in Indonesia, and table 6-5 does not clarify this matter at all. For instance, three H-1 facilities will produce about the same output as one K-1 facility, but the H-1 facilities have benefits and costs different from those of the K-1 facilities. For an objective analysis, it is thus necessary to compare the benefits and costs of the different processing facilities on the same output base. Normally, this can be done by calculating the least common multiple of the various output capacities. In this case, since the analysis concerns Indonesia's entire processing industry and not a particular plant, any output level can be taken as the basis for the comparison, and for ease of exposition the level has been set at 1,000 tons of milled rice. The net benefits and investments of the various processing techniques that could produce this output are shown in table 6-6.

There are now several possible ways to proceed. The usual textbook method of determining the most efficient method of production is to calculate the net benefits after allowance is made for recovery of the investments at the opportunity cost of capital. As

Table 6-5. *Basic Data on the Indonesian Rice Mills*

Item	Hand-pounding (Z)	Husker-polisher (C)	Japanese integrated rice mill (G)	Bulk satellite (H-1)	Bulk terminal (K-1)
Technical data					
Input of paddy (tons)	1,000	1,000	2,500	7,200	21,600
Output of milled rice (tons)	570	590	1,575	4,680	14,472
Market price per ton of milled rice (U.S. dollars)	105.26	118.42	126.31	130.26	131.57
Operative number of laborers	22	12	16	27	39
Value of output (U.S. dollars)	59,998	69,868	198,938	609,617	1,904,081
Operating costs (U.S. dollars)					
Paddy (US$47.37 per ton)	47,370	47,370	118,425	341,064	1,023,192
Wages (US$40 per laborer)	880	480	640	1,080	1,560
Maintenance, repair, insurance (2 percent of investments)[1]	0	161	1,810	9,066	52,119

Administration[a]	0	384	1,355	2,329	4,297
Fumigation (US$0.16 per ton of paddy)[a]	0	0	400	1,152	3,456
Bagging (US$0.26 per ton of rice)[a]	148	153	410	1,217	3,763
Fuel[a]	0	74	83	175	524
Opportunity cost of working capital at 24 percent per year[b]	478	478	1,194	7,105	23,684
Total	48,876	49,100	124,317	363,188	1,112,595
Annual net benefits (U.S. dollars)	11,122	20,768	74,621	246,429	791,486
Present value of net benefits during 15 years at 24 percent	44,502	83,099	298,581	986,035	3,166,968
Investment costs (U.S. dollars)	0	8,049	90,511	453,283	2,605,926
Benefit-cost ratio	—	10.3	3.3	2.2	1.2

— Not applicable.

a. According to the consultants' original estimates.

b. The consultants estimated that for the G, H-1, and K-1 facilities the average holding period of paddy is one and one-half months (that is, average stock is one-eighth of storage capacity) and that the average cost of paddy held in storage is US$52.63 per ton. To put the Z and C technologies on a comparable basis, I have assumed that working capital costs per ton of paddy are approximately equal to those of the G facilities.

Table 6-6. *Evaluation of the Indonesian Rice Mills According to Three Economic Criteria*

Item	Hand-pounding (Z)	Husker-polisher (C)	Japanese integrated rice mill (G)	Bulk satellite (H-1)	Bulk terminal (K-1)
Basic data per 1,000 tons of milled rice output per year					
Investments (U.S. dollars)	0	13,642	57,467	96,855	180,067
Operational laborers (number)	38.6	20.3	10.1	5.8	2.7
Value of output (U.S. dollars)	105,260	118,420	126,310	130,260	131,570
Paddy input (tons)	1,754	1,695	1,587	1,538	1,493
Value of paddy input (U.S. dollars)	83,087	80,292	75,176	72,855	70,723
Labor cost (U.S. dollars)	1,544	812	404	232	108
Other operating costs (U.S. dollars)	1,098	2,119	3,335	4,497	6,070
Benefits before capital recovery (U.S. dollars)	19,531	35,197	47,395	52,676	54,669
Net benefit criterion					
Capital recovery cost (U.S. dollars)	0	3,409	14,362	24,206	45,002
Benefits after capital recovery (U.S. dollars)	19,531	31,788	33,033	28,470	9,667
Incremental rate of return and incremental benefit-cost criteria					
Incremental benefits before capital recovery (U.S. dollars)	0	15,666	12,198	5,281	1,993
Incremental investments (U.S. dollars)	0	13,642	43,825	39,388	83,212
Incremental rate of return (percent)	—	>100	28	11	negative
Incremental benefit-cost ratio	—	4.6	1.1	0.5	0.1

— Not applicable.

may be seen in table 6-6, the net benefits of the G type of facility are higher than those of any other method of production; the G type of facility is, therefore, the most efficient one. A slightly more sophisticated method is to calculate either the incremental rate of return or the incremental benefit-cost ratio of the facilities. Again, it is clear that the G type of facility is the preferred one because the incremental rate of return would drop below the 24 percent which, being the assumed opportunity cost of capital, would be the cut-off point; similarly, beyond G, the incremental benefit-cost ratio would drop below 1.0.

That the three methods are equivalent may be shown with the help of figure 6-1, which presents the investment benefit graph of the various processing methods as well as the capital recovery line CR, the slope of which corresponds to a rate of return of 24 percent and a benefit-cost ratio of 1.0. Clearly, G is the optimization point since the vertical distance between G and the capital recovery line CR is greater than at any other point so that net benefits are at a maximum at G. Similarly, the slope of the line segment CG is greater than the slope of the CR line, so that the incremental rate of return and the incremental benefit-cost ratio at G is greater than 24

Figure 6-1. *Investment Benefit Graph of the Indonesian Rice Mills*

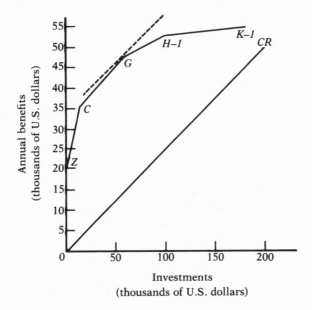

Investments
(thousands of U.S. dollars)

percent and a benefit-cost ratio of 1.0, respectively. The situation at H-1 is the very opposite, and G is therefore clearly the preferred choice.

A glance at table 6-6 shows that the value of the paddy inputs is the most important cost element and that total costs are therefore very sensitive to the price of paddy. It is, however, easy to calculate that over a wide range of paddy prices, the G facilities remain the optimal ones. This is so, of course, because of Timmer's assumptions regarding the paddy input coefficients. For 1,000 tons of milled rice output, the savings of the G facility compared with the C facilities are 108 tons, whereas the savings of the other facilities compared with their next best alternative are only of the order of 50 to 60 tons. Hence, an increase in paddy prices above Timmer's assumed market price of US$47.37 a ton, given the output price, makes the G facilities more attractive. By contrast, a decrease in paddy prices results in lower additional benefits, and it is at a paddy price of less than US$32.03 a ton that the C facilities become optimal.

What is the correct paddy price? Since paddy is an intermediate product, its price depends on what the consumer is willing to pay for the final product, that is, milled rice. If markets are perfectly competitive, then the actual market price would present the true value of the product, but perfect competition is not to be expected in the real world. A more probable situation is that monopsonic elements operate in the paddy markets, so that the market price of US$47.37 a ton of paddy will be somewhat below the real economic value. It may thus be concluded from Timmer's and the consultants' input and output coefficients that the G facilities are probably the most efficient in the Indonesian context.

The calculations have been simplified in that variations in construction periods and life spans of the different facilities were not taken into account. If these were known, one way of calculating the optimal processing technique would be to draw up for each technique cost-benefit streams inclusive of reinvestments, over a period long enough that time discounting would not affect the results. Alternatively, one could attach a terminal benefit to the last year of each facility's life to put them on a comparable basis. These terminal benefits are found by deducting from the present value in the last year of all subsequent net benefits the present value of all subsequent investments, the calculations again to be done over such a period that extension of the period would not affect the value of the terminal benefit because of the arithmetic of discounting. By drawing up the differential cost-benefit stream of two alternatives, it is then possible to calculate the incremental rate of return of the more capital-intensive alternative. By doing this for all alternatives, the optimal facility is found, that is, the facility whose incremental rate of return just exceeds the assumed opportunity cost of capital. This method also has the advantage that the opportunity cost of capital does not enter directly into the calculations so that there is no need to estimate it precisely, something that in reality is extremely difficult to do. Furthermore, this method allows immediate concentration on these facilities whose incremental rates of return are likely to be in the range of the assumed opportunity cost of capital so that the choice is narrowed down. Sensitivity testing of the assumed parameters, that is, varying their values to the extremes of the likely ranges, is then useful to refine the analysis further. Since the relevant data are not available, this type of analysis has not been followed here. It is likely, however, that the conclusion that the G type of facility should be preferred from an economic point of view remains unchanged in this more refined analysis.

Much has been written about the choice of technology in the developing world, and much confusion exists as regards the right technology. It is hoped that this paper has shown that methodologically the analysis is not difficult if the choice is based on purely economic considerations. On purpose, the analysis was based on assumptions biased toward the choice of labor-intensive techniques. The assumption of an opportunity cost of capital of 24 percent is certainly on the high side, and a labor cost of US$40 a year is certainly on the low side. Nevertheless, the analysis is not affected much by the values of these variables, and the relative paddy savings and the milled rice premiums are the dominant variables in the technology choice. Contrary to Timmer's contention, the moderately capital-intensive integrated rice mill is economically the most efficient, basically because the higher valued rice output and the paddy savings of this facility more than compensated for the increase in capital costs. This conclusion is reinforced if the self-sufficiency objective goes beyond the purely economic objective and is considered meritorious in itself.

It is also possible that the choice of technology will be influenced by the objective to increase the incomes of the poorest income classes, an objective that has become more and more important in the developing world. The assumption, therefore, is that the Indonesian government attaches a higher value to a dollar of income accruing to a poor person than to a dollar of income accruing to a middle-class or rich person and that it actively intends to increase the incomes of the poorest group. As may be seen in table 6-7, for 1,000 tons of milled rice output the net benefits of the G facilities are US$1,245 higher than those of the C facilities, while the C facilities in comparison with the G facilities would increase the incomes of an additional ten laborers from US$40 to US$80 a year. Can the C facilities be justified because of this income increase? In the traditional economic analysis, it is assumed that benefits can be taxed away and transferred to the poorest classes, and the G facilities would thus remain the optimal ones. In many developing countries, however, such tax cum transfer mechanisms are not feasible. Assuming that this is also the case in Indonesia, would the C choice of technology be justified? Because the C facility has a very satisfactory rate of return, it seems that, in principle, some efficiency losses relative to the G technology could be accepted. To what extent such losses are justified depends, however, on what the Indonesians consider a minimum target income and what social marginal utility of income schedule, that is, social weighting function, they have in mind. I am not sufficiently familiar with the Indonesian scene to make any definitive comments on these issues but have calculated, as shown in table 6-7, that the premium to be attached to the annual income increase per laborer from US$40 to US$80 would have to be more than about 300 percent to make the C facilities preferable to the G facilities. Elsewhere, I have discussed in detail possible social weighting functions, and it might therefore suffice to

Table 6-7. *Social Analysis of the Indonesian Rice Mills*

Per 1,000 tons of milled rice output	*Hand-pounding (Z)*	*Husker-polisher (C)*	*Japanese integrated rice mill (G)*	*Bulk satellite (H-1)*	*Bulk terminal (K-1)*
Operational laborers (number)	38.6	20.3	10.1	5.8	2.7
Income increase of laborers (U.S. dollars)	1,544	812	404	232	108
Net benefit after capital recovery (U.S. dollars)	19,531	31,788	33,033	28,470	9,667
Premium on income increases (300 percent)	4,632	2,436	1,212	696	324
Social benefits (U.S. dollars)	24,163	34,224	34,245	29,166	9,991

state that premiums of 300 percent are indeed on the high side.[2] It must be concluded—albeit with some hesitation because of the lack of data—that if income distribution objectives are considered, the G facilities should probably remain the preferred ones.

How would the G facilities fit in with a basic needs strategy? As is well known, such a strategy aims to achieve a certain specific minimum standard of living for the poorest income classes in the developing countries before the end of the century. An important instrument for attaining this goal would be increasing the volume and productivity of employment, especially for the production of basic goods and services.[3] The G facilities would produce with the same paddy input as in the case of the C facilities some 1,068 tons of milled rice instead of the 1,000 tons that the C facilities would produce (1,695 tons of paddy produced in the G facility $\div$ 1,587 $\times$ 1,000 = 1,068 tons of rice). This gives rise to the interesting proposition that, to provide additional incomes for ten laborers per 1,000 tons of milled rice production annually, some 68 tons of this staple food would be irrevocably lost. If properly distributed, 68 tons of rice could sustain annually some 375 persons (on the assumption of a basic need for a rice intake of one pound per person per day). This analysis seems to confirm that the G facilities are probably the optimal ones in the Indonesian context. In passing, it may be noted that even in a basic needs strategy, tradeoffs enter into the picture and that, contrary to the contention of some writers, such tradeoffs cannot be evaluated without the use of distributional weights.[4]

Finally, it should be emphasized once again that this chapter should be seen as a methodological exercise rather than as a comprehensive study of the rice-milling technology in Indonesia. Although the consultants' and Timmer's data are precise, one must doubt that such precise data can be correct, and it would have been preferable to work with a range of values to determine the economically optimal technology. Of course, the choice of the right technology is also a matter of social concern, and it is here that in the final analysis only the consensus of the Indonesians counts, notwithstanding all the good advice of foreigners.

Notes to Chapter 6

1. Peter C. Timmer, "The Choice of Technique in Indonesia," in Peter C. Timmer, John W. Thomas, Louis T. Wells, and David Morawetz, *The Choice of Technology in*

Developing Countries: Some Cautionary Tales, Harvard Studies in International Affairs, no. 32 (Cambridge, Mass.: Harvard University Center for International Affairs, 1975).

2. F. Leslie C. H. Helmers, *Project Planning and Income Distribution*, Series Development and Planning, Erasmus University, Rotterdam, vol. 9, 2d ed. (Boston, The Hague, and London: Martinus Nijhoff, 1979).

3. International Labour Office, *Employment, Growth, and Basic Needs: A One World Problem*, Report of the Director General (Geneva, 1976).

4. Arnold C. Harberger, "On the Use of Distributional Weights in Social Cost-Benefit Analysis," *Journal of Political Economy*, vol. 86, pt. 2 (April 1978), pp. S87–S120.

Part IV

Promotion and Innovation

APART FROM THEIR PRINCIPAL ACTIVITY of providing long-term finance to viable investment projects, development banks perform a variety of tasks that are often lumped together and characterized as promotional or innovative functions. These terms are rarely defined. But they are generally applied to the nonfinancing activities of a development bank, or to those of its activities not directly related to the selection and protection of its own portfolio of loans and investments. That is, they are activities designed to create the business the development bank handles or to help create an environment conducive to such business, and—more particularly—to do so with an eye toward serving the institution's underlying developmental purpose.

The innovative tasks a particular development bank may choose, or be required, to perform depend on the specific environment in which the development bank operates and on the structure of financial institutions in the country. The choice is also affected by the views of the sponsors (whether private or government), the policies of the government, and the experience, dynamism, and personality of the chief executive. Development banks may range from institutions operating behind guarded doors reacting coolly, if not coldly, toward potential clients who happen to knock on the door, to aggressive institutions involved in activities far beyond simple lending and equity investment. Most development banks fall somewhere between these extremes.

In general, the promotional or innovative functions of a development bank comprise several activities. First, appraisal and follow-up, although designed primarily to minimize the risks the development bank takes in making an investment and in looking after the health of its client thereafter, can be creative activities which help shape a project and can decisively influence its evolution.

Second is the application of the experience a development bank accumulates in the process of its day-to-day work. The obvious first such application is to the activity of the development bank itself. But a development bank can also make its experience available to the business community and to the government, thereby educating the former and improving the policies of the latter. Third is the deliberate direction of the development bank's efforts toward specific geographical or economic sectors, sometimes as the result of top management's far-sighted detection of emerging opportunities. Fourth is the active search for investment opportunities and the formulation of specific projects, and the creation, alone or in partnership with others, of enterprises to carry them out. This traditional entrepreneurial type of promotion is the most difficult and the most risky of a development bank's promotional activities, not only because its own funds are at risk, but also because it calls for attracting others to invest in projects or enterprises it has devised. Fifth is financial innovation, that is, the creation of new financial instruments or new financial institutions to broaden the services a development bank provides.

The following three chapters touch on all these aspects of promotion and innovation. Chapter 7, by William Diamond, discusses all but the fifth item just mentioned. Chapter 8, by Jayarajan Chanmugam, focuses on three particular aspects: the identification and support of new entrepreneurs, the sponsorship of new enterprises, and the provision of services designed to support the business community. He also raises the important question of institutionalizing promotion, that is, so organizing the development bank that innovation becomes a normal part of the activity of the entire staff, rather than depending on a few appropriately gifted individuals.

In Chapter 9, V. V. Bhatt focuses on the one particular opportunity for promotion that can be seized by aggressive, development-oriented financial institutions. He sees them taking a central role in the adaptation and diffusion of modern technology in the developing world. He suggests a conceptual framework for an organic link between research and consultancy (both foreign and domestic) and financial institutions and the production system. Because of the leverage provided by their resources, he assigns to financial institutions, and to development banks in particular, the lead role in ensuring smooth and effective interplay among the various institutions dealing with the twin problems of technology choice in the developing world: the upgrading of traditional technology and the adaptation and improvement of modern technology consistent with the environment and development strategy of each country. Mr. Bhatt illustrates his schematic framework with specific cases drawn from the nineteenth as well as the twentieth centuries.

Chapter 7

The Impact of Development Banks on Their Environment

WILLIAM DIAMOND

THIS CHAPTER discusses how development banks modify the environment in which they work, as well as provide finance for it. I had originally planned to sum up the process in the word "promotion," thus equating promotion with the entire developmental role of a development bank. There is hardly a discussion of development banks these days that does not refer to promotion in that broad sense, and many annual reports of development banks refer to their promotional activities with an aggressiveness that borders on defensiveness—with good reason. Most development bank charters contain the word "promote" or its near equivalents "encourage" and "stimulate," and their public declarations and policy statements generally express their intention to encourage, stimulate, or promote development in one sector or another. More important, development banks are often criticized by those who watch them most closely—the governments and international institutions, which usually help sponsor them and which almost always help finance them—for apparently falling short of their objectives. This apparent shortfall from expectations is often linked to the inadequacy of their promotional activities. Promotion and the activities related to it are invoked not only as criticism but also as inspiration in exhortations to development banks to pursue their developmental duties.

Originally titled "The Inter-Play between Financial Institutions and Economic Development," IFCI Silver Jubilee Memorial Lecture at the Industrial Finance Corporation of India, New Delhi, October 16, 1974. The first five paragraphs have been omitted.

Used in this broad sense, the word "promotion" covers a wide range of activities—from studies of industrial structure to financial packaging, from project formulation to influencing businesses to adopt new practices and governments to adopt new policies—so broad a range of activities, in fact, that promotion loses its precise meaning, certainly its original economic meaning. In that narrower, more conventional sense, promotion is the process of enterprise creation. It involves the formulation and development of a proposal, the mobilization and organization of the various elements that are needed to give life to it, and, finally, its execution. Promotion is, in effect, the carrying out of the entrepreneurial function.

On reflection, I prefer to use the word "promotion" for that specific entrepreneurial process of enterprise creation. And I shall apply the word "innovation" to the broader range of functions. I do so because I believe that, while few development banks have been involved to any extent specifically in promotional activity, many have been involved to some extent, and often to a large extent, in innovative activity. In evaluting a development bank's performance, it should be kept in mind that it is possible to score high in innovation while doing little in promotion, with an overall result that can still be very creditable to the institution.

Of course, you will recognize in the word "innovation" what, in less sophisticated days, was called the developmental role of a development bank—precisely that mix of functions or tasks that called for linking the words "development" and "bank" together and that justified governments in sponsoring and financing them. On this old subject, I cannot hope to say anything new. Nevertheless, I believe the subject is sufficiently important to justify continuous reminders to those engaged in the business—reminders that their business goes far beyond the daily bread and butter of providing capital on a "yes" or "no" basis to entrepreneurs who apply for it.

The Creative Role of Bankers

The words "banks," "bankers," and "financial intermediaries" carry, in some quarters, a burden of onerous connotations and evoke images of usury, of middleman, and of being cold-blooded and analytical rather than imaginative and creative. Such is the power of words that a banker-president of the institution with which I am associated once tore the phrase "development bank" from our vocabulary and substituted for it the phrase "development finance company," thus symbolizing the distinction we wished to make between an aggressive, creative, financial institution and a traditional bank, and the emphasis we wished to give to the developmental aspect of the institutions we were trying to promote, encourage, and finance around the world.

Among historians and economists there continues to be debate about whether financial institutions, banks, and bankers have been, or can be, innovative or are simply followers and exploiters of economic reality. My own reading of the historical record is not so equivocal. Financial institutions have two essential functions: to mobilize savings and to allocate them. There is room for dynamism and creative imagination on both sides of the financier's balance sheet—dynamism in expanding the limits and improving the quality of both assets and liabilities. I mean something much more here than the aggressive search for additional business, which itself can be a creative process. I mean innovation as well—the invention of new instruments and inducements to encourage and attract savings, the energetic search for newer, better, more productive, and more socially useful investments, and the creation of new institutions to provide specialized services and to carry out specialized functions as the economic environment becomes more complicated. Among the latecomers in the process of industrialization, whether on the European continent, or in the United States, or in Japan, banks played a crucial role in the creation of industry and not simply in financing it. It is indeed this example that has led so many of the still developing countries of Latin America, Asia, and Africa to sponsor or create new financial institutions for the precise purpose of spurring the nation to get ahead and catch up. In certain circumstances, the financial sector has been, and can still be, a "growth-inducing" sector.

Of course, financial institutions and their managers are not entirely free agents. They are limited by environmental inhibitions to savings and investment with which we are all familiar: poverty, lack of knowledge, cultural blocks, and so on restrict the savings that can be mobilized as well as the demand for their use. And, since increasing the quantity and improving the quality of savings and investments have a profound social as well as economic significance, financial institutions find themselves the objects of continuing government attention. Governments exercise a strong influence through policies that affect the incentive to save, the channels through which savings move, and how they are used. The frequently noted conservatism of bankers and their aversion to risks and new ideas are too often an entirely rational reaction to environmental factors and to the policies of government.

Even in this context—one might almost say because of this context—there remains room for imaginative, innovative financiers to try to transform their environment rather than simply to provide the finance required to help operate the economy. In the last analysis, the creativeness of the financial system depends on the people who make it up and on their interplay with their environment, that is, on the opportunities and the freedom to maneuver that exist in circumstances in which they operate. There are always some financiers who are "development-minded"—the result sometimes of their deliberate, conscious reactions to the needs of their countries, and sometimes of the imperatives of their own creative entrepreneurial spirit.

Creative Appraisal and Follow-Up

The provision of capital to finance investment is the hard core of the activities of development banks. Their day-to-day business is evaluating investment proposals and, if investments are made, looking after them. These tasks may sometimes seem routine and humdrum. I submit, however, that doing these jobs well is a creative, not a routine, process.

From my reading of the experience of the best-known development bank, the World Bank, in which I work, I believe its principal influence on the world has been through the "project," which is its colorless word for investment proposal. True, the World Bank tends to surround the project with an aura of sanctity. But the fact is that the Bank has had a decisive role in the conception, formulation, and execution of most of the projects it has financed in its member countries, and a significant influence on the ways in which the governments and citizens of those countries look at their investment plans and proposals and the institutional arrangements through which they are carried out. This influence is not the result of a conception that existed full-blown when the Bank opened its doors for business in 1946, much less a few years earlier in Bretton Woods. It is rather the result of a learning process which is still under way and which included, first, the realization that the only way to ensure that the Bank would get its money back and that its member countries would benefit from its money was to try to ensure the success of the project and, second, the continuing evolution and refinement of ideas about what constitutes the success of a project. That is, the Bank's view of its business evolved in the light of its experience and of its own and the world's changing perceptions of the problems of the developing countries.

It is no longer necessary, as perhaps it once was, to state that a development bank's decisionmaking task—indeed, the task of any bank that is putting out capital on a long term—is more complicated than giving a "yes" or "no" answer to the applicant who enters the bank. Sound appraisal requires the development bank to go through virtually the same kind of examination of the proposal that the entrepreneur himself goes through, asking much the same questions about, and applying much the same tests to, the product mix, the scale of operation, the technology, the plant facilities, the financial structure, the marketing arrangements, the managerial arrangements, the financial results, and so on. Constructive bankers thus find themselves molding, modifying, and advising on the proposals before them to minimize the risks of failure. If there is a difference between the postures of the financier and of the entrepreneur, it results not from the thought processes and skills they bring to bear on the environment, but rather from their degree of commitment to it and the amount of risk they are prepared to assume.

Although wise bankers recognize that their clients generally know much more about their business than they do, wise clients in turn recognize that they get much more than capital from their banker. At best, they get a constructive partner; at least, they get a second diagnostic opinion from one whose critical view can be trusted precisely because it is an outside opinion, not committed to the investment proposal in advance, and hence more likely to be objective. And, indeed, with the passage of time, the development bank itself develops a breadth of experience, which its clients can rarely match.

If appraisal is to contribute to the formulation of an investment proposal and to minimize the risks of failure, then it must comprise much more than the description and the relatively simplistic financial analysis that often go under the name of appraisal. These are but the beginnings of appraisal, not simply because they produce some of the facts that must underpin analysis, but also because the staffs of new development banks may not be capable of going further. The skills that are required for effective appraisal do not come easily. Most development banks begin with some financial expertise and experience. They acquire more slowly the ability to put to the test the technology and engineering used in a project and to advise their clients on both the engineering and the financial aspects of their proposals. And only recently have development banks begun to realize the potential of economic analysis, both for improving the financial attractiveness of an investment proposal and for making it a more efficient project. Although this is a tricky area, which risks collision with clients and government alike, it is difficult to see how a development bank—concerned with the long-range prospects of its clients as well as with its developmental role—can avoid involvement in these delicate matters. It must, however, have the expertise and the experience on which to base the judgments that carry it into this dangerous field.

In the appraisal process—even at its simplistic beginning, and certainly in its more complicated and sophisticated forms—development banks force their clients to reexamine their plans, to spell them out in unaccustomed and explicit detail, and to understand more clearly their implications and, particularly, the available options. They thus affect the working habits, thinking, and attitudes, not only of their clients, but of the business community in general. This quiet revolution in the techniques of project formulation and appraisal is a major innovation for which development banks can take some of the credit. They cannot take all the credit. Necessity itself—the increasing complexity of modern industry, its increasing capital cost, and the demand for more sophisticated management—often makes it vital to introduce new techniques. But if they are not the originators of the new ideas and techniques, development banks encourage those who have the ideas and give them special impetus by linking their adoption to the provision of finance.

Not every entrepreneur welcomes such scrutiny. This is especially so of the larger ones, who do not always realize or will not admit that they too are not immune from disastrous miscalculations and misjudgments. But the innovation is of particular value to smaller and newer entrepreneurs and to enterprises changing from the family to the corporate form and which therefore must introduce more systematic techniques of forecasting, decisionmaking, and accounting. This is not surprising, since a developing economy by definition lacks experience. The crucial role of the development bank, in my judgment, is to help bridge that gap of experience.

The development bank's creative role does not stop with the decision to finance a project. Its relation with its client grows more intimate thereafter, if it is doing its job of supervision effectively. For supervision consists of more than the disbursement of funds and the collection of service payments. The submission of regular reports by the client is the start of the process of follow-up, not its end or objective. The reports provide simply the basis for the operational, financial, and economic analysis, which converts supervision from a simple clerical job to the complex task of operation evaluation. This task involves keeping a finger on the pulse of the enterprise, diagnosing difficulties that arise, and advising on their solution. It involves scanning the environment situations for factors that might affect the client, sensing problems before they become self-evident, and coming up with proposals to deal with them. It leads the way to improving a client's accounting, auditing, and budgeting systems; to improving management; and to identifying possibilities for economies of scale in production and management through mergers, backward and forward integration, and marketing arrangements.

This constructive follow-up is one of the most delicate areas with which a development bank must deal. There is only a very thin line between engaging in the variety of subjects I have mentioned and participating in management. But that line exists, and a development bank cannot ignore it. There is room, and need, for experimentation and innovation in the development of relations with clients, which permit a constructive contribution to broad management policy, with advice and support as needed, without creating a strain on, or interfering with, day-to-day operation.

To do these jobs of appraisal and follow-up well requires time. I am unaware of any development bank in a developing country that had the requisite skills and wisdom at birth. These can develop—given aggressive management with an appropriate orientation—only with the accumulation of precisely that daily work of appraisal and follow-up that often seems so unglamorous. With the growth of such experience, the bank would be expected to develop a capacity to make sound financial and technical appraisals of the projects that are presented to it. From this point, it would be expected to acquire the capacity to distinguish obvious economic losers at an early stage, and beyond this, the capacity, in due course, to improve project design. Then should come the capacity to give useful advice to clients on their continuing operations.

Of course, these stages in the development of skills may not in fact occur in such apparently rational order. Nor is it inevitable that a development bank will advance through these stages. It is possible to survive without doing so and to show an apparently satisfactory balance sheet and profit and loss account—in short, to seem to be a success without engaging in the kinds of activity that alone justify use of the name "development" bank. Some institutions have hardly begun to run this course, and a few have gone the whole way. Indeed, life is such that parts of the course must be continually rerun in the light of new knowledge and experience. Yet the development bank that perseveres in the course and becomes, and continues to be, effective in its critical tasks of appraisal and follow-up, safeguards its portfolio and profit and loss account, assures its clients a constructive partnership, and can justifiably consider that it is making an important contribution to the development of its country.

The Use of Experience

But this is not—or need not be—the end of the story.

Experience with the nitty-gritty of the development bank's daily work results in its becoming a repository of knowledge on the activities of the sectors in which it works, knowledge which is often unmatched by other institutions in developing countries and whose value goes far beyond its use to enrich the development bank's own investment decisions or to assist in the healthy growth of its clients. That work often places a development bank in an unusually good, if not unique, position to combine broad knowledge of the country's industrial structure with detailed familiarity with practical business problems; it can become an indispensible repository of factual information about costs, prices, and demand patterns and about ways in which previous investments have encountered difficulties. In addition, a development bank is in a position to attract, and to hold, the confidence of the private sector as well as of the government.

A dynamic development bank can take advantage of this unique position to advise the business community in matters going far beyond specific projects, and to advise governments on matters of general industrial policy. Some have reacted to their experience also by providing, or by stimulating the establishment of, new institutions to offer new services in a variety of fields.

What specific applications a development bank makes of its experience is the upshot of several factors: the condition of the business community in the country, the institutional framework that serves that community, the attitudes and policies of the government, and the reactions of the management of the development bank to the felt needs of the community as they emerge from its daily experience. In some countries or regions the development bank may find an active and energetic entrepreneurial community experienced in its business even though that business may be commercial rather than industrial. In such an environment, a development bank is likely to feel justified in assuming a relatively passive posture. If the case is otherwise, a development bank is likely to be tempted—and pressed—to be more aggressive. In a country or a region in which the standards of accountancy are low or nonexistent, in which there are no business schools or consultant services, and in which financial services are few and simple, a development bank management and staff are likely to feel frustrated and depressed and often overwhelmed by the need to do themselves all that a host of individuals and institutions are ready and able to do elsewhere. In such an environment there is no end to the services a development bank is likely to be tempted to undertake, even with an inadequate staff, or to stimulate and to sponsor. In some countries the government lacks an adequate awareness of the problems affecting industrial growth and of the instruments and policies needed to induce and sustain productive investment. Or the government may wish deliberately to shape industrial patterns in ways that may not be conducive to industrial growth. In such circumstances, a development bank has to struggle to do the job it was created to do, must work as best it can within the constraints of government policy, and must try to inform and advise the government from the lessons of its own experience.

There are few among the older and more experienced of the development banks that have not felt impelled to take action in one way or another to try to deal with such situations—to contribute a clearer concept of the problems faced, if not solutions to them. The following are a few examples.

First, there are many activities involving what I might call the education of the community. For instance, the managing director of an Iranian development bank felt acutely the absence of first-class business training facilities in his country. Quite outside his company's normal work, he interested local and foreign educational institutions in the establishment of a school of business administration in Iran, which is now in operation, closely linked to one of the most advanced schools in this field in another country. In the fullness of time this will no doubt prove to be a far more important contribution to the development of Iran than many of the multi-million dollar investments in which he and his development bank have been involved.

In India, where there are many research and training facilities, the Industrial Credit and Investment Corporation of India, Ltd. (ICICI) nevertheless felt the need for a specialized research and training facility in the field of finance and stimulated the creation of the Madras Institute; and the International Financial Corporation of India (IFCI), sensing the need for better management training, established the Management Development Institute in 1973 to provide training in modern management techniques, particularly to new entrepreneurs. Indian development banks have sponsored conferences not only for their clients but also for the business community in general to sharpen perceptions of what goes wrong with industrial projects and how to deal with those problems. The more experienced development banks have been active in the establishment of training facilities for less experienced financial institutions, which should greatly improve the quality of their influence on their clients. IFCI has begun to create chairs in financial and industrial management in various educational institutions and has seconded staff to less developed development banks. In other countries, development banks have extended such training also to the staff of commercial banks and even to governments.

Second, there is a broad range of activities that provide services to the business community. As noted earlier, development banks are often overwhelmed by the absence of many of the services normally required by a business community. Moreover, as an economy develops, the need for such services multiplies. No single institution is capable of providing all the services a sophisticated economy requires, and certainly a development bank is not in a position to do much more than to perceive the gaps and to try to find means of bridging them.

Thus, development banks in various countries have been instrumental in setting up consultancy companies, accounting firms, leasing companies, and industrial estates. A Turkish development bank has done much to promote the sale of industrial bonds. Iranian and Greek development banks, in part because of problems arising from their own operations, but also because of broader national considerations, have stimulated the creation of mutual funds. India's principal development banks have joined in creating industrial and technical consulting organizations in several states. Some of its development banks pioneered in providing underwriting facilities; and some have recently set up merchant banking units to provide services required for company creation, expansion, or merger. A Korean development bank, troubled by chaotic and unhealthy conditions in the unorganized money market, took the lead in creating a new institution to attract funds away from the unorganized money market to make them available to enterprises on a sounder basis.

Third is the development of an effective dialogue between development banks and the government. It is absolutely crucial to the integrity of a development bank (whether publicly or privately owned) that its relations with its clients be confidential. In referring therefore to a useful dialogue with government, I am not by any means referring to the provision of information about specific investments or specific clients. I am referring, rather, to making available the development bank's accumulation of knowledge affecting important government policies; for instance, taxes, investment incentives, protection, and policies affecting the efficiency of industry. A government ignores such information at its peril, if it is available; and a development bank, if it has such information, is ignoring a great opportunity to stimulate sound economic growth if it does not make it available. After all, government policies are generally conceived and made by persons without direct experience in industry, and those persons are often astonished by the subtle adjustments the business community is able to make to frustrate such policies. A development bank, because of its deep immersion in the daily operations of firms, has an intimate knowledge of the marketplace. That knowledge can be of great service to the government in devising effective policies based on the realities of the marketplace. Opportunities should be sought by both participants in the dialogue to exchange views as frequently as possible on the formulation of new policies and on the implementation of old ones.

I have the impression that in India the dialogue has become more extensive and more fruitful than in some other countries in which I have worked. If this observation is correct, it is the result both of the maturity of many of India's development banks and of the realization by the government of the importance and relevance of the experience of those banks. This is not to say that that dialogue cannot be broadened and made even more intensive. There can be no end to this two-way interaction. Arrangements under consideration in India would further institutionalize cooperation and interaction between government and the development banks and put their relations on a more systematic footing, without, I hope, undermining, or threatening to undermine, the integrity or autonomy of the individual development banks concerned, and without reducing the opportunities for competition among the banks in achieving excellence if not in acquiring business.

Directed Efforts

There is still another path of innovative effort that I should like to mention. A moment comes, sooner or later, when a development bank has the knowledge and experience, and the self-confidence, to look actively for, or to encourage, investment opportunities of a particular kind—specifically those which might contribute to the national development effort by acting deliberately to remove critical bottlenecks of one kind or another. This process is sometimes called laying out a "development strategy." That phrase implies a level of knowledge of wider opportunities, an entrepreneurial capacity, a systematic overview of alternatives that few development banks have, and a role for a development bank that goes far beyond the realities. I prefer the more modest characterization of this process: directing the development bank's efforts toward new opportunities for investment and for service, which are both profitable and economically sound.

This is not a new concept in India. Although IFCI was set up with a very broad and undifferentiated mandate, most of India's development banks were designed—by statute or by explicit policy—to meet specific needs as understood at a specific time. Thus, ICICI fixed for itself at the start the policy of financing the newer, rather than the traditional, industries in the conviction that this was a developmental path from both demand and supply viewpoints. The State Finance Corporations were designed to provide for the financial needs of smaller-scale industry, and to help decentralize industry. The State Industrial Development Corporations were given a more specifically entrepreneurial, rather than a financial, role. The Industrial Reconstruction Corporation of India was created to cater to enterprises in trouble. IFCI, as a matter of deliberate policy, has concentrated on the cooperative movement in India and helped put new life into it.

If the concept of focusing on specific development objectives by seeking special new opportunities is not new, the thought that the direction of effort should change from time to time might be. This focus should be reviewed periodically and should be reoriented in the light of the development bank's own experience and of the changing public view of the country's needs. The public perception of requirements gives rise to new opportunities or to clues as to where to search for new opportunities; and a dynamic development bank will be ready to reorient its efforts to search for, and to exploit, them—always, of course, within the limits of technical and managerial capacity and of financial prudence.

For example, regional aspects of economic development and, in a broader sense, a more equitable distribution of income are not new concerns. They have long been of much concern in the industrially advanced world, as well as to those in the developing world who have been alarmed by the seemingly inevitable concentration of economic progress in and around a few commercial centers, with corresponding backwardness elsewhere, and by the apparently unbridgeable gulf between the rich and the poor. But it is only relatively recently that these questions have been brought directly into the mainstream of thinking about the economic development process and have come to loom large in the minds of all who are concerned with the progress of developing countries. Inevitably, these issues surface in a discussion of a development bank's activities, both because of the bank's underlying objectives and because it is a continuing object of public attention. A development bank cannot avoid being judged in the light of its contributions in dealing with those problems, however much it points out that awareness of the problems played no role in its establishment and that a financial institution can play only a very limited role in this largely political area.

But a development bank can play a role in dealing with these matters—a role, moreover, which was very much in the minds of the sponsors of many development banks, certainly those with which I have been associated. Wherever the question of decentralization of economic activity looms large, or where there is a significant problem of concentration of economic power, a development bank's efforts can contribute much to development by seeking investment opportunities outside the main business concentrations, or by deliberately looking for new entrepreneurs, or by ensuring that project designs have a capital-labor mix that is in line with the factor endowments of the economy.

In India, much attention has been directed to these areas. For instance, IFCI has been quite active. In its past fiscal year, twenty-nine of the ninety projects it sanctioned were in areas the government has declared less developed, and almost a third of its total assistance since inception has gone to such areas. Moreover, a substantial proportion of its financing has gone to new entrepreneurs. Other development banks have done as much, as the result of deliberate effort. In a very large country, such as India, with an elaborate framework of financial institutions, a development bank can contribute to regional development not only by direct investment outside the main centers, but also by helping to upgrade and to give technical and financial support to regional financial institutions, as India's national development banks are trying to do.

Another means comes to mind through which a development bank can contribute to a more equitable distribution of income. In economies or in regions where the unorganized money market is strong, a development bank can make a concerted effort to find and to finance financially and economically attractive projects, even though these may be in weak companies that are too poor to obtain conventional financing. It was to help deal with the pervasive influence of the unorganized money markets to which such companies must normally turn that a Korean development bank stimulated the creation of the institution, to which I referred earlier, for channeling funds from the unorganized to the organized financial markets. Again, a development bank's effort to foster wider ownership of industrial securities also has a bearing on the question of better income distribution.

There are other areas that might fruitfully attract what I have called directed efforts. For instance, export promotion is critical in many countries. A development bank can contribute to export growth by an active search for investment opportunities in enterprises, which are, or can become, internationally competitive and which therefore have significant export potential, and by advising governments on an appropriate mix of incentives so that export will actually materialize. Still another area is the deliberate search among its own clients, or among other enterprises in the community of which it has knowledge, for opportunities where significant productivity increases can be achieved with relatively small inputs of capital.

There are no doubt other ways in which a development bank can reorient and redirect its activity in a fashion that will be economically beneficial. It would be presumptuous for someone not completely immersed in the local economy to make explicit suggestions. But it is not presumptuous to call attention to the fact that opportunities do exist for a development bank to contribute toward solving specific current development problems. A development bank manager, with his intimate knowledge of the business community, will be far better able to spot opportunities for developmentally directed efforts than any outsider—if the manager himself is sensitive to the need to do so, alert to the opportunities, and dynamic in their pursuit. Moreover, he will be more fully aware than any outsider both of the limitations of institutional experience and the imperatives of financial integrity. There is no rule that can be laid down with respect to when a development bank can push ahead and when it must hold back, or any clear line with respect to how much of its efforts should be directed toward new activities. A principal function of management is to know to what extent, and how far, the institution's efforts can be directed effectively, without risking its survival.

Enterprise Creation

I come now to the subject of promotion—narrowly and precisely conceived: that is, promotion as enterprise creation. It is common to say, as I did in 1958, that a development bank must engage in "uncovering new investment opportunities, including people to exploit them, and exploiting them by itself if no one could be induced to do so." Speaking to the Economists' Discussion Group in Bombay in 1959, I was prudent enough to say that a development bank "must even on occasion take the initiative in creating new enterprises." If I stressed the words "on occasion," it was because even then—and more so now—I considered the creation of a new enterprise the most difficult and complex activity a development bank can undertake. And that is why I have put it last among the innovative functions—not in importance, but in the sense that it should be tackled only when a development bank has acquired the technical skills, the financial strength, and the institutional repute to carry the risks and the costs of the process.

I need not elaborate on the well-known process by which a new enterprise is typically promoted, which is to say, the course it travels from conception to fruition. A notable example is the joint effort to promote and create enterprises in the backward regions undertaken in the past five years by the all-India development banks under the leadership of the Industrial Development Bank of India (IDBI). Together they made technoeconomic surveys of backward areas to develop detailed knowledge of the resources and problems of the areas and to bring to light investment proposals that should be given priority. These surveys are being followed up by the creation of the technical consultancy agencies mentioned earlier and by the creation of interinstitutional groups, each under the leadership of one of the all-India institutions, whose main task is to screen the ideas that emerged from the surveys, to pick those which should be subjected to detailed feasibility study, to identify potential entrepreneurs, and to develop a training program for them. These feasibility studies are in turn being discussed with entrepreneurs, state financing agencies, and institutions to bring the project to fruition. Some such proposals have already resulted in new enterprises; others are in various stages of study and development.

Needless to say, such promotional efforts can produce results only over a considerable period. But even before the physical results emerge, there are, and will be, by-products in the form of knowledge of local conditions, the development of the local institutional infrastructure, the stimulation of local initiative, and the pinpointing of governmental policies to encourage enterprise, which will no doubt yield benefits more far-reaching than the specific new enterprises that emerge from the process.

I would look to those developments, more than to the specific efforts to create enterprises, for the main results of the pioneering efforts of the all-India development banks, because usable ideas for creating enterprises are less likely to emerge from general resource surveys than from an intimate relation of the development banks with the business community and with the government. On the one hand, the business community is more likely to be impressed with its own ideas of what investments can and should be made, on the basis of its own knowledge of, and experience with, the market or the processes involved, than with suggestions from an institution not directly engaged in the business it is promoting. On the other hand, the government, in many developing countries, gives general orientation to the economy and establishes the incentives needed to point entrepreneurial energies appropriately. Indeed, the greater such central orientation, the less freedom of maneuver there is likely to be for a development bank in its specifically entrepreneurial efforts.

Aside from directly encouraging others to invest, a development bank, whether for profit or for service, sometimes takes a central position (as equity holder and in management) in the new enterprises which it promotes. In short, the development bank itself sometimes carries the principal burden of bringing the investment proposal to fruition. This is the role of the development bank in the classic environment of underdevelopment in which there is no entrepreneur or not enough sponsorship to carry the burden, or in which sponsors require an important involvement by the development bank for one reason or another. Here is the acme of development bank activity, one to be strongly encouraged—but only if the development bank enters the process fully aware of implications of the entrepreneurial role. Some of those implications are described in the following paragraph.

Studies and other activities to create enterprises are costly, and there is no assurance that the outlay will be recovered. At best, the payoff will be long delayed. When promotion carries with it an equity investment, the investment risk is far more important than the original administrative outlay. Moreover, sooner or later, the promotion brings other investors into the picture, either at the start, as participants in the original financing plan, or later, as purchasers of the development bank's investment. In either case, the development bank carries a heavy moral responsibility for seeing the project through and ensuring good management, and the responsibility, when it reduces or gives up its equity in the enterprise, for leaving the enterprise in the hands of interested, competent, and devoted parties.

These financial and moral risks have implications for the capital structure and ownership composition of a development bank. The bank must have a capital structure capable of carrying the burden of risk for an indefinite time, and a flow of revenue capable of sustaining the company while awaiting the return on promotional efforts. This means that promotion must be financed, not with borrowed capital, but with equity or from special funds that have been set aside for the purpose (such as IFCI's new Benevolent Fund). It also calls not only for a capacity but for a will to wait for returns for an indefinite period.

Above all, promotion imposes a heavy drain on manpower and on management. Company promotion is seductive, for staff is often more interested in creating something new than in processing someone else's plans; and the result may be "pet" projects that interfere with financial judgment. Promotion is also time-consuming. Project appraisal is a task that can perhaps be put aside at closing time, but the person engaged in promotional work is more likely to take the work home and to bed with him. The staff and management of a promotional institution are not necessarily the kind of staff and management that a financial institution should have. The bureaucracy and the commercial banking system, as well as schools of economics and engineering, from which most development bank managers and staff are drawn, might well produce a first-class entrepreneur; but it should be clear that, as a class, they are not entrepreneurs and not necessarily capable of becoming entrepreneurs.

It is precisely because of these costs and risks—the ease with which staff may become overinvolved in promotional activities and overinvolvement may slide into overcommitment, and the moral risk of putting others into commitment—that management must be personally involved in promotion and maintain a tight control over it. Enterprise promotion involves a commitment that a purely financial commitment cannot match, and hence it must involve management as no other activity does.

As I said before, I refer to these implications of entrepreneurial activity, not to discourage it, but to note that it is, in the best of circumstances, a risky business, which should be undertaken with full awareness, on the basis of experience, and with first-class management.

A Summing Up

My first point is that financial institutions need not be passive instruments of economic activity. With dynamic management and an adequately permissive environment of available opportunities and of favorable policies, they can be active engines of economic development, as they have been in the past.

Second, if among financial institutions, the development bank has been singled out for discussion, it is not because it is unique in the opportunities it has to foster economic development. It is rather because the development bank has, aside from the conventional function of providing finance, an explicit, special task. It has been created, generally with community support, to do something to foster development, which is not being done by others. The development bank cannot avoid the responsibility to behave accordingly.

Third, the provision of finance must remain the hard core of a development bank's activity. Capital is its stock-in-trade, and it must use that capital well if it is to survive financially and if it is to live up to the objectives of its sponsors and of the community that supports it. It follows from this that the ability to choose sound projects is the basic skill the staff and management of a development bank must acquire. This sounds simpler than it is in fact. For we have all learned, over the years, that the simple financial and technical analysis with which we started to appraise investment proposals is not enough either to assure viability in the longer run in a changing world or to give some assurance of the economic benefits a development bank should seek to achieve. Financial and technical analysis is thus only the groundwork on which other, more subtle skills and instincts must grow. If these skills and instincts are developed to the point where a development bank has a portfolio of financially profitable and economically sound investments, the institution can indeed be pleased with its performance.

Fourth, to reach this point, however, a development bank will necessarily have engaged itself in, or put itself into a position to become involved in, a host of activities that have an important developmental impact on the community. These range from the improvement of investment proposals in the interest of both economic efficiency and financial profit, to advising clients in difficulty. And these in turn lead to influencing the thinking of the business community, to helping develop some of the many services which an industrial economy requires, and to advising government on aspects of industrial policy.

Fifth, a development bank does not inevitably proceed on this path. There are development banks that survive, and seem to have satisfactory accounts, without doing so. I submit that their portfolios are likely to be suspect and their profits and losses illusory, and that in a broader sense they are missing out on the development task for which they were established. By contrast, most experienced development banks with dynamic management are engaged, to a greater or lesser extent, in such activities, which might originally have seemed peripheral to the specific task of investing capital, but which are in fact central to both sound investment and the development process.

Sixth, with the refinement of its skills and the growth of its experience (and the self-confidence that comes from the two), a development bank will also find it possible to direct its efforts toward contributing directly to solving some of the major development problems of the country. Among them, in most countries, will be regional development, international competitiveness and promotion of exports, a more equitable income distribution, and the improvement of industrial efficiency.

Seventh, a development bank has the opportunity to promote enterprises, that is, to conceive investment proposals and to stimulate others to pursue them or itself to carry them through from conception to realization. In principle, a development bank is well suited to assume this kind of role. Yet enterprise creation is fraught with costs and risks that a development bank cannot neglect. Development banks can prudently undertake them only when they have the requisite financial strength, technical expertise, and the managerial skill to deal with them effectively.

This brings me back to a point I made before and on which I would like to close. Investment opportunities and a favorable climate are in a sense passive factors. Dynamic management is needed to exploit them. An experienced board of directors is not difficult to acquire, and skilled staff can be acquired or developed in due course. But a dynamic management is needed to weld these into an innovative institution capable of perceiving and exploiting opportunities for development investment. Finding out and pursuing the right line between developmental dynamism and financial and institutional integrity is the delicate, yet crucial, task that gives development bank management its peculiar challenge. That challenge changes with the times, for as the environment changes so do the opportunities. Dynamic management calls for continuing reappraisal of the opportunities offered to a development bank and a continuing reconsideration of the programs it could pursue to exploit those opportunities. In the final analysis, in any given environment, the difference between a developmental bank that is dynamic and one that is not, is to be found in its manager. His personality and qualities of leadership are crucial.

Chapter 8

Promotion and Innovation
in Development Banks

JAYARAJAN CHANMUGAM

IN OCTOBER 1965 the World Bank organized a conference of the chief executives of the development banks to which it had made loans (or in which the International Finance Corporation had equity investments). After the conference, essays were published on each of the agenda items. The essay based on the discussions on the first item on the agenda concerned promotion. The introductory note to that essay succinctly summarizes the views expressed by the conference participants.

"The provision of capital is the hard core of the function of a development finance company. But, should it also help formulate, initiate, and organize a proposal for industrial investment? Does it have such an entrepreneurial role to play, as well as a financial one? What are the circumstances and the ways in which a development finance company can appropriately and prudently take the initiative and the leadership in conceiving and fashioning proposals for new enterprises, organizing the finance for them, and carrying them out? What are the costs and risks of such activity?

A variety of views was expressed on these questions, views which tended in general to reflect the level of economic development in the country concerned. Those who were most reluctant to take the lead in promoting enterprises were from countries in which there was already a large and active entrepreneurial class, while those that stressed most vigorously the need for promotional activity came from countries where investment opportunities existed but where entrepreneurs to grasp these opportunities were conspicuously absent or were hard to convince of the merits of new proposals in new fields.

Yet even the managers of companies in the more underdeveloped countries considered that the primary function of their institutions was to provide finance and to organize the provision of finance. There was a general reluctance to take the primary responsibility for the formulation and execution of a project and an awareness of the moral as well as financial risks involved, of the danger of spreading staff capacities too thinly, and of the seductive effects of promotion on staff, which tended to find promotion much more exciting than the more pedestrian activity of appraising the projects of applicants. Some criteria emerged from the discussion to cope with these risks and dangers. For instance, promotion should be undertaken only in industries which are of national importance and should involve operations which are large enough to make considerable risks worthwhile.

Mr. N. M. Uquaili, then Managing Director of the Pakistan Industrial Credit and Investment Corporation, chaired the discussion of promotional activity. In summing up his reaction to the discussion, he said that the main functions of development finance companies, with respect to promotion, were to suggest improvements in projects submitted to them for approval, to assist in finding technical and entrepreneurial partners, to assist in finding funds for large projects, to arrange for the preparation both of industrial surveys and of feasibility studies for specific projects, and to make equity investments and carry out underwriting operations and thereby attract other private investors. Since development finance companies were primarily financial institutions, their promotional role had to be limited. But sometimes the objective situation called for promotional activity. The cost should be borne by the sponsors of the project which emerged from the promotion, that is by the new enterprise itself, although such expenses might also be shared by development finance companies, national governments, and friendly foreign governments."[1]

Since then, there has been much progress, much growth, more opportunities, and more difficult and diverse issues facing development banks in their attempt to fulfill their mandate to contribute to development, allocate resources in an efficient manner, and manage their portfolio effectively. No financial institution can play a merely passive role with respect to industrial investment opportu-

nities. The role of a development bank in particular is not simply to
wait for well-conceived proposals to arrive, then check them out
and say "yes" or "no" to the financing. Nearly everyone involved in
development banking has, at one time or another, heard criticism of
the relatively cozy situation of their institutions. In the course of
these criticisms development banks are confronted with descrip-
tions of the activist role of investment banks located in New York,
London, Paris, Frankfurt, and Tokyo. These financial houses play a
vital promotional role in arranging mergers, attracting international investments, financing new enterprises, reorganizing existing enterprises, and helping to raise capital. But what is often
forgotten is that, by and large, they operate in countries where there
is no shortage of entrepreneurs, where there are many alternative
opportunities for investment, and where the role of governments in
the conduct of the business of the banks is regulatory rather than
participatory.

Development banks in developing countries operate in a quite
different environment. Over the years they have drawn upon the
experience of financial institutions in the advanced countries in
establishing their basic structure and institutional framework. But
for many other aspects of their activities, development banks must
try to find their own solutions. One of these aspects—perhaps the
most creative—is the charting of a promotional and innovative role.

Promotion is a broad-ranging subject. It would be futile in a short
discussion to try to cover the entire spectrum of activities included
therein. I shall therefore limit my remarks to three aspects of the
promotional and innovative role. These are the promotion of entrepreneurship, the promotion of project proposals, and supportive
innovation. Finally, I shall comment on the institutionalization of
promotion work.

Promotion of Entrepreneurship

The promotional function, whether it is undertaken by development banks, by governments, or by individuals, is undoubtedly the
engine of growth. But in developing countries, there are far too few
entrepreneurs to discharge that function adequately.

People looking for a new business fall into one of two groups.
Some have technical knowledge (some special ability) to sell, and
the record shows that many successful businesses have been spun

off from larger companies by people who had good ideas their employers would not take up. The other category of people does not have specialized knowledge, but has one great quality (so difficult to define), the aptitude to do business and a determination to succeed. The entrepreneurs from developing countries have little time for, nor do they understand, such matters as feasibility studies, market surveys, corporate planning, budgetary control, and cash forecasts. They simply want to manufacture, supply their products or services to their customers, and make a profit. More often than not, they make no careful overall assessment of the difficulties, but overcome them one by one as they arise. If the enterprise is successful and plans to expand, it will in time need the careful introduction of sophisticated management techniques and of professionals who understand them. But to introduce them in the initial stages is very likely to stifle the entrepreneurial spirit at birth.

To succeed, entrepreneurs have to gain knowledge of the environment in which they are going to do business; they have to understand the conventions of commercial life and what is acceptable; they have to be familiar with the methods of employing labor and the methods of payment; they have to learn to take advantage of incentive schemes; they have to appreciate the influences of the government and the bureaucracy on the conduct of their business. In this general context, a development bank has a fundamental role to play in identifying, stimulating, and encouraging entrepreneurs. Without them, all other promotional activities by a development bank are academic exercises.

Promotion and Investment Proposals

A second aspect of promotion concerns a development bank's activities in formulating project proposals of its own and in inducing others to join in implementing the undertaking. It is useful here to distinguish between two types of promotion. One is the kind that any development institution ought to do and, in general, is doing rather well. It consists of examining a proposal brought to the development bank and modifying it so that it is economically sound, has good prospects of commercial profitability, and is worthy of investment by the bank. Essentially, the development bank does the analytical work of reshaping somebody else's project, so that the project takes a more desirable form. To a large extent, this is the bread-and-butter business of most of the development banks. In making such promotional modifications, a development bank is considering proposals that have already been thought through by others to some extent; it is dealing with sponsors who already have a substantial commitment to the undertaking.

The second type of promotional work originates in the development bank itself. It stems from a recognition by the bank of a particular gap in the country's productive capacity and a desire to fill that gap by establishing an industrial plant. Having identified this need, the development bank then conducts some sort of sector survey, evaluating the market prospects, estimating requirements for capital, raw materials, skills, and so on, and makes a preliminary feasibility study. All this has to take account of government policy, strategy, and directives.

Too often, such surveys and feasibility studies sponsored by development banks are not very persuasive to the businessmen at whom they are directed. Perhaps this is because the studies often start from the premise that a certain project is desirable from the standpoint of the national economy, and then proceed to make the case for its being undertaken without sufficiently detailed or critical analysis of the difficulties and risks. Potentialities may be stressed more than actual experience, economic reasoning more than practical realities, and the crucial bottom line—the financial result—sometimes seems almost an afterthought. In a sense, the conventional relation of banker and project sponsor is reversed; in this type of promotion, the former seeks to persuade and to sell the project, and the latter becomes a hard-eyed skeptic. It is therefore essential that a development bank's promotional feasibility studies be even more solid and realistic than its most careful appraisals.

The cost of undertaking these studies is a matter of great concern to all development banks, largely because, in promoting a proposal of its own and in inducing others to join in, a development bank has to be even more sure of the prospects of success than when it is financing somebody else's project. The first study may lead to additional and more detailed studies, which are likely to stretch over a long period and to involve protracted discussions with government authorities. It is often difficult to recover the cost of the studies, for the potential investors are likely to resist the inclusion of this cost in the total cost of the project.

These comments are particularly germane in dealing with the private sector and the kinds of projects that private entrepreneurs are likely to be interested in. By contrast, when sector and feasibility studies are made for large projects of national significance, involving a substantial government commitment in one form or another, different issues arise. Such studies usually need to be undertaken by the development bank in collaboration with the government.

Supportive Innovation

Development banks have achieved a great deal during the past decade in finding ways to support the industrial community. These include trying to fill the technological gaps within the country and between the country and the industrialized nations; introducing modern business administration techniques; mediating between businesses and governments; incorporating economic benefit considerations into financial decisionmaking; introducing environmental and pollution control measures; responding to government stimuli in developing backward regions; using local raw materials and increasing employment generation; and, in general, assuming the mantle of leadership in the business community, all of which contribute to the innovative role of a development bank. There are, however, two areas in particular to which development banks should pay much more attention and which have much potential for innovative impact on the character and pace of industrial development. These are the feedback mechanisms by which government leaders and planners become aware of the industrial situation, and the new financial mechanisms to meet the new needs of industry.

To a large extent, development banks deal with issues of industrial activity generally at the level of the firm, while government decisionmakers deal with the macro policy side of industrial growth and the strategy of development in the sector as a whole. In the absence of a dynamic and widely dispersed industrial community whose views and concerns are actively sought by government leaders, such as often occurs in the advanced countries, development banks have a major innovative role to play in supplying information, describing operating experience, commenting on problems, and identifying the constraints faced by their client enterprises to government, so that corrective measures may be appropriately taken at the policy level. Many development banks seem reluctant or hesitant to establish this kind of relation with government. Some of the reasons advanced for this reluctance are maintaining autonomy from the government; difficulties in presenting the development bank's point of view to government; reluctance of government officials to listen to complaints from the industrial sector; lack of a central office in government with which the development bank can discuss such matters; and lack of government directors who are aware of the problems. Some of these reasons may have a measure of validity, but they do not outweigh the potential benefit that can accrue to the community when a development bank takes an active part in changing or amending the industrial policy and strategy of a country. How else can the micro issues be brought to the attention of macro planners?

In the area of capital market development there are several financial market innovations that development banks can usefully exploit to meet the needs of the industrial community. These include, for example, leasing and hire purchase, setting up mutual funds, providing short-term credit for working capital requirements, export financing and guarantee operations, providing financial arrangements for subcontracting and government procurement activities, assisting (through refinance or guarantee operations) rural and cooperative institutions, syndication activities with other financial institutions, merchant banking, and cooperating with commercial banks for term transformation of deposits. Some development banks have already ventured into one or more of these activities. It is time for many development finance institutions to expand their financial horizons beyond borrowing long-term and lending long-term, but this expansion requires an innovative and fresh outlook.

Institutionalization of Promotional Activity

The primary impetus for the development of innovative and promotional activity comes, of course, from skilled people. The dynamic element is enlightened management. But this is not enough; only the institution itself can engage in promotional work in a systematic, consistent, and enduring manner. Proper institutional arrangements are necessary to ensure effective promotion. No institution can survive in the long run on the basis of a few individuals making ad hoc decisions in an isolated and insulated fashion.

There is no need to dwell on the importance of well-defined decisionmaking processes, or on the need for clearly established corporate policies and objectives, since these are discussed in previous chapters. It is vital, however, to establish promotion and innovation on a permanent basis by giving them a place in the organizational framework. Innovation and promotion imply new levels of investigative, analytical, and creative skills, which are not easy to come by, least of all by development banks in a competitive market. Furthermore, innovational and promotional activities are not one-shot affairs but explicitly involve further dimensions of continuing responsibility.

Considerable thought needs to be given to how the promotional function relates to the other activities of a development bank. How does one ensure that enthusiasm for promotion does not impinge on institutional objectivity? For instance, in sponsoring a new entrepreneur or promoting a new project, difficulties may arise for the enterprise, which require the development bank to become even more intimately involved in the new enterprise. Lines of distinction, usually between the financing role and the management role (which are generally articles of faith for a development bank), become blurred, and the bank can get into the precarious situation of taking on functions of a holding company or managing agency.

How should the functional responsibilities be assigned? Many development banks have problems in dealing with the human and psychological preferences of staff for appraisal rather than for follow-up work. Promotion and innovation are generally considered even more stimulating and enticing. Institutionally rational solutions are not easy to find, but with a conscientious and dedicated staff, development banks can manage, with a minimum of trauma, the organizational and administrative measures needed to institutionalize promotion.

Note to Chapter 8

1. William Diamond, ed., *Development Finance Companies: Aspects of Policy and Operation* (Baltimore, Md.: Johns Hopkins Press, 1968), pp. 5–6.

Chapter 9

Financial Institutions and Technology Policy

V. V. BHATT

THE FINANCIAL SYSTEM (including the government, when it acts as a financier) has a pervasive influence on the processes and patterns of resource mobilization, allocation, and use. Quite logically, therefore, considerable attention is paid in the literature to its criteria for selection of projects for financing. The major emphasis has been on the "right" system of relative (accounting) prices and social cost-benefit analytic techniques. The significant choices with regard to products, processes, and machines, however, are made at the project design stage. Once these choices are made, the financial system has merely the option of accepting or rejecting the project; its criteria cannot, however, affect the real choices to any meaningful extent.

Even at the project design stage, the use of accounting prices can have a rationale only if complete information about the range of technology choices is available to the project designer.[1] It is not possible to have such information without an active and intelligent search and even research—in fact without an institutionalized technology policy.[2] Thus project selection criteria would serve the intended purpose only if the range of technology possibilities were actively widened through an appropriate technology policy. It is the purpose of this paper to indicate the major elements of such a technology policy and to emphasize the crucial role of Technical Consultancy Service Centers (TCSC) and the Financial System (FS) in providing organic links between modern technology and domestic and foreign Technological Research Centers (TRC) on the one hand and the Production System (PS) on the other.[3]

The broad outline of a technology policy is presented in the first section. The catalytic leadership function of the FS in such a policy is emphasized in the second section, and how this function has been performed by banks in some countries is suggested in the final section.

Broad Outline of a Technology Policy

The developing countries, with all their handicaps of a late start, have one critical advantage—the growing accumulation of scientific and technological knowledge. But to use this knowledge creatively for solving their own problems, they need to develop competence in choosing technology through an institutionalized technology policy. Sophisticated techniques of planning or project evaluation are not—and cannot be—a substitute for a technology policy; the former in fact have relevance only when a policy is in place.

Such a policy is essential because the present-day developing countries face problems of technology absorption and diffusion that are qualitatively different from those faced by developing countries in the nineteenth century, such as France, Germany, and Czarist Russia. Modern technology has long outgrown the stage of being based largely on engineering practice and invention; it has now become immensely complex and knowledge-based, requiring high-level scientific and technological manpower for both its growth and operation. It is capital-, scale-, and skill-intensive; and, further, because of economic development and increasing real incomes, it is geared to the production of sophisticated goods and services intended to meet simultaneously a wide variety of functional, aesthetic, comfort, and status needs and wants.[4]

Thus both technology and consumer products are oriented toward meeting the complex dynamic want pattern of the richer countries and are out of tune with the initial conditions, resource composition, and basic functional want pattern of the poorer countries. Hence, the developing countries can take advantage of accumulated and growing knowledge only if they have the capacity to search, select, and adapt modern technology creatively to their own environments and development objectives. Further, they have a problem of upgrading technology in their traditional sectors to improve the living conditions of people with traditional skills. This problem cannot be identified by the technological systems of the developed countries; developing countries must first formulate the problem in concrete terms before they can benefit from the knowledge accumulated so far.

Of course, those countries are in a position to obtain assistance from the TCSC and the TRC of the developed countries. But such help can be fruitful only after identifying the problem for which solutions are being sought. The ability to ask questions and identify technology problems is essential to making correct technology choices. Further, in the case of small to medium-size enterprises, it would not be economically feasible to rely on foreign TCSC. What then are the basic elements of a technology policy for the developing countries?

One has to start with the human problem of poverty and try to solve it through means directly related to the problem. It is neither practical nor desirable to provide a progressively rising decent minimum of physical security to each family without providing employment as well. So poverty can be removed only through the full employment of each family at progressively rising levels of productivity. From this focal point, and given natural resources, the problem becomes very specific and concrete: how to choose organizational forms and technology to employ fully the available and growing labor force and at the same time ensure each family initially a decent minimum level of living and later a progressively rising level.

In this context, one has to start from the traditional sector with its skills, techniques, and organization. In many developing countries this sector employs about 80 percent of the labor force (60 percent in agriculture and related activities and 20 percent in traditional industry, such as rural transport and trade, food processing, dairies and cattle breeding, forestry, poultry farming, piggeries, fisheries, and the manufacturing of organic fertilizer, agricultural implements, and household utensils and appliances). About 10 percent is employed in the modern sector, and the remaining 10 percent is either underemployed or unemployed. With population growing at about 2.5 percent a year, even if the modern sector grew at 20 percent a year, it would not be able to provide enough jobs even to meet the increase in the labor force, let alone to hire those at present unemployed. Thus the traditional sector would have to absorb the currently unemployed as well as a part of the increase in the labor force.

The crucial issue, therefore, is to promote the viable growth of the traditional sector and to link organically the growth of the modern sector with that of the traditional, to supplement and reinforce the growth and development of the latter. It is not possible to supplant traditional skills and techniques by modern ones; the latter cannot solve the poverty problem.[5]

There are therefore two problems in technology choice: the problem of upgrading traditional technology, and the problem of adapting and improving modern technology consistent with development objectives, changing institutional structures, and natural resources. Without such upgrading and adaptation, it is not possible to provide a rising minimum level of living to each family.

To accomplish both tasks, it is essential first to identify the concrete ideas relating to the projects or project complexes that have to be undertaken. For both the traditional and modern sectors, this identification process needs to be institutionalized in, say, Project Identification Centers (PIC). Once such project ideas have been identified, the search for appropriate technology should begin. This is the design and engineering function that needs to be institutionalized in TCSC.

It is the function of a TCSC to design machines, processes, and products. This requires knowledge of the initial conditions of both the production and the organizational structures. It requires identification of current knowledge and the current ways in which it can be applied. It requires identification of specific research problems and the ways in which they can be tackled within the country or abroad, and so on. Once experimenting begins with the design of projects or project complexes that are to be implemented (which is how the design-engineering function is crucially linked with that of the PIC and FS), search for relevant knowledge as well as relevant research is set in motion. This is a cumulative process of innovation and one that is self-reinforcing.

As an integral part of development and technology policies, the developing countries need to develop TCSC with the capacity to identify technology choice problems; to search for their solutions with the assistance, when necessary, of foreign TCSC and domestic and foreign TRC; to adapt creatively the suggested solutions to actual project making; to upgrade technology in the traditional sectors (agriculture and cottage and small industries); to identify technology research problems and thus link the TRC with the production system. Thus a TCSC can function as a vehicle for absorbing relevant modern technology, serving as an effective communication link with the foreign as well as the domestic sources of technology. At the same time, it can support and improve machine-building capacities by providing machine industries with designs as well as links with the evolving production structure. In the process, it can generate a wide variety of new project ideas.

Thus TCSC are an essential link between modern technology and domestic and foreign TRC on the one hand and the FS and the PS on the other. Quite a number of countries (such as Brazil, Mexico, and India) have TRC, but they function in a vacuum and are not in a position to tackle relevant problems of the PS; this has caused both internal and external brain-drain and irrelevant research.[6] Some countries have tried to evolve TCSC but have not been able to forge a link between them and the FS and the PS, with the result that such TCSC remain stillborn. Unless one starts from the focal point of actual project ideas—consistent with a country's resources and development strategy—and hence from the PS and the FS, the TCSC also function in a vacuum and become obsolete.

Such TCSC should be functionally linked with the PIC, the FS, and the PS; without an organic functional link, they would become obsolete and operationally irrelevant. They also should be organically linked with the TRC; without this link, technology research would become irrelevant. A research setup—a TRC—is essential; but such a setup can derive meaning and purpose only if it is related to the design-engineering function, which is, in turn, intimately and vitally related to actual projects or project complexes, which again have to be an integral part of a development strategy.

From strategy to project ideas to design and engineering (TCSC) to financial system (FS) to project implementation to new project ideas (PIC) is a single sequence that organically relates one function to the other. Another organically related sequence is from strategy to project ideas (PIC) to design-engineering (TCSC) to technological research (TRC) to design-engineering (TCSC) to financial system (FS) to project implementation (PS) to new project ideas (PIC). A third sequence is from design-engineering (TCSC) to product, process, and machine ideas to project ideas (PIC) to design-engineering (TCSC) to financial system (FS) to project implementation (PS) to new project ideas (PIC). The important point, however, is the central and crucial significance in these chains of the design-engineering function (TCSC). In agriculture (for instance, high-yielding varieties of seeds), there is some appreciation of the significance of these organically related functions; but in other areas, this obvious and more or less self-evident function of technology policy is still not understood.

What is the role of the international community in general and of international development institutions in particular in this field?

- They can urge developing countries to set up PIC, TCSC, and TRC in relevant fields linked with the FS and the PS and assist them in the initial stages in a variety of ways.
- For certain complex fields, they can set up regional-institutional TCSC.
- They can start on their own international-regional TRC, which should work primarily on research problems identified by the national-regional TCSC and which should also function as clearinghouses for relevant information for the national TCSC and the TRC.

It is only thus that national and international efforts can be effectively integrated for solving the urgent and immediate problems of poverty and socioeconomic development.

Catalytic Leadership Function of the FS

So far I have identified the technology problem and outlined the institutional structure and functions for a sound technology policy. The next issue to be discussed is which institution should play the catalytic leadership role to ensure effective interaction among functions, as suggested in the technology policy outline. Since a project cannot be implemented without finance, the vital decision rests with the FS (including the government, when it acts as a financier). Hence, the leadership function has to be assumed by the FS; and its leadership is more important, the more the FS—as in the case of development banks—has to play a promotional role in the development process.

Currently, the FS in many developing countries is trying to perform this function by inducing enterprises to make "right" technology choices through its project selection criteria based on social cost-benefit analysis or economic evaluation of projects. Since the FS tries to evaluate an already formulated project, however, it obviously cannot affect technology choices, which are made at the project design and formulation stage. The project formulation task is performed, by and large, by foreign TCSC or their domestic counterparts for large enterprises. For small to medium-size enterprises, project formulation is based largely on the knowledge acquired by entrepreneurs from machinery suppliers, large enterprises, or past experiences in the field. Here again, the technology choice at one remove is in fact made by the foreign TCSC or their domestic counterparts. The latter normally do not use accounting prices in their project design work, and their choices are largely governed by their experience in the developed countries. This basic limitation of mere economic evaluation of projects is emphasized by Little and Mirrlees in a very illuminating way:

> In other words, a large number of economic choices will have been made already, either at the level of the initiating department, commission, or other decentralized public authority, or by the designing engineers ... Now industrial engineers—good ones, any way—are economists, but they are not usually the kind of economists who are trained to look at matters from the point of view of the economy as a whole. They will, or should, have profitability very much in mind. But they will, of course, assess profitability in the light of actual prices.
>
> The value of choosing from a list of projects according to a criterion using accounting prices, supposed to reflect real scarcities and benefits better than actual prices, is clearly greatly reduced if each such project has in effect been chosen from a long list of variants by a criterion (profitability) which uses actual prices. For instance, if it is desirable to put stress on employment by using low accounting prices for labor, then clearly *this stress should take effect at the level of project design and not merely at the level of final project selection.* Indeed, it may be at the former level that a low accounting price for labor would have its main effect ...
>
> Of course, the sheer unfamiliarity will make for difficulty at first . . . where outside, especially foreign, firms of consultant engineers are involved, the difficulties may be greater. First, their psychological objections to accounting prices may be stronger as a result of private enterprise laissez-faire training, which does not sufficiently admit the possible divergence of social and private interest. Secondly, they generally have something to sell, which has usually been evolved in the light of actual prices. Designs are not all made afresh, from the bottom up, for the project on hand ...
>
> *Only very few western firms appear to have made any effort to adapt their designs to the different scarcities prevailing in developing*

countries . . . Sometimes, indeed, the plant which western engineers design for a developing country is more "modern"—i.e.,
capital intensive, potentially labor saving—than anything that
exists in their own country. There are two obstacles to overcoming the problem. *The first, and possibly more important, is often the
lack of an informed and critical client, determined to get a plant
which will be very profitable* . . .

For the reasons given, it may not be easy to get foreign engineers to adapt . . . However, it must be admitted, when everything in favor of accounting prices has been said, that communication between . . . departments, etc.; between departmental
administrators and engineers and scientists; and between the
local client and the foreign firms; is easier in terms of (predicted)
actual prices . . . it is certainly best to keep the use of accounting
prices as limited as possible.[7]

It must be emphasized, as Little and Mirrlees do, that it is not
merely a question of the project designer's using accounting prices
for making technological choices. Even if he did use them, the range
of choice is usually limited to actual alternatives already in use in
the developed countries, especially with regard to the core processes and products.[8] Of course, this does not mean that there do not
exist additional alternative core processes and products even within the range of modern technology. These alternatives, however, can
be known only as a result of active search and creative adaptation of
the various alternatives, "and in so doing, one ought to go beyond
those best-practiced technologies on the shelf, given open-minded
consideration to discarded laboratory results, as well as to technologies now considered obsolete by today's major industrial
concerns.[9]

Foreign TCSC or their domestic counterparts would not be inclined
for obvious reasons to undertake such processes of search and creative adaptation of modern technology as well as upgrading traditional technology. To induce them to do so would require "an
informed and critical client, determined to get a plant which will be
very profitable."[10] This means that the FS (say, development banks)
should actively support or help promote TCSC that have adequate
technological competence to ask the right questions to all the possible sources of technology—TCSC, TRC, and enterprises anywhere in
the world—and evaluate the suggestions for upgrading traditional
technology and creatively adapting modern technology. The FS
without domestic TCSC would not be able to induce and enforce

"right" technological choices, the very purpose for which it is using economic evaluation techniques to select projects for financing.

This vital link between the FS and the TCSC is even more essential when the development banks must play a promotional role in initiating a viable and widely diffused process of industrialization through the development of small and small to medium-size enterprises. This development is essential for several reasons: to develop latent entrepreneurial and managerial ability on a wide functional and geographical basis; to create employment opportunities on a viable basis for whole families and particularly for workers without much training and literacy in rural and semiurban areas (to save on overhead and distribution costs); and to improve the distribution of wealth and income. Such small enterprise development requires institutional machinery (that is, TCSC), linked to the FS, to identify project ideas, prepare feasibility studies, make appropriate technological choices, formulate detailed projects with specification for machines, processes, and products, and provide assistance in project implementation and operation.[11]

Such TCSC can help the FS in its promotional role as well as in appraising projects that the FS would get directly from the project promoters. They should be autonomous; the FS should support or help promote them, but should not interfere in their functioning. Further, the FS should not finance projects formulated by the TCSC without an independent evaluation of its social cost-benefit criteria. Such independent evaluation by the FS serves the essential function of appraising the soundness of the TCSC themselves. The latter would have a compulsion to be up-to-date and alert; for, since the FS personnel would have experience in appraising a wide variety of projects, they would be able to judge effectively the performance of the TCSC with regard to technology choice. Many government-operated TCSC, such as the Indian Small Industry Service Institutes, have not been effective in their main purpose because they lacked this vital link between them and the FS.

Another point needs to be emphasized. If the TCSC function successfully, they should be able to increase the profitability of projects that obtain their assistance. This is, in fact, their very purpose. Thus, they should be self-supporting in their operations as well as in their growth and should therefore charge reasonable fees to both the promoters and the FS. Free advice is never valued and, more important, those who give free advice tend to become obsolete and irresponsible. Further, the capacity of the TCSC to generate their own resources is a good index of their fruitfulness and efficiency.

Leadership Role of the FS: Some Examples

A catalytic leadership role for the FS is not a new phenomenon. This section indicates how some banks performed this function in different contexts.

Describing development banking during the nineteenth century in the then developing countries of Western Europe, Gerschenkron wrote of the "truly momentous role of investment banking of the period for the economic history of France and of large portions of the Continent. The relative shortage of both capital and entrepreneurial talent was made good by the creative response of the banking systems to the challenge of development. The continental practices in the field of industrial investment banking must be conceived as specific instruments of industrialization in a backward country."[12] He later said that in Germany,

> the various incompetences of the individual entrepreneurs were offset by the device of splitting the entrepreneurial function: the German investment banks—a powerful invention, comparable in economic effect to that of the steam engine—were in their capital supplying functions a substitute for the insufficiency of the previously created wealth willingly placed at the disposal of entrepreneurs. But they were also a substitute for entrepreneurial deficiencies. From their central vantage points of control, the banks participated actively in shaping the major—and sometimes even not so major—decisions of the individual enterprises. It was they who very often mapped out a firm's path of growth, conceived far-sighted plans, *decided on major technological* and locational innovations, and arranged for mergers and capital increases.[13]

Quite often, the problem of creatively adapting tax and financial technology is not even identified. The Universal Bank in Germany was a creative adaptation of banking technology. Thus, Gerschenkron says,

> In particular, the story of the Credit Mobilier of the brothers Pereire is often regarded as a dramatic but, on the whole, rather insignificant episode . . . It seems to be much better in accord with the facts to speak of a truly momentous role of investment banking of the period for the economic history of France and of large

portions of the Continent . . . But more important than their slavish imitations was the creative adaptation of the basic idea of the Pereires and its incorporation in the new type of bank, the Universal Bank which, in Germany, along with most other countries on the Continent, became the dominant form of banking. The difference between banks of the credit mobilier type and commercial banks in the advanced industrial country of the time (England) was absolute. Between the English bank essentially designed to serve as a source of short-run capital and a bank designed to finance the long-run investment needs of the economy, there was a complete gulf. The German banks, which may be taken as a paragon of the type of the Universal Bank, successfully combined the basic idea of the credit mobilier with the short-term activities of commercial banks . . . the banks acquired a formidable degree of ascendancy over industrial enterprises, which extended far beyond the sphere of financial control into that of entrepreneurial and managerial decisions.[14]

Development banks need to adapt creatively the modern technology in finance if they are to function as catalysts of development, as their counterparts in Europe did during the nineteenth century. In those days, the banks could perform the tasks of identification, design, and formulation of projects with the available design-engineering talent, supplemented when necessary by foreign talent. Now, with the much greater complexity of these tasks and with the imperative need for domestic technological capability to adapt, modify, and improve both traditional and modern technology, the banking system cannot perform these tasks without establishing TCSC in relevant fields.

The Swedish financial institutions early in the century seem to have perceived the chain relation necessary for technological advance. High-voltage transmission, an automobile combining passenger-car styling with ruggedness for poor roads, and an aircraft capable of landing and taking off on very short runways were some of the technological needs identified by bankers. As Drucker states:

Yet Swedish technological strategy had not been formulated by technologists. It seems to have come mostly from the industrial development bankers who head the country's three large banks. Not one of them is a scientist or an engineer; all of them, however, apparently understand the need for technological strategy that is appropriate to a small country where available resources have to be concentrated on filling gaps in a few areas rather than in providing the main advance. When World War II ended, Sweden was still largely a mining and lumbering economy. Now she has become, in terms of per capita output, Europe's leading industrial economy and has attained a standard of living second only to that of the United States.[15]

The Industrial Development Bank of India (IDBI) clearly perceived the need, in the Indian context, to establish TCSC to perform the various tasks related to project design work and to establish close and direct links between them and the banking system to enable the latter to perform its promotional role in stimulating a viable yet diffused process of industrialization in the backward parts of the country. As the IDBI Annual Report for 1971–72 puts it:

> The IDBI has been keenly aware of the limitations of financial and fiscal incentives in promoting industrial development in backward areas. It has been recognized that it would be essential to undertake a considerable amount of project work for the purpose. This work comprises identification of project ideas, preparation of preliminary feasibility studies, search for managerial and entrepreneurial talents, preparation of detailed project reports, managerial, technical and financial assistance for project implementation, critical evaluation of projects from the national point of view and finally project supervision.[16]

Since 1970 the IDBI has initiated action in this field by coordinating the functioning of the FS and by linking this system with the TCSC established at its initiative. So far, nine have been established, each in a different state. Given dynamic and imaginative leadership, these initiatives are pregnant with great possibilities. The IDBI has got out of the rut of the banking models borrowed from the rich countries.[17]

The IDBI's role in creative adaptation of modern technology can be illustrated by the case of the Swaraj tractor.[18] For the small farms in India, it was essential to have a low-horsepower, multipurpose tractor suited to their needs as well as resources. The multinational companies were producing tractors of 30 horsepower and above, using obsolete technology. Russian assistance was sought in 1965, but this implied a large foreign exchange cost and a large number of Russian experts. At any rate, the Russians suggested the purchase of 20-horsepower tractors from Czechoslovakia. Mr. Suri, the director-in-charge of the Central Mechanical Engineering Research Institute (CMERI), convinced the planners that India had the capacity to design, engineer, and manufacture a 20-horsepower tractor suited to the specific Indian conditions. The Swaraj tractor was thus devised and passed the tests of the Tractor Testing and Training Station (TTTS). Out of six other tractors, only two passed this test.

The Ministry of Agriculture and the public sector Hindustan Machine Tools (HMT) still favored Zeteor, a 20-horsepower tractor of Czech design, on the grounds that Zeteor was a production model, while Swaraj was still a prototype. HMT decided to produce Zeteor on a turnkey contract with Czechoslovakia. The Swaraj tractor thus was left without a promoter. Fortunately for the Swaraj, the Punjab Industrial Development Corporation (PIDC) became attracted by the idea at the persuasion of Mr. Suri and his team. The design-engineering tasks were offered to Mr. Suri (who was responsible for the tractor design) and his consulting firm, the technical personnel for the project being drawn from CMERI staff who had worked on the design. The financing problem was solved at the initiative of IDBI, which appraised the project, was convinced of its viability, and was attracted by the fact that the tractor was indigenously designed and that its manufacture was based on skills, materials, and equipment available in India. The IDBI supported the project also because of the project's vital and organic links with small-scale ancillary industries, from which the Swaraj tractor project was to buy a substantial number of parts. This project has been successfully implemented, and the firm has already introduced two new designs of tractors based on its own research and development.

This project has relevance to the process of creative adaptation of modern technology. The success of this experiment was primarily due to the organic and sequential relations among the following tasks and functions. Identification of a project idea was the critical first stage. This was done by the Planning Commission in this case. The identification of available technological choices for the project was the second; this was the function of a TCSC, and in this case CMERI performed this function. Identification of a research problem by a TCSC (in this case, CMERI) was the third stage. The research on this problem by a TRC (again CMERI) and the transmission of the research result to the TCSC (M/S Suri and Associates) were the fourth stage. The detailed project report by the TCSC to the project promoter (PIDC) and the FS (IDBI) was the fifth stage.

In this organic sequential relation, the critical functions were performed by the TCSC and the FS (in this case, the IDBI, which identified relevant problems, embodied the research results meaningfully into a concrete project, and facilitated its implementation). Without the TCSC, neither the relevant research problem nor a concrete project would have been identified; and without the link between the TCSC and the FS, the project would not have become operational. It appears from a priori reasoning as well as from this case study that the critical links in the process of creative adaptation of modern technology are the TCSC and the FS; these two provide the essential links between the PS on the one hand and the TRC and modern technology on the other. Without these two functional agencies, the production system and technological research system are likely to evolve on parallel lines—as seems to have happened in several countries with TRC.[19]

The vital significance of these links is again borne out by the Korean experience. Korea is one of the few countries that emphasized the relevance of a technology policy.[20] It started in 1966 with a TRC—Korea Institute of Science and Technology (KIST)—which in some respects also performed the role of a TCSC. Its major emphasis, however, has been on technological research, which has yielded valuable results. But in its research function, KIST had not established links with the TCSC or the FS. Its research effort, hence, lacked operational relevance.[21] This situation was rectified by the establishment in 1974 of a TCSC—Korea Technology Advancement Corporation (K-TAC); and K-TAC established links with the FS, in this case the Korea Development Finance Corporation and Korea Credit Guarantee Fund (KCGF). As a result, out of the forty research results from KIST, about ten have been embodied in concrete projects, some of which have been implemented by K-TAC itself.[22]

Notes to Chapter 9

1. See chapter 4.

2. V. V. Bhatt, "On Technology Policy and Its Institutional Frame," *World Development*, vol. 3, no. 9 (September 1975), pp. 651–63; also available in World Bank Reprint Series, no. 29.

3. These are not the names of specific, existing institutions, but rather generic names for institutions created to carry out functions described in the text. They may be public or private, and in some countries there may be more than one of each.

4. Bhatt, "On Technology Policy and Its Institutional Frame."

5. V. V. Bhatt, "Development Problem, Strategy and Technology Choice: Sarvodaya and Socialist Approaches in India," a paper presented to a symposium sponsored by the U.S. Pugwash Committee on Social Values and Technology Choice in an International Context, Wingspread, Racine, Wisconsin, June 1978 (February 1978; processed).

6. Jack Baranson, *North-South Transfer of Technology: What Realistic Alternatives Are Available to the U.S.?* (Washington, D.C.: U. S. Department of State, December

1977); see also Charles Cooper, "Science Policy and Technological Change in Under-developed Economies," *World Development*, vol. 2, no. 3 (March 1974), pp. 55–64.

7. Ian M. D. Little and James A. Mirrlees, *Manual of Industrial Project Analysis in Developing Countries* (Paris: Development Centre of the Organisation for Economic Co-operation and Development, 1968), pp. 64–66.

8. V. V. Bhatt, "Capital Intensity of Industries," *Bulletin of the Oxford University*, vol. 18 (1956), pp. 179–94.

9. Development Centre of the Organisation for Economic Co-operation and Development, *Choice and Adaptation of Technology in Developing Countries* (Paris, 1974), p. 81.

10. Little and Mirrlees, *Manual of Industrial Project Analysis*.

11. "A satisfactory arrangement, in the World Bank's limited experience, is a technical assistance agency outside, but closely linked with, the financial intermedi-ary for *SSE*; the financial institution would thus act as a sponsor of technical assist-ance to its clients (actual or prospective) and of its clients to the technical assistance agency. The entity that provides or controls financing seems often to have the most leverage (or catalytic influence) on the other two parties." See World Bank, *Employ-ment and Development of Small Enterprises* (Washington, D.C.: 1978), p. 40.

12. Alexander Gerschenkron, *Economic Backwardness in Historical Perspective* (Cambridge, Mass.: Harvard University Press, 1962), p. 12.

13. Alexander Gerschenkron, *Continuing in History and Other Essays* (Cambridge, Mass.: Belknap Press, 1968), p. 137; italics added.

14. Gerschenkron, *Economic Backwardness in Historical Perspective*, pp. 12–14. On the role of financial innovations see V. V. Bhatt, "Interest Rate, Transactions Costs and Financial Innovations," World Bank, Domestic Finance Studies, no. 47, January 1978.

15. Peter F. Drucker, *The Age of Discontinuity* (London: Pan Books, 1971), p. 71.

16. Industrial Development Bank of India, *Annual Report 1971–72* (Bombay, 1972).

17. V. V. Bhatt, "Industrial Development Bank of India: A Decade of Perfor-mance," *Commerce*, Annual Number (January 1975); also available in World Bank Reprint Series, no. 18.

18. For details about this project, see V. V. Bhatt, "Decision Making in the Public Sector: Case Study of Swaraj Tractor," *Economic and Political Weekly*, vol. 13 (1978), pp. 30–45.

19. Baranson cites the experience in Brazil, Mexico, Colombia, and Venezuela: "These programs are generally associated with Latin American universities and government-sponsored research institutes . . . These programs have met with varying degrees of success, but their scope has traditionally been limited to topics and areas of scientific investigation and exploratory research. Rarely have the programs con-centrated on designing and engineering technologies with immediate and direct application to problems in industrialization." See Baranson, *North-South Transfer of Technology*, p. 14. Also see Cooper, "Science Policy and Technological Change."

20. Hyung-Sup Choi, "Adapting Technology—The Korean Case," in *Views of Science, Technology and Development*, eds. E. Rabinowitch and V. V. Rabinowitch (Oxford: Pergamon Press, 1975).

21. Korea Technology Advancement Corporation, *K-TAC's Role in Commercializa-tion of New Technology in Korea* (Seoul, 1978).

22. Ka-Jong Lee, "Technology Transfer and Development Strategies: The Role of Large Firms in Korea," Ph.D. thesis, University of Hawaii, 1977, pp. 53–54.

Part V

Development of Small-Scale Enterprises

THE FIRST CHAPTER in Part V opens with the statements that "the contribution made by small-scale enterprises (SSE) to employment and production is broadly recognized" and "so also are the economic and social implications of SSE development for ironing out regional disparities and for the creation of a new entrepreneurial class." These certainly are recognized, and long have been. It is fair to say, however, that recognition has become widespread and has engaged the energies of policymakers only in recent years.

In the first fifteen to twenty years of the emergence of new nations after World War II, during which economic growth became the principal policy objective of the developing countries, other matters loomed larger. Belief in the simplicity of the development process and confidence in the tractability of the obstacles to that process predominated. Capital investment was, generally, emphasized, particularly for infrastructure, as was the introduction of modern (Western) technology, and so forth. Large-scale irrigation projects, power, steel mills, fertilizer plants, airlines, and the like were foremost in national plans. The developing countries in general made important advances in this period and some made spectacular advances. But the evidence is that the "big push into self-sustained growth" had relatively little effect on unemployment and poverty and left large segments in most countries unaffected. That experience has led to changes in perceptions of the development process, awareness of its complexity, and a shifting of development priorities.

One result of the evaluation of recent development experience and the consequent resetting of priorities has been to focus attention on small enterprises. Their importance is seen, of course, in the contribution they can make to economic growth. More important, however, is their potential for striking more directly at the problems of unemployment and poverty and for enhancing and speeding the development of human resourcs by making fuller use of indigenous talents and technologies and by bringing new segments of the population into the productive process. Large-scale factory production is almost always—at least in the beginning—an enclave operation. A small enterprise, with its grass-roots origins, is indigenous in its origins, is often linked to local traditions and the rural community, yet can develop technological, market, financial, and other ties with the more modern and large-scale sector of the economy. Hence, it eases the transition from traditional to modern society, avoiding the disruptions that so often accompany this change.

Most development banks must face up to the necessity of participating in the financing of small enterprises. Some have no choice, for they have been set up for that specific purpose, or are ordered by government to do so. Others may have a choice but are likely to heed the persuasions of government and of external financiers to direct some of their efforts to the more neglected segments of society as part of their developmental contribution. And still other development banks, specifically assigned to deal with large-scale enterprises within the national network of development finance institutions, may decide to devote some resources to small-scale enterprises in recognition of their emotional and political appeal or as a contribution to the public welfare.

Whether the efforts of development banks are required by charter or law, or are influenced by government or providers of capital, or are free responses to community problems, they will find themselves confronting a particularly difficult sector. To start with, they must decide what is meant by small enterprise. Its definition varies from country to country and sector to sector and covers quite different activities: from one-man or one-family enterprises operating with no, or virtually no, equipment in the unorganized sector of the economy to small-scale factories fully integrated into the modern production system. Development banks entering the field of small-scale enterprise must determine where within that spectrum they want to operate and then devise a strategy for doing so.

The following chapters attempt to lay out some of the elements that must go into such a strategy. In the first, V. S. Raghavan and T. A. Timberg briefly sketch the principal problems faced by small-scale enterprises, which they sum up as money, management, and markets. They then discuss various mechanisms for dealing with those problems. In the second paper, A. H. M. Kamaluddin focuses on small enterprises in one country, in which it is by far the predominant form of enterprise. He thus provides an extensive discussion of the issues and solutions that Raghavan and Timberg have illustrated from the experience of a variety of countries. Of particular interest to development banks are the comments of the authors on the transaction costs of financing small enterprise and the means of reducing them.

Chapter 10

Notes on Financing
Small-Scale Enterprises

V. S. RAGHAVAN AND T. A. TIMBERG

THE CONTRIBUTION made by small-scale enterprises (SSE) to employment and production is broadly recognized. So also are the economic and social implications of SSE development for ironing out
regional disparities and for the creation of a new entrepreneurial
class. Nevertheless, few development banks (other than those specifically created for that purpose) have devised programs for SSE
financing either because other institutional arrangements exist in
their countries for SSE development or because the risk and cost of
administering SSE programs inhibit them from entering the field.
Now, however, as a result of public policy or other pressures, including the priority attached by several international lending agencies to programs designed to alleviate urban poverty, development
banks are increasingly becoming involved in SSE financing.

The provision of finance is only one element in the program for SSE
development, though this is the aspect that concerns development
banks most. The provision of technical and management assistance,
establishing markets for the products of SSE, promoting linkages
between SSE and larger-scale industrial enterprises, and entrepreneurial development are other aspects which are likely to figure
in a successful program for SSE development.[1] The purpose of this
paper is to explore the role of a development bank in various aspects
of such a program.

Handicaps of SSE

The International Labor Office (ILO) "basic needs" model of development asserts that, in labor-surplus economies, SSE employ

labor-intensive technologies and produce primarily goods for mass consumption.[2] They are, the ILO contends, more efficient in their use of capital, create more employment, and fit with a more equitable and labor-intensive consumption pattern than do large-scale enterprises. The evidence on ILO's assertions is mixed, but it is likely that these advantages do obtain in some industries and in some countries. A recent World Bank study points to industries in Korea and Taiwan, where SSE are clearly superior on the basis of economic census data.[3] Some analysts place entrepreneurship at the center of economic growth, emphasizing the importance of tapping entrepreneurial drive, savings, and motivation; this view supports SSE both because they mobilize savings and motivate managers and because they promote competition, provide training grounds for starting medium- and large-scale enterprises, increase economic flexibility, and disperse economic power and wealth. SSE have served these purposes to varying extents in economies as diverse as Japan, Korea, Taiwan, Israel, and India.

It is, however, generally accepted that SSE entrepreneurs find capital scarcer and more expensive than do large-scale enterprises because of the higher real and perceived risks and administrative costs of lending to them. In many countries, including the United States and the United Kingdom, SSE find themselves forced to borrow heavily in unorganized or unofficial financial markets at far higher rates than are charged by commercial banks and other financial institutions. SSE often have difficulty in obtaining access to raw materials, which may be cornered by their larger competitors because of their superior buying power. They may also be excluded by larger enterprises from potential market channels for their products. SSE may find it difficult to recruit and retain skilled labor, and they often pay a premium to skilled labor at the same time as they use relatively cheap unskilled labor. SSE management may also lack skills in production and finance and thus operate at low overall levels of efficiency.

If money, market, and management are the three main constraints of SSE, it follows that, to be effective, any program for SSE development should attempt to deal with these handicaps. In the field of finance, this means finding ways of reducing the transaction costs of lending, which appear to be the main factor that has inhibited the flow of funds to the small-scale sector.[4] Other solutions might be changes in the requirements and procedures for credit; a simplification of forms and a reduction of information required; a relaxation of requirements for collateral; an increased reliance on the evaluation of the personal characteristics of the entrepreneurs; and help in preparing their projects and advice on the selection of equipment and on the solution of technical problems in the production of their goods. In rare cases, the financing agency may have to be directly involved in organizing markets for the products of SSE.

Precisely what constitutes a small-scale enterprise depends either on the general scale of enterprises or on the legal definition in a particular country. The enterprises covered by small-scale programs range from artisans and rudimentary shops using traditional technology, with a capital outlay of less than $100 and the owner as the principal worker, to enterprises that employ more than a hundred workers, with investment of nearly $250,000 and sophisticated technology. The problems of financing the latter (larger) category of SSE units are not very different from those of medium- and large-scale enterprises, though they may call for simplification of procedures and perhaps involve somewhat higher costs. It is the smaller units—the artisans or cottage industries—that differ both in scale and in kind and that pose peculiar challenges to agencies entrusted with the task of SSE development.

The difference in the nature of the problems faced by the artisanal or cottage industry enterprise—which is often characterized as the informal sector—and the modern, factory-type small industrial units in the organized sector may necessitate the adoption of two separate delivery systems for financial, technical, and management assistance in many countries. It is clearly not possible to develop or suggest a model that is applicable to all countries or, for that matter, to all parts of the same country, because the programs to be initiated need to take into account the problems peculiar to the locale. The problems faced by small-scale units and the policy options available for dealing with them in India, for instance, are not the same as those in, say, Mauritius. Even within India, the problems of SSE units in hilly regions in northeast India may have to be dealt with differently than those in the city of Bombay. Likewise, the role assigned to development banks in the delivery system for SSE will differ from country to country, depending on, among other things, the size of the country and the existence or absence of a network of institutions capable of providing the financial and advisory services referred to earlier.

An attempt is made in the following paragraphs to describe the essentials of a good delivery system for SSE development and its links with development banks. The issues relating to finance, management assistance, and marketing are discussed in separate sections, with the principal emphasis on the provision of finance.

A Strategy for SSE Financing

It is almost axiomatic that to acheive a satisfactory level of SSE financing, vigorous government or central bank direction (by incentive or fiat) is needed. The choice of the financial intermediary (or intermediaries) for lending to the sector will, of course, depend on the size of the country. In relatively large countries, the appropriate institutions are commercial and cooperative banks that have a wide network of branches. But even in smaller countries, where a development bank may be entrusted with the task of financing the SSE sector, it will be necessary for the development bank to create a network of local offices, with a measure of autonomy in granting loans, subject, of course, to centrally set standards. To illustrate how these issues are handled in some countries, we have chosen to discuss the cases of India, the Philippines, and Mauritius, because of their varying sizes.

Institutional Arrangements

In a country such as India, the various State Financial Corporations (SFC), which are state development banks, are expected to confine their attention to small- and medium-scale industrial units. To facilitate this—and to maintain the financial viability of the SFC—there is a limit of Rs2 million on the size of loans they may grant to any individual borrower. As a result, more than 90 percent of the number and 60 percent of the amount of loans granted by SFC have been directed to small-scale units.[5]

Since all the major commercial banks in India are government-owned, the monetary authorities have decreed that a predetermined percentage of commercial bank credit should be channeled to what is known as the priority sectors. At present, agriculture, small-scale industries, and small businesses constitute the priority sectors. With this emphasis on SSE lending, bank credit to small industries and businesses jumped from Rs3 billion in 1969 to nearly Rs25 billion in 1978;[6] the SSE share of total bank credit increased from 8.8 to 16.7 percent during the same period. About 80 percent of commercial bank credit to small industries is for working capital.[7]

Several development banks in India operate on a national basis, but all of them confine their attention to medium- and large-scale units. The only exception is the Industrial Development Bank of India (IDBI), the apex institution for term finance, which plays a crucial role in SSE lending through refinancing term loans granted by primary lenders such as commercial and cooperative banks and SFC.[8] The interest rates under the scheme are fixed in such a way that the primary lenders get a spread of about 3.5 percent, which is adequate to cover their transaction costs. IDBI has issued a few guidelines on eligibility criteria, and loans fulfilling these criteria are approved automatically. Because of the simplicity of procedures, the refinancing scheme has become popular; by the end of 1978 IDBI had provided nearly Rs5 billion to about 50,000 small-scale units under the scheme.[9] Although precise estimates are not available, IDBI's cost of administering the refinancing scheme is estimated to be approximately 0.5 percent of the portfolio. Since the average transaction cost of the primary lenders is about 3.5 percent, the total transaction cost is about 4 percent. This is only one example of how a development bank in a very large country can evolve an efficient delivery system to reach thousands of small-scale units scattered all over the country by using local intermediaries.

The general pattern of the institutional network for SSE financing in the Philippines is very similar to that in India, though there are differences in detail. The Development Bank of the Philippines (DBP), which is the largest development bank in the country and which finances virtually every economic sector, was until 1973 virtually the sole institutional source of term credit for small entrepreneurs. Since 1973, however, mainly as a result of the program of assistance for small industry suggested by a working group composed of all important agencies connected with the sector, several institutions have been assigned a role in SSE financing, although DBP continues to be the biggest single lender to the sector. DBP now provides both fixed capital and working capital to small industry. The Private Development Corporation of the Philippines (PDCP), the largest private institutional source of long-term finance, and a network of Private Development Banks, a special breed of private institution that was promoted with equity participation by DBP, are making special efforts to finance small-scale industries. These efforts are strengthened by the Industrial Guarantee and Loan Fund, owned by the government and administered by the Central Bank, which provides funds to primary lending institutions at concessionary interest rates (7 percent in 1979) and in addition guarantees for a fee 60 percent of the losses that may be incurred on small-scale loans.

DBP functions through a network of branches and agencies spread all over the country. Before its procedures were streamlined in 1973, its loan-processing procedures suffered from bureaucratic complexity and duplication of work, with the result that it took an average of six to eight months to process loans. It was found that this lag could be reduced to one to two months if authority were decentralized to branch managers, team appraisal projects were replaced by one-man appraisal, appraisal reports were shorter and more succinct, and assistance were given to entrepreneurs in filling loan applications—and if, in addition, the communication system between the head office and the branches were improved. Similarly, the large arrearage in the small-industry portfolio was directly attributed to inefficient project supervision. With the decentralization of the follow-up function to the branches and a stricter enforcement of supervision requirements, it was possible to reduce the arrears.

To effect the recommendations of the working group, DBP set up a separate department for handling small loans in 1973, and since then there has been a demonstrable improvement in the efficiency of its SSE operations. The volume of its lending increased from ₱132 million (US$18 million) in 1975 to ₱384 million (US$52 million) in 1977. The arrears decreased from 16.5 percent of portfolio in 1975 to 10.5 percent in 1977.

In contrast to India and the Philippines, Mauritius is a small country with an area of 750 square miles and a population of 0.8 million. The Development Bank of Mauritius (DBM) stepped in to provide direct loans to very small enterprises in the informal sector. Its program covers a category of enterprises that are, by and large, untouched by the rest of the banking sector. These enterprises are engaged in such occupations as tailoring, garmentmaking, furnituremaking, shoemaking, metalwork, jewelry, fishing, pig and poultry farming, printing, and service-related activities such as garages, repair shops, and small construction. Typically, the owners of such enterprises are also the principal workers who are assisted by other members of the family or by a few employees—less than five in 90 percent of the cases. Rarely does the capital investment exceed Rs5,000 (US$830). DBM's loans normally cover about 80 percent (and in rare cases as much as 95 percent) of the expenditures on the acquisition of fixed assets—in most cases, machines and tools or a simple shed for the workshop. These are far smaller enterprises than those covered in the Indian and Philippine programs.

The program of assistance to these very small enterprises started in 1966 and was administered by the Small-Scale Industries Branch of the government. Until 1970 only some twenty loans for a total of Rs100,000 had been sanctioned. DBM took over the scheme in 1971 and, in six years, granted about Rs11 million to more than 1,600 enterprises. All loans are guaranteed by the government; similarly, all administrative and legal expenses incurred in the program are reimbursed by the government.

Until 1973 DBM functioned from one office in Port Louis, the capital. When DBM took over the SSE lending program, it soon realized that this work could not be effectively handled unless it built up an extensive field organization. Accordingly, DBM opened twenty-two one-man field offices (subsequently reorganized into twelve offices) to act as initial points of contact with small enterprises. Since DBM's standard appraisal procedures for medium- and large-scale industries resulted in delays of several months for sanction and disbursement of SSE loans, the work relating to scrutiny of SSE loan proposals was decentralized and entrusted to field officers. These field officers were high school graduates without special financial or technical skills; but they were given simple guidelines regarding the purpose of assistance, eligibility, promoter's contribution, procurement, estimation of profitability, debt service capacity, and security requirements. It became the field officer's responsibility to complete his information-gathering (including verification of costs and markets) within a week of receipt of the requests for assistance. The field officers worked five days in the allotted areas and, on the sixth, came to the head office to prepare final reports with the help of the head office staff. The decentralization of a major part of the appraisal work thus reduced the time lag between application and sanction to a matter of days.

The extensive field organization was also useful in vigilantly pursuing defaulting clients. Although SSE loans are covered by a blanket government guarantee, no occasion has arisen when the government guarantee has had to be invoked. Although it would be wrong to generalize on the basis of experience of one institution, DBM's record contradicts the belief of many bankers that "small is risky." Small can be safe, provided lending institutions do their follow-up with some vigor.

Transaction Costs of Lending to SSE

But vigorous follow-up to reduce the risk of default can lead to enormous increases in the administrative costs of lending. Precise information on transaction costs for various categories of borrowers is hard to come by, though studies by the development policy staff of the World Bank have begun to remedy this gap. According to a study completed in December 1978 on the transaction costs of credit to the small-scale sector by various financial institutions in the Philippines, the administrative costs of lending to small-scale enterprises are 3 percent for DBP and PDCP and 4 percent for the private development banks compared with less than 0.5 percent for large-scale enterprises.[10] The default risk expenses of SSE are 2.5 percent for DBP, 3.7 percent for PDCP, and 2.3 percent for private development banks. The comparable figures for large-scale enterprises are 1.3 percent for DBP, 2.3 percent for PDCP, and 1.7 percent for commercial banks. Thus, the transaction costs for SSE are almost three times those for large industrial loans. DBP makes a profit of about 5 percent on its loans to large-scale enterprises compared with a loss of about 1 percent on small-scale loans.[11] This indicates that, with cross-subsidization from other bank programs, the transaction costs for SSE loans are quite manageable.

Similar studies in India estimate the total transaction costs of all lending by commercial banks to be slightly in excess of 4 percent of the portfolio; most of this cost is for administrative expenses and very little for bad debts.[12] The administrative cost of lending to very small enterprises (receiving loans of less than Rs10,000, or US$1,250) are in the range of 30 to 40 percent, but this is balanced by the lower costs of servicing larger clients.

Although both the Philippine and India data relate to small-scale enterprises, it should be remembered that the classification is based on the legal definitions in each country. The average size of the loan to which the Philippine data pertains is approximately US$10,000; this category of enterprise (as well as the typical SSE client of the Indian SFC) would in all probability be a modern factory-type enterprise, even though small in scale, and quite different from the artisanal type, which is preponderant in the informal sector lending program of Mauritius.

The administrative costs of the small enterprise program in Mauritius, which was about 20 percent of the outstanding portfolio in 1974, came down to 13 percent in 1977, a period in which, while the portfolio volume grew, the average loan remained stable at Rs5,000, or US$830. This is still a high figure, but quite reasonable in comparison with other similar programs directed to the informal sector. The average size of DBM's other industrial investment, that is, other than artisanal financing, was slightly in excess of Rs600,000, or US$100,000. In several developing countries a major portion of this latter portfolio would fall under the definition of small-scale enterprises. The cost of administration for the portfolio as a whole worked out to less than 1 percent. In the four years from 1974 to 1977, DBM had to write off only one-tenth of 1 percent of its portfolio as bad debts in respect to its non-SSE lending. (As mentioned earlier, DBM did not incur any loss in respect to SSE lending during the same period.) With annual profits (before provisions) in the region of Rs6 million in fiscal 1977 and 1978, DBM could have undertaken the SSE lending program on its own without undermining its financial viability, even if the government subsidy for the administrative costs of the SSE lending program stopped.

To eliminate some of the risk element and reduce to that extent the transaction costs of lending to SSE, credit guarantees of all or part of SSE loans are often provided either at the cost of the borrower, as in Korea, India, and the Philippines, or at the expense of the government, as in the United States and Mauritius. In some countries, the guarantee is provided by an independent extension agency serving SSE; and in others, the central bank undertakes the guarantee function.

The response of financial institutions to any guarantee scheme is conditioned by the cost of the cover and the procedures for obtaining the cover and for settlement of claims. In the Philippines the effective cost of the guarantee is 1.2 percent. In Korea it is 0.25 percent. In India the credit guarantee scheme (administered by the central bank on behalf of the government) for small-scale enterprises charges a fee of 0.1 percent, while a parallel scheme operated for small-farmer advances and other advances to small borrowers in the informal sector operated by the Credit Guarantee Corporation (jointly owned by the central bank and commercial banks) charges a fee of 0.5 percent.[13] Recent studies show that these fees are quite adequate to make the schemes self-supporting, even after taking into account the administrative costs, which, under the present arrangements, are borne by the central bank. The Philippine and Korean guarantee funds appear to have accumulated large surpluses, which perhaps point to the possibility for some reduction in the guarantee fee.

The guarantee schemes in various countries differ in the ease with which claims for losses are actually paid, and thus the effectiveness with which they encourage SSE lending. The World Bank sector policy paper "Employment and Development of Small Enterprises" refers to some criticisms of the Indian guarantee scheme "principally because the conditions for compensation are uncertain." Two observations appear to be in order. One is that the use of the central bank (which has supervision functions over commercial and cooperative banks) as the guaranteeing agency perhaps inhibits lending agencies from invoking guarantees for fear the central bank will conclude that they are careless in their lending operations. If this is so, it would be worth exploring whether it is feasible to separate the guarantee function from the central bank, although such an action is bound to increase the cost of administering the program. Any new organization would have to incur additional costs in reviewing the credit programs of lending agencies, whereas this task is now being undertaken by the central bank as part of its normal supervisory work. The second point is whether it would not be worthwhile to liberalize the procedures for settlement of claims, even if it results in a somewhat higher guarantee fee than the present nominal rates. A claim in case of default does not mean that the amount is to be written off; if it is to be written off, the guarantee organization has to pay the claim in any case. Since the guarantee covers only 75 percent of the loss in most cases, the lending institution continues to have a vested interest in recoveries. This is the underlying principle in all co-sharing arrangements in insurance. What is important is to inspire confidence among the various levels of decisionmaking in lending institutions in the policy and program for lending to small borrowers; any procedure that impairs this confidence deserves to be modified.

Delivery System for Lending to SSE

On the basis of this brief review of institutional arrangements and of transaction costs in a number of countries, it should be possible to suggest some points for a strategy for SSE financing. Since the financial services required by the SSE sector are radically different from those for units in the large-scale sector, it would be useful if this work is undertaken by a specialized cadre, which could be located either in existing institutions or in a specialized institution set up for the purpose. Irrespective of the agency chosen, it is imperative to develop a network of local offices that can reach the large number of clients in the SSE sector. This may suggest that in large countries, commercial and cooperative banks, with their extensive branch office networks, may be more appropriate channels for SSE financing than would development banks, which tend to function from one office or a limited number of offices. There are several advantages in using commercial and cooperative banks. First, banking facilities could be integrated, since the same agency could meet both fixed capital and working capital requirements of SSE, thus avoiding the need for small, unsophisticated clients to deal with more than one institution for their limited requirements. Second, using local institutions that have an intimate knowledge of the clients would result in a gradual reduction of transaction costs of SSE lending, through administrative economies and efficient recovery procedures. It does not follow that development banks should not involve themselves in SSE lending at all. But in some situations the financing role of the development bank should be limited to a refinancing and supervisory role.

Quite often the creation of specialized institutions for financing the SSE sector is justified on the ground that traditional bank—even development bank—personnel are not prepared to make the adjustments in practices and procedures that SSE financing would require. Nevertheless, many programs have proven successful with such personnel. It is also alleged that established institutions will find the new tasks onerous and will shrink from them; but through government fiat or subsidies, several established institutions have been encouraged to play a significant role in SSE financing. The advantages of specialized institutions for SSE financing are their single-minded devotion to SSE development, the operational expertise they accumulate, and the absence of competitive demands on their funds. By contrast, this very identification with one, often neglected, sector, which carries emotional appeal, may occasionally lead to the encouragement of poorly chosen enterprises. Further, as has been noted earlier, the relatively higher transaction costs of SSE financing would require cross-subsidization from funding programs directed to large-scale enterprises. If institutions to finance SSE exclusively are set up, some form of government subsidy is inevitable.

Whatever the institutional channel adopted for SSE financing, it will be necessary to simplify reporting and application requirements. Even the requirement for "proper" accounts can often be dispensed with in relatively primitive enterprises such as one- or two-man workshops. Notional accounts can be generated by lending officers themselves. Larger enterprises can be expected to keep accounts, but since the scarcest resource in many small enterprises is entrepreneurial time, reporting requirements should not be time-consuming. In particular, requirements for clearances and certifications from various authorities (land-use authorities, title recorders, and so on) should be kept to a bare minimum. These clearances rarely affect materially the viability of the loan and on occasion much cost and time are expended by entrepreneurs.

Another shortcut in project evaluation is to develop profiles of the more common type of enterprise. Since SSE tend to fall into a narrow range in most developing countries—for instance, tailors, bakers, carpenters, handloom operators, and shoemakers—profiles can often be prepared quite economically. Units proposed for finance can then be judged against the profiles, with appropriate allowances for their size or other factors that differentiate them from the norm. In some cases, these profiles have been used to develop scoring systems that measure how fully the proposed unit shares the characteristics of the successful units in its product category.

Another area in which there is scope for relaxation is the security requirements for SSE loans. Demands for guarantees and large amounts of collateral typically discriminate against the smaller entrepreneurs who usually have few initial assets or influential friends. Many varieties of SSE involve little fixed, but substantial working, capital, and are usually those the banks have the greatest difficulty financing because of the difficulty in finding appropriate collateral. But some forms of security-oriented business finance, such as deferred payment, lease of equipment, factoring, or accounts receivable finance provide a relatively easy way of relieving SSE needs. Lending agencies would have to explore constantly whether any new type of financial instrument can be introduced to facilitate the flow of funds to the SSE sector.

If the information and security requirements of financial institutions are simplified, it will be essential to exercise careful, subjective judgment about the reliability of SSE debtors and close and continuous supervision of their operations. In the realm of supervision, much can be learned from informal credit markets. The sources of informal credit base themselves on close and continuous involvement with their clients in the market. Sometimes it may be appropriate to use these informal credit sources themselves as brokers or intermediaries. For example, the shroffs in India—bankers in the unorganized sector—have traditionally lent their funds to SSE and rediscounted their bills with the commercial banks. The smaller Philippine banks, which have been very successful in SSE financing, are also dominated by local magnates, comparable to the bankers in the unorganized sector in India.

Management Services

It has been noted earlier that finance is only one of the requirements of SSE. In addition, SSE clientele will need a considerable amount of service, especially in production, marketing, financial management, and inventory control. The managerial inadequacies in SSE in these areas can be approached by either specialized training for potential entrepreneurs or extension services suitable for the managers of operating enterprises. In a few cases, both these services are provided by the same agency that is entrusted with the task of providing funds for SSE; but the more common practice is to separate the lending and what may be loosely called the technical assistance functions in two distinct agencies, which cooperate with each other.

In India the technical assistance functions for SSE are now supposed to be coordinated through the government-run District Industries Centers and at the higher level by the state and central industries ministries. But technical assistance is in fact provided by a variety of institutions including "lead banks," which have set up multiservice agencies in selected districts, and the central government-sponsored small industries service institutes, which maintain offices in all the states to guide small-scale entrepreneurs in production, management, and marketing. In addition, specialized boards and commissions have been set up for handlooms, cottage industries, and so forth. Training courses for entrepreneurs are sponsored by several state finance corporations.

While most of the above agencies concentrate on the SSE units in the traditional sectors, the more sophisticated and relatively larger small-scale industrial firms are expected to be served by the Technical Consultancy Organizations (TCO) set up by the Indian development banks under the leadership of the Industrial Development Bank of India. The principal objectives of the TCO are to identify viable project ideas, prepare feasibility reports, select and train potential entrepreneurs, and provide assistance to entrepreneurs in project implementation and operation. The first TCO was set up in 1972 for Kerala, the southernmost state of India; and, in the following seven years, eight more were set up to service practically all the backward regions in the country. Since a majority of these TCO have been operational for a very short period, it is not possible to judge their effectiveness; but the experience of those started in the early years indicates that this type of institutional measure has the potential to promote a viable process of small-enterprise development.

In the Philippines the promotional effort for SSE is headed by the Commission on Small and Medium Industries in the Ministry of Industries. Under its direction there are small business advisory centers, which provide technical and managerial assistance, trade assistance centers, which help with marketing, and entrepreneurial training conducted by the University of the Philippines Institute of Small-Scale Industry.

The extension service appropriate for very small artisanal units normally focuses on teaching elementary bookkeeping and the rudiments of marketing and business planning. One such program is administered by UNO (Uniao Nordestina de Assistencia a Pequenas Organizacoes), a private, autonomous, nonprofit organization established in Recife, Brazil, in 1972 to assist the very smallest enterprises.[14] Today, 85 percent of UNO's funding comes from the Brazilian government. To be eligible for assistance, an enterprise must have annual sales of less than US$36,000, and the proprietor's total assets (business and personal) must be less than US$800. Proprietors must also be "workers," and the enterprise must be an "integral part of the community." The program is controlled by an elected board of community members, advised by volunteers from local government and business.

UNO actively recruits entrepreneurs in the community, interviews them to establish their eligibility, prepares proposals for commercial bank loans, and advises the enterprises so assisted. Sixty to 90 percent of the loans that UNO supports are made by commercial banks, which are required by law to lend to SSE an amount equal to 12 percent of their demand deposits at a maximum rate of 18 percent—about their normal lending rate. Actual rates charged to UNO borrowers average from 12 to 13 percent. UNO also provides a 100 percent guarantee on each loan, as against a legal requirement of 130 percent collateral on Brazilian bank loans. Extension workers visit enterprises every three months, and UNO runs in addition a full-scale program of training and technical assistance open even to enterprises that are not assisted. The technical assistance concerns primarily bookkeeping, simple marketing, and business planning.

From 1973 to 1977, 715 enterprises secured bank loans averaging US$1,583—three-quarters for working capital purposes. The UNO program costs are now roughly 50 percent annually of loans extended, and it is hoped to reduce them to 30 percent. Despite the high costs, and the admittedly marginal nature of the enterprises, the UNO model is being widely copied in Brazil and Latin America.

Partnership for Productivity (PFP), also a voluntary organization, runs a somewhat similar operation, primarily in Africa.[15] In this case, the emphasis is on using secondary school graduate extension workers to teach simplified accounting and business management techniques. The Kenyan PFP was established in 1970. After several other strategies were tried, it began, in 1974, to use "schoolboy consultants"; by 1976 twenty such consultants were in the field serving some 600 businesses. These schoolboy consultants were selected on the basis of interviews and tests of their commercial aptitudes. They were then trained in small groups for several weeks in a course that included field training. Their skills were thereafter upgraded in monthly and other meetings with their supervisors, who had considerable authority over them.

The consultants' training course—and thus the advice they are able to give small entrepreneurs—covers such matters as maintaining cash, credit, and expense records; stocktaking and control; preparing profit and loss accounts and balance sheets; surveying market demand; deciding on prices, promotion, and shop presentation; and dealing with banks. Some attention is also paid to specific needs of manufacturers, such as factory layout, quality control, and costing products.

The firms assisted are mostly small and commercial rather than industrial. There is no regular cycle of visits, nor any fixed duration for assistance. Businesses are generally visited at least twice a month and, in most cases, six months are adequate to achieve a significant improvement. According to PFP, the profits of assisted enterprises increased by $2.66 and their sales by $22 for every dollar of program costs.

Many efforts have been made to promote entrepreneurship, especially in India. To help identify and develop potential entrepreneurs, a variety of training courses has been organized by development agencies. The bulk of these courses concentrate on the simple accountancy, marketing, and managerial tools needed to run a small business. A smaller number do try to apply the work of psychologist David McClelland in increasing the level of a certain measurable psychological trait called "N-achievement," which has been demonstrated, in some cases, to be causally related to entre-preneurial success.[16] Training programs of both sorts are run by banks and other promotional agencies and are often prerequisites to funding and support.

A recent study of one such training exercise in Gujarat in India (using McClelland's techniques) shows striking success among its graduates.[17] The Small Industries Extension Training Institute (SIET) in Hyderabad in India, which pioneered N-achievement train-ing, has embarked on a comprehensive evaluation of it.

It is also possible to assist in the actual entrepreneurial tasks themselves. For example, promotion agencies can and have re-searched and written up prototype investment projects, helped in securing physical accommodation (for example, in industrial estates), and introduced the potential entrepreneur to marketing and financial sources. Many SSE promotional agencies provide funds for project preparation—"front-end money." In Tanzania prospective entrepreneurs are taken to Arusha and introduced to standard prototypes of machines and then financed to launch their enterprises. In Kenya the industrial estates perform a critical pro-motional role for many larger SSE, providing prototype equipment and advice as well as work space.

Assistance in Marketing

In a few countries, some items are reserved for production exclu-sively by the small-scale sector to provide protected markets. In India more than 800 products are now reserved for the SSE sector, and the government prohibits expansion in the production capacity of large-scale units for these items. The more usual practice is for governments to give some preference to products of SSE in govern-ment procurement through quotas, subsidies, or preferential purchases, even if at slightly higher prices, to enable them to com-pete with large-scale units.

Direct assistance in marketing is usually confined to units pro-ducing handicrafts and similar items. Several countries have cre-ated marketing agencies for this category of SSE. The artisanal centers in Tunisia provide workshops as well as marketing outlets for Tunisian craftsmen, though there is criticism of their high marketing margins. In India an elaborate system of cooperatives for handloom weavers involves a network of credit and marketing cooperatives, which provide looms, credit, and yarn and market the

cloth produced. More than one-fourth of all handloom cloth produced in India is handled by these cooperatives, and roughly one-
third of all looms are affiliated with them. Various marketing networks have been set up in India, Bangladesh, Sri Lanka, and
Malaysia to market handicraft items.

Because marketing has often been the weakest link in the various
efforts to promote productive enterprises in Africa, the Fund for
Research and Investment for the Development of Africa (FRIDA), a
privately funded group in Europe, has set up a market outlet for the
handicrafts of the least developed African countries (and to some
extent other African and non-African countries). In the next stage,
FRIDA will actively promote the creation of enterprises to produce
goods for which markets have been developed. In general, a large
marketing network—whether publicly or privately owned or organized as a cooperative venture of the artisans—is a prerequisite to a
large-scale artisanal production.

The relatively larger and more sophisticated of the small-scale
enterprises need much less assistance in their marketing, but they
may require some help in export marketing. One way to tackle this
issue would be to encourage the formation of export houses to
channel the products of many small-scale units.

Some Concluding Observations

The role of a development bank in the promotion of SSE varies
according to the specific country environment in which it operates.
While some may opt (or be required by national policy) to deal
exclusively with large-scale enterprise, most will feel constrained
for one reason or another to devote a part of their manpower and
financial resources to financing SSE. Those that do may find in the
early part of this chapter a sketch of the ways in which they can
participate in SSE development and ideas for adoption or for adaptation in the light of their own environment.

Beyond these suggestions, however, development banks might
consider the following points:

• If the project selection criteria of development banks are based
on economic and social cost-benefit analysis, that is, the systematic
"pricing" of inputs and outputs to reflect their scarcity or social
values, the result in most developing countries will be to encourage
projects based on labor-intensive, rather than capital-intensive,
technology. Since small-scale enterprises are, by and large, labor

intensive, this might mean that SSE will figure more than hitherto among the clients of a development bank.

• It should also be possible for development banks to make a systematic effort to promote linkages between small-scale units and the large-scale enterprises that seek financial facilities, for instance, by encouraging subcontracting wherever feasible. In the process, many SSE might emerge as ancillaries to larger factories, each specializing in the operations in which they are most efficient. This would, to some extent, solve the problem of inadequate access to markets, which is at present a major obstacle for the small-scale sector.

• Where existing arrangements for work space, extension facilities, and various other services the SSE sector requires are inadequate, the development bank may have to undertake some of these functions until other institutional arrangements can be made. To maintain a measure of objectivity, however, it might be desirable to separate what may be broadly described as the promotional function from the financing function, so that the institutions engaged in these different functions will serve as a check on one another. Of course, they will also have to cooperate with each other if they are to be successful in the tasks assigned to them. Development banks must join hands with other development agencies in the country in funding and staffing such institutions, within reasonable limits.

Whether a development bank undertakes operations in the SSE field directly or works through other agencies, it is in a unique position to provide central direction and guidance to the various institutions entrusted with the task of SSE development. It combines the development bias and the intimate connection with the financial and industrial communities that are necessary to promote a viable process of economic development.

Notes to Chapter 10

1. For a comprehensive discussion of many of these issues, see "Employment and Development of Small Enterprises," Sector Policy Paper (Washington, D.C.: World Bank, February 1978).

2. Ed P. Neck, *Small-Scale Industry Development* (Geneva: International Labour Office, 1975).

3. Samuel P. Ho, "Small-Scale Industries in Two Rapidly Growing Less-Developed Countries: Korea and Taiwan—A Study of Their Characteristics, Competitive Basis and Productivity," Studies in Employment and Rural Development no. 53, Employment and Rural Development Division, Development Economics Department, World Bank, Washington, D.C., 1978.

4. V. V. Bhatt and Alan R. Roe, *Capital Market Imperfections and Economic Development*, World Bank Staff Working Paper no. 338 (Washington, D.C., 1979).

5. Industrial Development Bank of India, *Annual Report, 1977–78* (Bombay, August 1978).

6. One billion equals one thousand million.

7. C. Rangarajan, *Innovations in Banking: The Indian Experience*, Part I: *Impact on Deposits and Credits* (Ahmedabad: Indian Institute of Management, 1978), pp. 123–24, and 128.

8. IDBI also operates a scheme for rediscounting bills and promissory notes for the deferred payment of domestically manufactured machinery. The procedures under the scheme are very similar to those of the refinancing scheme. Although until 1978 only Rs73 million had been used by small-scale units under the scheme, the volume is expected to increase substantially in view of the reduction in rediscount rates for SSE at the end of 1978.

9. IDBI, *Annual Report, 1977–78*.

10. The actual figures for large-scale enterprises are 0.5 percent for DBP and 0.2 percent for PDCP. The private development banks do not, by and large, assist large enterprises, but the commercial banks which are active in financing this category of enterprises incur administrative costs of 0.4 percent.

11. Katrine Anderson Saito, and Dan P. Villaneuva, "Transaction Costs of Credit to the Small Scale Sector in the Philippines," Domestic Finance Studies no. 53, Public Finance Division, Development Economics Department, World Bank, Washington, D.C., 1978.

12. Paul Mampilly, *Innovations in Banking: The Indian Experience*, Part II: *Cost and Profitability of Commercial Banking* (Ahmedabad, Indian Institute of Management, 1978), pp. 135–56, 180–98, and 257–62.

13. Rangarajan, *Innovations in Banking*, pp. 175–211.

14. Jose Bentil Schreiber, *Small Business Development in Brazil: A Study of the UNO Program* (New York: Interbook, 1976).

15. Malcolm Harper, *Consultancy for Small Businesses: Training the Consultants* (London: Intermediate Technology Publications Ltd., 1976).

16. David McClelland, *The Achieving Society* (Princeton, N.J.: D. von Nostrand, 1961); Ed McClelland and David Winter, *Motivating Economic Achievement* (New York: Free Press, 1969).

17. V. G. Patel, "Innovations in Banking: The Gujarat Experiment," Domestic Finance Studies no. 51, Public Finance Division, Development Economics Department, World Bank, Washington, D.C., August 1978.

Chapter 11

Financing Small-Scale Industrial Enterprises in Bangladesh

A. H. M. KAMALUDDIN

SMALL-SCALE INDUSTRIAL ENTERPRISES (SSIE) have a vital role to play in any developing economy. They act as an excellent vehicle for employment expansion, decentralized economic development, and rational distribution of wealth and income. The economy of Bangladesh is largely dominated by agriculture, but there is hardly any opportunity to increase substantially productive employment in agriculture. Furthermore, the scarcity of investible capital and constraints of technology and management severely limit employment expansion through large industrial enterprises, where investment cost per job created is much higher. Any effective development program in a developing country such as Bangladesh should, therefore, seek to increase the employment potential through the expansion of small-scale enterprises, which have great potential for generating direct and indirect job opportunities.

SSIE provide opportunities to talented, enterprising individuals of limited financial means to participate actively in the development of the national economy. Besides, small-scale enterprises stimulate personal savings, promote agroindustrial linkages, are ancillary to large enterprises by supplying components and subassemblies at comparatively less cost, and help improve rural welfare. Recognizing these facts, the policymakers of Bangladesh have emphasized the need for appropriate strategies to develop this vital sector of the economy.

SSIE development is a continuous process requiring coordination by several agencies (governmental, semigovernmental, and nongovernmental) and a package of assistance and incentives. This development has to be viewed against the backdrop of general

181

industrial development. The intention of this chapter is not to cover the entire gamut of ssie development, which in itself is a vast subject, but to concentrate primarily on the problems of financing ssie and to suggest appropriate courses of action to minimize, if not eliminate, the problems confronting ssie. This chapter also gives an overview of the ssie sector in Bangladesh and the experiences gained by the Bangladesh Shilpa Bank (BSB) over the past few years in financing ssie.

The Bangladesh Economy and the Role of ssie

The manufacturing sector has been heavily influenced by the scarcity of natural resources, and the major industries of the country are based on agriculture. The growth of industry is thus dependent on the performance of agriculture. The industrial sector contributes 8.5 percent of gross domestic product (GDP) and more than 6 percent of total employment. The contribution of industry to the country's exports is well over 50 percent. The major manufactured products exported are jute goods, tea, paper, frozen food, semiprocessed tanned leather, and timber.

ssie are composed mainly of cottage enterprises and account for more than 40 percent of the total contribution to GDP of manufacturing. The contribution of ssie to GDP has more than doubled between 1972–73 and 1976–77, while during the same period the contribution of large and medium-size enterprises increased by about 45 percent. Between the two ends of the industrial spectrum are medium-scale enterprises processing food, tobacco, hides and skins, metal, oil, timber, paper products, and engineering goods.

ssie produce a wide variety of goods, particularly consumer goods, such as textiles, leather goods, salt, food, cosmetics, tobacco, furniture, clay products, and light engineering goods, as well as many kinds of services. In fact, more than 80 percent of the domestic supply of cloth comes from ssie, and a similar proportion of leather goods and footwear. About 100 percent of the country's salt requirement is met by ssie.

Statistics relating to ssie are scanty. According to a survey conducted by the former East Pakistan Small Industries Corporation in 1962, there were about 22,000 small enterprises and 356,000 cottage enterprises in Bangladesh. The current estimates put the figures between 45,000 and 50,000 for small enterprises and between 425,000 and 450,000 for cottage enterprises.

There is no single satisfactory definition of SSIE in Bangladesh, and the border line separating SSIE and medium-scale industry is often indistinguishably thin. In fact, in the past two decades the official definition of SSIE has undergone several changes. According to the currently accepted definition, any industrial undertaking that has a total investment of less than Tk2.5 million[1] in fixed assets (for example, land, building, machinery, tools, and equipment) may be classified as SSIE. Cottage industries, by contrast, have been defined in the first five-year plan (1973–78) as:

- Enterprises carried on wholly or mainly by the members of a family, either as a full-time or as a part-time occupation
- Enterprises using family or hired labor, or both, which do not use motive power for any operation and employ fewer than twenty hired workers
- Enterprises, using either family or hired labor, that use motive power for any operation and employ fewer than ten hired workers

In this chapter, both small enterprises and cottage or household enterprises have been referred to as SSIE, without making any fine distinction between the two.

Problems of SSIE

SSIE are plagued with a host of chronic problems more or less similar to those experienced by other developing countries, such as India, Indonesia, the Philippines, Malaysia, Thailand, Korea, Fiji, and Papua New Guinea. The major problems of finance, marketing, raw materials, technology, and infrastructure are discussed briefly in the following paragraphs.

Marketing

Marketing of products at reasonable prices is one of the serious problems of SSIE. Organized outlets are absent, and terms are dictated by the middlemen. The individual SSIE are financially incapable of holding their products for better prices and for the same reason are not in a position to adopt modern marketing techniques, such as advertising and employing showrooms and skilled salesmen. Moreover, surveys to determine the market situation and trends, changes in consumer demand, and so on, are conspicuously absent in this sector.

In any developing country, the government is the principal buyer of many varieties of goods and services. SSIE, because of the information gap, lack of organization, and limited financial means, fail to participate in government tenders directly. Institutional arrangements to bridge this gap could be devised, which would allow participation in government tenders on behalf of SSIE, as has been done in India. A list of items or commodities produced by SSIE could be reserved for purchase from SSIE. If necessary, preferential price treatment could be given to SSIE products for government purchase. Collective efforts by SSIE through cooperatives or associations would place them on a better footing in dealing with government tenders and in finding other market outlets. Some institution, perhaps Bangladesh Small and Cottage Industries Corporation (BSCIC), could, in association with the Export Promotion Bureau, find export markets for SSIE products. Linkages with larger enterprises through coordination by development banks would help deal with the marketing problems of ancillary SSIE.

Raw Materials

SSIE in general suffer from difficulties in procurement of enough raw materials and spare parts of the right quality, at the right time, and at reasonable prices. The chain of middlemen in the case of the handloom industry, for example, raises the cost of weaving to an unprofitable level. In many cases, bargain prices cannot be enjoyed because of the small size of individual purchases. The majority of SSIE have no entitlement for the import of spares. One of the functions of BSCIC is to ensure the supply of raw materials to SSIE. BSCIC therefore maintains a stock of imported raw materials for distribution among SSIE and supplies them with scarce local raw materials. These activities are to be expanded. A more dynamic and progressive attitude on the part of the financial system to augment the funds required by SSIE for the purchase of raw materials would reduce the problem substantially.

Technology

Machines, tools and equipment, processes, and so on, employed in SSIE are by and large outdated. Because of the general poverty and often illiteracy of the entrepreneurs and the disorganized nature of ssɪᴇ, the latest technological developments in manufacturing industry are yet to be recognized and adopted. Many ssɪᴇ are not only poorly located and have inappropriate plant layouts, but also lack innovative product designs and pay little attention to quality control and training. Field operations take place on an uneconomic scale. The redeeming feature, however, is that workmanship in general is quite good. Given technological support and extension facilities, ssɪᴇ have great potential for significantly contributing to the industrial development of the country. Development banks could effectively assist ssɪᴇ, particularly those belonging to the organized sector. The government should, however, take the initiative in building up centralized factories and workshops under institutional control to produce appropriate tools and equipment to meet the requirements of the ssɪᴇ sector. Appropriate tools, dies, and molds at low cost would facilitate production of quality goods. These centralized factories could also be used as a training ground for ssɪᴇ workers. Such institutional assistance could be provided by appropriately organizing ʙsᴄɪᴄ, which could also undertake research on product and equipment design, production planning, and quality control. Common central facilities providing technical and processing services to ssɪᴇ should be made more effective.

Management

Most ssɪᴇ are either under one-man management or are a closed family affair. Managers are also owners. As a consequence, planning and decisionmaking are very often influenced by personal considerations to the detriment of the enterprise. This gives rise to a host of related problems. General surveys reveal that lack of good management is one of the principal causes of the high failure rate of ssɪᴇ in Bangladesh. Appropriate advisory services by development banks and ʙsᴄɪᴄ could offer entrepreneurial and management training and help solve some of the management problems of ssɪᴇ.

Infrastructure

In Bangladesh, transport and communication systems are not yet fully developed and electricity is yet to be made available in many rural areas. This low level of infrastructural development seriously handicaps ssɪᴇ, which are scattered all over the country. The government, however, has taken in hand an ambitious plan for electrification of the rural areas of Bangladesh.

Finances

The inadequacy of funds from institutional sources, particularly credit, is in itself a serious problem. A committee constituted by the government to recommend ways of promoting, organizing, and running cottage industries said, in its report of July 1977, that a third of the total working capital requirements of cottage industries, amounting to Tk1,000 million, should be met "primarily by the banking system." The figure would be much higher if the requirements of other small-scale enterprises not covered in the report were also taken into account. The Bangladesh Bank, the central bank of the country, under the small-loan scheme introduced in 1976, asked the banking system to advance 2 percent of its demand and time liabilities to small-scale industries, traders, and businessmen. This means that about Tk350 million to 400 million might have been made available to small businesses in 1977–78, with no assurance, however, that the credit would in reality reach SSIE. In fact, the attitude of the banking system has so far been unfavorable to financing SSIE because of such obvious reasons as the high cost of lending and of loan supervision, the inadequate number of competent and experienced personnel, and the traditional pattern of security-oriented lending policies, all implying a high risk for the banks.

The position is no better for the supply of long-term funds. Although development banks such as BSB can lend up to 70 percent of the total investment in fixed capital, mobilization of the remaining 30 percent in equity funds poses a real problem for small entrepreneurs. The equity base of many SSIE is almost nil. Besides, for SSIE, whose major investment consists of working capital, development banks can be of little help because of statutory restrictions on their financing of working capital. Because of the inadequacy of the financial system of Bangladesh to meet both the short-term and long-term financial requirements of SSIE, noninstitutional sources such as mahajans (moneylenders) or middlemen fill the gap. SSIE, however, have to pay a heavy cost for borrowing from these sources.

The problems highlighted above do not cover all the difficulties of SSIE; nor are they equally applicable to all SSIE now operating in Bangladesh. Nevertheless, they should be recognized in planning at the macro level and appropriate measures developed to deal with them.

Government Policies and Strategies for Promotion of SSIE

Government policy has been to give due priority to SSIE both in the allocation of funds and in the development of necessary infrastructure. The first five-year plan (1973–78) specifically provided for reorganizing and strengthening the Small and Cottage Industries Corporation and developing twenty industrial estates, sericulture and the silk industry, the salt industry, the handloom industry, and the handicraft and cottage industry.

One of the main objectives of the Two-Year Approach Plan (1978–80) was to achieve socially desirable equity in income distribution through promotion of cottage and rural industry. The strategy outlined for this purpose was to favor "labor-intensive technology and small and cottage industries." The plan also envisaged the continuation of existing promotional services and the development of new programs. The plan document stated that "a vigorous program of cottage and rural industry development will be undertaken all over the country and promotional services like training, extension services, marketing facilities and supply of designs, etc. will be provided."

The total plan allocation for industry as a whole was Tk8,160 million, of which Tk2,460 million, half in foreign exchange, was meant for private sector investment. Private sector investment is primarily for SSIE based on modern technology in the fields of edible oil, food processing, specialized textiles and garmentmaking, leather goods, chemicals and pharmaceuticals, metal products, small-scale engineering and repairs, furniture, various types of consumer goods, printing and publishing, and so on. Study tours abroad and surveys have been made and are being undertaken at the request of the government to formulate appropriate policies for SSIE. Clearly the government's intention, as reflected in national planning and investment strategies, is to give high priority to the development of SSIE.

Institutional Arrangements for Financing SSIE

At present there are four sources of institutional credit to SSIE, namely, Bangladesh Small and Cottage Industries Corporation

(BSCIC), Bangladesh Shilpa Bank (BSB), six nationalized commercial banks (NCB), and Bangladesh Jatiya Samabaya Bank (BJSB). The role of BSCIC is to act as a financial intermediary to SSIE, to provide extension services, technical and management advisory and training services, and infrastructure—and, above all, to promote the growth of SSIE. The current thinking is to utilize the resources of BSCIC primarily as a promotional institution and as an agency responsible for providing technical and management development services, extension services, and such other services as are needed for the growth and development of SSIE. The NCB have thus evolved a consortium arrangement with BSCIC to finance (on long- and medium-term) projects promoted by BSCIC. In addition, NCB have been providing mainly short-term working capital to SSIE. The BJSB, which deals primarily with cooperatives, usually provides short-term credit. BSB, as one of the two conventional development banks in the country, provides long-term credit both in local and foreign currencies.

As a development bank, BSB has been playing its dual role in promoting and developing SSIE, although the beneficiaries of BSB's assistance by and large remain confined to somewhat organized urban-based small enterprises. Cottage industry and the rural-based small (informal) sector continue to be ill-served by BSB. Being more or less a centralized institution, BSB has found it hard to extend its services to very small enterprises, mainly because of the high cost of such services and organizational inadequacies. Nevertheless, about 46 percent of the total number of loans and about 50 percent of the projects sanctioned by BSB up to the end of September 1978 were in the SSIE category. This, however, represented only about 8.4 percent of the total amount sanctioned by BSB up to that time.

Before December 1971, BSB, under an agreement with BSCIC, acted as a financial intermediary to SSIE projects sponsored by BSCIC. The responsibility of project appraisal, follow-up, and monitoring, however, remained with BSCIC; consequently BSB had very little or no influence on the repayment performance of the units sanctioned. As a result, 84 percent of the total loans sanctioned to BSCIC-sponsored SSIE projects were in arrears by September 30, 1978.

BSB is now entertaining proposals directly from SSIE. These proposals are subjected to BSB's standard appraisal criteria. The World Bank is, however, conscious of SSIE's difficulties in fulfilling its standard criteria. Efforts are therefore being made to develop simplified lending criteria and procedures that will permit rational allocation of funds and loan supervision without undue delay. BSB's branch network is being expanded to cope with the situation.

According to its charter, BSB has no restriction regarding the minimum amount of loan it can sanction. It is using this privilege for financing SSIE proposals, particularly from less developed areas, and for projects with distinctive labor-intensive technology for providing consumer goods and intermediate goods and subassemblies for larger enterprises. In line with the national objectives of developing agro-based labor-intensive SSIE, BSB has sought to identify and develop viable projects on the one hand and to select and train entrepreneurial talent on the other. BSB's efforts in this direction have so far remained a beginner's attempt to promote SSIE, mainly because of constraints of professional and technical expertise. Success in promoting SSIE will depend on BSB's ability to develop the required expertise and on its dynamism in evolving and adopting appropriate operational policies and procedures.

BSB has consciously adopted a policy of promoting more labor-intensive technologies wherever feasible and of assisting smaller enterprises in the modern sector. Its ability to influence the choice of technology is still limited, however. Evolving more appropriate technological solutions is a difficult task that requires government assistance in the form of research and the development of alternative product designs, production processes, and equipment designs to suit local needs. Assistance of the international agencies is considered very helpful in the dissemination of information on appropriate technology.

Commercial banks have a relative advantage as effective financial intermediaries to assist the growth of SSIE, particularly those of the informal sector. They have a wide network of branches penetrating deep into the remote corners of the country, which can profitably respond to the needs of SSIE. Development banks, by contrast, are handicapped by the centralized nature of their activity. Given awareness and motivation, commercial banks are better suited to assess the personal qualities of the entrepreneurs and local business conditions. Monitoring and supervision of projects by commercial banks are relatively easy and inexpensive. Moreover, commercial banks can effectively deal with both long-term and short-term credit requirements, since they have an easy access to the day-to-day operation of SSIE, which depend almost entirely on them for their working capital. Recognizing these facts, the World Bank, in its recent report on the development of SSIE in Bangladesh, placed heavy reliance on commercial banks as the main financial intermediaries for promoting the growth of SSIE.

Commercial banks are, however, traditionally security oriented and are often reluctant to finance small enterprises because of the costs and risks involved. It may therefore be necessary for the government either to bring pressure on the banks or to provide incentives for their increased participation in financing SSIE, as has been done in India, where commercial banks have been serving a wide range of SSIE clientele. The government may consider providing cheaper resources to commercial banks for such purposes. Often the government or the central bank is called upon to provide partial guarantees against loss to minimize risk. As mentioned earlier, the Bangladesh Bank has launched a countrywide small-loan scheme operating through the commercial banks. The Bangladesh Bank has also sponsored and formulated a scheme to guarantee a portion, not to exceed 30 percent, of the bona fide loss that a commercial bank has incurred in any advance given under the small-loan scheme. The incentives of this guarantee scheme are likely to intensify commercial bank efforts in assisting SSIE, although the results still remain to be assessed. Ways must now be explored to find substitutes for collateral security. In many SSIE, prospective cash flows may serve as a better safeguard than conventional collateral.

While SSIE belonging to the modern manufacturing sector are likely to continue to be the main objective of development bank operations, the commercial banks are expected to assist other kinds of productive activity offering equal or greater job creation in relation to investment costs. Transport, construction, fisheries, maintenance and repair facilities, personal services, arts and crafts, and tourism are such sectors of economic activity.

Conclusions and Some Suggestions

Although the flow of institutional finance to SSIE in Bangladesh has been inadequate, there has been growing awareness in financial circles that the traditional pattern of financing cannot fulfill the national objectives of economic development. The coverage of financing institutions must be broadened, alternatives to conventional collateral devised, and organizational and procedural snags removed. All these are possible through sustained efforts by the banks and other financing institutions. NCB, BSCIC, and BSB are working individually and jointly with such foreign aid and international agencies as the World Bank, the United States Agency for International Development (USAID), and the Swedish International Development Agency (SIDA) on a number of action cum research programs. A breakthrough in evolving effective financing of SSIE is likely in the coming years.

The financing and development of SSIE in Bangladesh is a gigantic undertaking and cannot, of necessity, be by a single institution, through one approach, and a one-time affair. It is essentially a specialized job and calls for a great deal of patience, dedication, and idealism. Concerted and coordinated efforts are required from all the financial institutions and government agencies and departments; international support is also necessary. There is no dearth of good intentions in any quarter. In this regard, the following recommendations merit consideration.

First, projects should be formulated with strong potential links between the agricultural and industrial sectors and within or between various subsectors of industry. Small industry should complement and cooperate with both agriculture and large-scale enterprise. Development banks are better placed to emphasize this aspect by formulating a series of small projects complementary to the large projects they finance. In the same way, they should refrain from financing large projects that would wipe out existing smaller units in the field. All possible efforts should be made to assist clients to explore possibilities for subcontracting.

Second, time should not be wasted on debates over advanced technology, intermediate technology, appropriate technology, and the like. The choice of technology should be based primarily on the employment-generating capacity of the projects, including their forward and backward linkages. In the context of Bangladesh, the choice should favor labor-intensive, simple, and cheap technology.

Third, there is perhaps no need to add new institutions to finance SSIE exclusively. Existing institutions should be in a position to meet the demand effectively if the reasons they perform poorly at present are properly diagnosed and corrected. Financial institutions should be assured a fair return on their SSIE portfolios, which will in turn ensure better service to the customers. A better return on savings, by contrast, would facilitate mobilization of savings, which would augment the financial resources of the banking system. In other words, interest rate policy should be rationalized and institutions should be allowed to operate on a self-sustaining basis.

Fourth, industrial estates for SSIE should be complete with buildings, and space should be provided for ancillary industries in the neighborhood of the larger enterprises that will support the ancillaries. This suggests the desirability of having industrial estates with enterprises of differing size, both small and large. Entrepreneurs should be required to install machinery only in buildings already constructed for them. This will enable them to save time as well as capital.

Fifth, machinery could be made available by various methods, including deferred payment. If necessary, it should be possible for the development banks and government agencies to offer guarantees to the suppliers of machinery, both local and foreign, for the deferred payment of equipment.

Sixth, SSIE should be encouraged to form formal or informal associations. This will improve their bargaining power with regard to both the purchase of inputs and the sale of their outputs.

Seventh, specific quotas of government purchases should be earmarked for the SSIE. Similarly, development banks might exert their moral influence on the large-scale enterprises they finance to give preference to SSIE products, if available—and to sell their products to SSIE on a preferential basis.

Eighth, promotional organizations such as BSCIC, the Bangladesh Industrial Technical Assistance Centre (BITAC), and the Investment Advisory Centre of Bangladesh (IACB) should expand and intensify their efforts to provide training, technical assistance, and extension and consultancy services to SSIE. Development banks should in turn concentrate on their existing as well as prospective clients.

Ninth, there should be a central controlling and monitoring authority in the country for SSIE. This body should formulate realistic and effective policies and programs for SSIE, harmonize and coordinate activities of various agencies operating in the field, conduct surveys, collect and evaluate field data on a continuous basis, and ensure that government policies and programs with regard to SSIE are implemented fully and on schedule.

Note to Chapter 11

1. 1 U.S. dollar = 16.75 taka (approximately).

Part VI

Financial Management

THE CHIEF EXECUTIVE who addresses the issues of financial policy cannot do so in a single-minded fashion. He is caught in a web of different and sometimes conflicting interests: he might be interested primarily in steady and orderly growth; the bank's creditors will be concerned above all with the security of their loans; and its shareholders might be interested in the prospect of dividends or in some combination of dividends and capital gains. Hovering over these three parties is government, sometimes a shareholder, often a creditor, and always in its capacity as "regulator" (in any one of several senses) of the economy. These various parties are not necessarily in conflict, but neither do their views exactly coincide. Of all the matters with which top management must concern itself, it may well be that financial policy is the one in which there is the least likelihood of a "logical" solution to problems to which one is driven, and the one in which tradeoffs and the compromising of differing viewpoints are unavoidable.

The complex of issues from which financial policy is derived has taken on new dimensions in the light of the changes in the past few years in the economic environments in which development banks operate. These changes mainly relate to the high rates of inflation most countries are experiencing, which affect project costs above all but also administrative costs; unstable exchange rate regimes; new functions being taken up by development banks, which tend to increase the transactional costs of their portfolio (administrative costs and default risks); and increasing pressure on more experienced development banks to "stand on their own feet" financially.

In the first of the following two chapters, V. S. Raghavan has taken growth as the central theme to which to tie his discussion of the key issues in financial policy. One objective of financial policy, he argues, is survival in adverse circumstances. The other is to ensure that the development bank can mobilize in a timely fashion and at a minimum cost the resources it requires to sustain or to expand its investment program. What combination of financial policies, in a given environment, will contribute most effectively to that objective? Management's response to the components of that main question will determine whether and how the institution can finance itself.

Most development banks have so far depended on official sources of finance for a variety of reasons. But increasing demands on official sources from other legitimate claimants for finance as well as vulnerability to political pressures and changing official views make it inevitable that few development banks will want or can expect to rely on official sources for the finance they need to expand, let alone to sustain, their positions as instruments of economic development. The crux of the problem of resource mobilization for development banks is, therefore, how to tap new, nonofficial sources of finance, and thus progressively to reduce the preponderance of official sources.

Exploring and developing alternatives to official assistance, for both domestic and foreign resources, calls for coming to grips with "the market." On the domestic side, this means "creating" a market, adapting a development bank's financial policies to that market's requirements, and promoting new institutions; on the foreign side, it means achieving access to the market and adapting to its conditions. Both aspects involve government policies over which a development bank has no control, although it may have some influence. How these aspects present themselves to a particular development bank depends to a significant extent on the state of the economy of the country in which it is located. Objective conditions are not, however, the sole determinant. Vitally important are the goals and policies of government. And, of course, much depends on the creative imagination of management.

In dealing with the issue of resource mobilization, management has opportunities on two levels. It can work with government to identify the hard-core structural defects that inhibit the mobilization of resources and to devise policies and institutional reforms to deal with them. This will involve it in such matters as interest rate policy and taxation, the establishment of securities markets, and the promotion of new financial institutions. On another level, management can explore measures, feasible within the existing framework and constraints, to increase the flow of finance for both itself and its clients. This will call for new financial instruments, new institutional policies, and leadership in establishing new services and perhaps new financial institutions.

In the second chapter, David B. Gill explores both levels of opportunity—the broader, long-range policy issues government must cope with but development banks can help clarify, and the more immediate practical steps development banks can take within the existing legal and institutional infrastructure. Gill illustrates his discussion with specific cases in which development banks have acted effectively.

Chapter 12

Some Issues Relating to Financial Policies of Development Banks

V. S. RAGHAVAN

THE FINANCIAL POLICIES of any institution that has long-term investments as the hard core of its activities must serve two main objectives: survival in adverse circumstances and growth at all other
times. Growth in the case of a development bank is virtually
synonymous with increase in the volume of its investment operations. Thus, in normal times, the principal objective of financial
policies is to ensure that the development bank can mobilize sufficient resources, when required and at a minimum cost, to sustain
its investment program.

Since the resources of a development bank are raised mainly by
share capital and borrowings, it follows that its financial policies
need to be attuned to the ideas and expectations of its shareholders
and creditors. The main concern of the creditors is the safety of their
investments. They need to be convinced that the development bank
always has the funds necessary for servicing its debts. The concern
of the shareholders goes beyond this. They need to be convinced
that a development bank conducts its affairs in such a way that it
not only covers its costs of administration and bad debts but also
earns a surplus sufficient to offset any unforeseen contingencies
and, if possible, to compensate for the erosion, because of inflation,
in the value of the share capital. If the shareholders are private
investors, they expect, in addition, a reasonable return on their
investments by way of dividends.

In other words, to attain its objectives of growth and survival the
development bank has to devise policies that contribute to its financial viability. This is true irrespective of the ownership pattern of
the development bank or the debt-equity mix in its capital struc-

ture. It is true even of the rare institution that is funded entirely by equity.

This does not mean that the financial policy problems faced by all development banks are identical. The problems and the options available in resolving them vary with the economic environment in which the development bank operates, the sources of its funds, the nature of its activities, and its experience in business. In spite of these differences, there are also some similarities. The purpose of this chapter is to identify the common set of problems and the variety of policy responses that may be appropriate in particular circumstances. The first section deals with the financial policy issues, which are relevant to the growth of the development bank. The second section discusses the specific problem of exchange risk, an issue not directly related to the development bank's growth, but of prime interest to every development bank that has contracted foreign currency loans.

Financial Policy and Resource Constraint

Any discussion on the financial policies of a development bank will ultimately focus on two issues: capital structure and profitability. When a development bank is established, the main questions are: What is a prudent debt-equity mix? In what form and on what terms should debt be arranged to satisfy both shareholders and lenders? What should be the exposure limits of the development bank in individual transactions, in a particular category of assistance, or in a particular industry? What interest spread will achieve an acceptable level of profitability? When the development bank has been in business for some time, other issues come up. For instance, what should be the policy for providing for bad and doubtful debts? How much of the profits should be allocated to reserves and how much paid as dividends to shareholders, and so on?[1]

In one sense, these questions are easy to deal with at the time a development bank is established and in the initial years of its operations. When all is said and done, there is no generally agreed formula for determining the appropriate level of debt a development bank may incur. If there is absolute certainty that all the loans granted by a development bank will be repaid according to schedule, and it is assumed that the development bank can lend out all its funds at an interest rate that will give the bank a spread adequate to cover its own financial and administrative costs, as well as a modest profit margin, there is no need to place any debt-equity limit on the development bank. The only limitations in this situation would be the availability of funds for borrowing and the ability to use those funds. Unfortunately, this happy state is not attainable because of the risks inherent in long-term investments. A rational decision on the capitalization structure of the development bank and the various exposure limits will have to be based on an assessment of these risks. But such an assessment is not an easy matter even for seasoned development banks, which have their own records upon which to base their judgments. For new institutions, the only course open is to resort to some rule of thumb based on the experience of similar institutions elsewhere.

Debt-Equity Limits

One such rule of thumb is the debt-equity limit of 3:1, which has been used for several development banks when they were first launched. This may at first glance look restrictive, but in actual fact it is not. With few exceptions, the capital structure in what is frequently referred to as the World Bank model included interest-free or low-interest long-term loans (typically granted by the government or the United States aid agencies at the request of the government), which were subordinated either to share capital or to other term debt. Since this quasi equity amounted to anywhere between one and a half to three times the share capital, the effective leverage worked out to nine to fifteen times the share capital.

This does not mean that every development bank has reached these levels of debt. Although generalization is always difficult, given the diversity of institutions, the debt-equity limit has usually not proved to be an important issue for development banks that have been in operation for less than fifteen years. It takes several years for an institution to build up its portfolio and to reach the limits of its debt. Nevertheless, the limits set have not proved too "permissive," in the sense that there has been no case of serious default, though some development banks may have had to face temporary liquidity problems. In other words, the rule of thumb for capitalization of development banks has stood the test of time.

In cases in which the debt-equity limit has become an important issue, the reasons appear to be either the erosion of the borrowing base or the loss of leverage. Some development banks, whose initial capitalization included quasi equity in the form of subordinated debt, have reached a stage at which the subordinated loans are to be repaid. Although, over the years, they have increased the equity base through increases in share capital or accretions to reserves, they still face a diminution of their borrowing base—more so, if they have already used up the borrowing facility based on that increase in share capital and reserves.

Subordinated debt was a financial instrument invented to please lenders and shareholders alike. It acted as a safety net to senior lenders and it benefited shareholders by reducing risk and improving returns. It was created in recognition of the risk and uncertainty inherent in long-term investment and the consequent need for someone to support or to cushion a development bank in the initial years of its operation. It was never intended to be a permanent feature in the capital structure of a development bank, however; hence the inability of several institutions to obtain renewals of, or replacement for, subordinated loans that are due for repayment.

Even if the repayment of the subordinated loan is not yet due, the proportion of subordinated debt to total resources will decline every year with the acquisition of new resources by development banks. Since subordinated debt carries a nominal interest rate, if any at all, development banks naturally experience an increase in the average cost of funds. They try to overcome this disadvantage by improving the leverage in their capital structure. And since development banks have so far relied on official sources—both domestic and foreign—for a major portion of their resources, they have not experienced any serious problems in obtaining relaxations in their debt-equity limits. They have generally found their creditors to be accommodating.

Changes in the Environment

There are, however, several changes taking place in the economic environment in which development banks operate. First, because of the accent on economic expansion in developing countries, demand for assistance from development banks has increased both because of more applicants and because of the increase in the average size of industrial units being established. Another factor that has tended to push up the demand for funds is the phenomenal increase in investment costs because of higher rates of inflation in most developing and industrialized countries. A recent paper estimates that the unit price of machinery exported to developing countries rose by 15 percent a year, on average, between 1970 and 1975.[2] There were increases during subsequent years, though at a somewhat reduced rate. This general rise in prices, together with the depreciation in the value of local currencies against the strong currencies of Western Europe and Japan, has almost doubled investment costs in several categories of industry. As a result of these various factors, the volume of operations of development banks has increased at an annual rate of more than 25 percent during the five years from 1974 to 1978. There is no reason to assume that the demand for funds will abate in the foreseeable future.

This increase in the volume of operations of development banks is coming about when foreign and domestic official sources may not be in a position to provide the entire resource requirements of development banks, mainly because of competing claims for their assistance from other sectors. As a result, some development banks will have to explore the possibility of tapping the private capital markets at home and abroad on a larger scale than hitherto. This might necessitate readjustments in the financial policies of development banks to meet the requirements of capital markets.

The first such readjustment may very well have to be in the attitude of the development bank toward the issue of debt-equity relations. Instead of viewing the level of debt as a function of the net worth of the institution, as is most often done, capitalization decisions will increasingly need to be based on a rational analysis of the development bank's cash flow—an approach pioneered by the development banks themselves in their dealings with the industrial companies that sought their help.

It would thus become necessary to forecast the performance of the development bank over a reasonably long period to obtain a profile of the various levels of debt that can be serviced under both favorable and unfavorable circumstances. Since income from loans and equity investments and repayments of loan installments constitute the crucial elements in the inflow of funds of a development bank, any judgment about a prudent debt-equity relation would have to be linked to an evaluation of the portfolio risk.

Portfolio Risk

There is no objective or scientific method for making an evaluation of the portfolio risk. The risk of insolvency or default by an assisted concern is a commercial risk and can be dealt with as such if it arises because of difficulties connected with the specific project or concern. Quite often investments may go sour for reasons other than an inherent defect in the concept, execution, or operation of assisted projects. External factors such as changes in commercial or exchange rate policies at home or abroad, protracted interruptions in essential services, and political instability may affect the fortunes of enterprises in a particular industrial category or of all enterprises located in a particular region. When these occur, there will usually be a "bunching" of business failures. While these risks are real, and every development bank that has been in existence for the past fifteen to twenty years has had to face such a risk at least once, there is no accurate method for predicting such events or their consequences.

Evaluation of risk is thus a matter of cautious judgment—perhaps no better than a guess—by an experienced manager. Even then, to make an informed guess it is desirable to institute a procedure for portfolio evaluation, which may incorporate three different analyses, as follows:

CASE-BY-CASE STUDIES. In the course of its project supervision work, the development bank periodically receives performance reports and cash flow and profitability forecasts for each client. The officer in charge of the follow-up of the particular unit should assess the potential risk of default in respect of debt-service obligations to the creditors for the current and coming years. Tools such as interfirm comparison are useful for this analysis.

SECTOR STUDIES. Sector studies should be undertaken to identify problems peculiar to a particular industrial sector or subsector. Such studies (and on occasion, review of problems in a specific region) are also useful in initiating corrective measures before the situation gets out of hand.

ANALYSIS OF ARREARS. Development banks are most familiar with the analysis of arrears. All cases of arrears do not, fortunately, result in losses. In the light of its record of losses and its rescheduling experience, however, a development bank would have a reasonable basis on which to make an assessment of the portfolio risk, after allowing for the tendency of projects to flounder in bunches because of a general downturn in the economy or factors affecting a particular industry.

There is nothing novel in the above proposals. The principal problem is not in knowing what to do, but rather in ensuring that this task is not neglected because of staff preoccupation with other more glamorous and pressing tasks such as appraising and deciding upon new investments or overcoming obstacles to project implementation and disbursement.

A systematic evaluation of the development bank's portfolio would be useful in testing the appropriateness of several of its financial policies. What are the likely lags in the receipt of principal and interest payments from the clients and their effect on the cash flow and debt servicing ability of the development bank? Are any adjustments needed in the capitalization pattern in the light of this information? Is the level of the provision for bad and doubtful debts adequate? Are there any changes needed in the exposure limits for specific projects or for specific categories of assistance, and so on?

Profitability

If development banks increasingly resort to the private capital market for their future resource needs, one aspect of their operation that may receive greater attention than hitherto will be their profitability. This has all along been an important consideration for development banks with significant private shareholding, although it would be wrong to infer from this that private entities became shareholders of development banks merely, or even mainly, for reasons of profit. Actually, most private sector investors—whether local or foreign—were "roped in" by governments or international lending agencies, though occasionally private businessmen have taken the initiative to sponsor development banks. Whatever the motivations of their shareholders, private development banks have been conscious of their responsibility to their shareholders. So far development banks, as a class, have achieved reasonably satisfactory levels of profitability, partly because of the efficiency of their operations and partly because of concessional finance from government and various aid agencies. For understandable reasons, private development banks have been more inclined to distribute dividends than have development banks entirely owned by governments.

Because of the necessity to augment their resources rapidly and continuously and because of the expectations of the private corporate market of a greater measure of safety for its loans than official lenders would perhaps be prepared to accept, development banks—both public and private—may feel the need to make substantial additions to their share capital, precisely at a time when return on equity is declining because of loss of leverage and the higher average cost of funds. While government development banks may generally find it easier to raise share capital than those owned by private shareholders, both categories of institutions would have to pay closer attention to the profit margins in their operations than they have done hitherto.

Financial and Administrative Costs

The main factors that affect the profitability of a development bank, apart from its debt-equity relation, are its financial and administrative costs and its income, which derives chiefly from interest on loans and dividends on investments. The development bank has very little control over its financial costs, because it has no choice but to pay the charges set by the providers of funds. Nevertheless, it should always be alert to the possibility of alternative sources on more favorable terms. Accepting savings and fixed deposits from the public, selling participation certificates for some of its investments, and negotiating lines of credit through export financing institutions in countries that traditionally supply plant and equipment may be feasible propositions for some development banks and may reduce their financial costs.

Administrative costs can be controlled, to some extent, by the management of a development bank. Although these expenses will be high in the initial years, they tend to diminish as a proportion of the total assets as the development bank's portfolio builds up. Some of the large development banks that have been in operation for fifteen years or more have succeeded in containing these expenses to 0.5 percent of total assets. The ratios for other institutions are in the range of 0.5 percent to 8 percent, though 1 to 2 percent is typical for older and relatively large development banks and 3 to 4 percent for younger and smaller institutions.

Of course, administrative costs are determined not simply by the efficiency of financial intermediation. They depend also on how the development bank defines its task. If it devotes considerable effort to sector studies, promotion, advisory services, and technical assistance—activities that may have no early financial return—administrative costs will obviously be higher.

Interest Spreads

A major portion of the income of a development bank is derived from interest on its loans. Interest spreads available to a development bank determine the overall profitability of the institution and also the risks to which it would be willing to expose itself. Interest rate policy determines also the sources from which the development bank can mobilize its resources.

In such a crucial matter affecting its very character, or perhaps because it is such a crucial matter, a development bank cannot, except in the most unusual cases, decide the policy. Most governments, either themselves or through the central banks, determine interest rates, that is, deposit and lending rates in the country, as a part of their monetary policy. Even if decisions do not specifically cover lending rates of a development bank, the development bank, which is only a part of the financial structure, would have to fall in line, because it has to compete with other institutions, to a limited extent, for its resources and, to a large extent, for its clientele.

In its dealings with development banks, the World Bank has taken the view that the interest rates charged by development banks should reflect the cost of mobilizing resources either in domestic or foreign markets and the opportunity cost of capital in the country.[3] In the context of the high rates of inflation prevalent in recent years, this would mean that borrowers would pay positive real rates over the life of the loan.

One of the implications of this view may be that the interest rate on the development bank's loans to its clients would have to be indexed for inflation. Such indexation may not present serious operational problems; after all, commercial banks have for years been making term loans at variable interest rates that change with movements in the bank rate of the central bank. Development banks in Latin America have also considerable experience in linking interest rates to inflation. A corollary of charging variable lending rates would be that development banks should be prepared to pay variable rates on their own borrowings.

If a country continues to experience rapid rates of inflation, sooner or later an adjustment would need to be made in the exchange rate of its currency. The repayment liability of its clients for the foreign currency loans granted by the development bank would thus correspondingly increase. In a way, therefore, foreign currency loans are indexed for inflation, though only partially. Because of the practical difficulties in making frequent exchange rate adjustments, matching the timing and rates of these adjustments with the rates of inflation may not be possible. In discussing the appropriateness of a level of interest rates for foreign currency loans, one would need to take into account the extent of exchange risk borne by the development bank's clients. In view of the current importance of this question, it is treated separately in the next section.

Provision for Bad Debts

Some development banks prefer to make provision for bad debts only in those cases in which losses are imminent. There can be no objection to this on technical grounds. Because of the tendency for projects to flounder in bunches, however, it is preferable to spread the provisions over a longer period. This will guard against a severe drop in profits in a particular period because of the need for unusually large provisions and will even compensate for year-to-year fluctuations in the development bank's performance.

A related matter is the procedure for writing off bad or doubtful investments. Prudence requires that bad debts be treated as a cost item and charged to the income statement. In the balance sheet, there would be a corresponding reduction in assets. Some argue that, when provisions are made not for specific, identifiable losses, but generally, it is desirable to create a "reserve" for bad debts as an item allocated against profits. There can be only one objection to this. Every development bank will have some bad debts. Not to treat them as cost is tantamount to exaggerating the profit. In any case, the reserve for bad debts should not be available as equity for arriving at the borrowing base of a development bank. Indeed, to make the position quite clear, the funds allocated as protection against bad debts should more appropriately be called provisions rather than reserves.

Allocation of Profits

A question that is often raised is how much of the profits of a development bank should be paid out as cash dividends to the shareholders and how much transferred to reserves. In a development bank that has significant private shareholding, cash dividends may be a very important factor in its ability to attract additional share capital, while this consideration may not be relevant at all for a public development bank. The level of reserves has some relation to the level of debt incurred by a development bank, since it provides an additional cushion for both creditors and shareholders: for the former, against a disastrous fall in the flow of cash needed to service debt; for the latter, against impairment of share capital with its attendant legal implications. Building up reserves may also be an effective partial substitute for additional share capital since it provides a base for additional borrowing. Reserves also help maintain the financial integrity of share capital by compensating for the erosion in its value because of inflation.

Although a development bank's policy for allocation to reserves may vary from year to year, there appears to be a general consensus among development bankers that a good policy would be to transfer, over a period, approximately 50 percent of profits to reserves.

Management of Liquidity

Another aspect of financial policy that will affect profitability is the amount of liquid funds maintained by a development bank. It is difficult to estimate the precise timing of the various elements that make up the flow of funds of a development bank. Disbursements are invariably linked to progress in the implementation of projects, while receipt of interest income, loan installments, and dividends on share investments depend on a project's fortunes. If a development bank accepts savings and fixed deposits, their levels may be subject to day-to-day fluctuations. To provide for the contingency that inflows and outflows may differ in amount and in time from estimates, it is necessary to maintain adequate liquidity. What is a safe limit for liquidity and how much is too much are matters for each development bank to decide, through trial and error, over time. What should be remembered is that the cost of an overcautious policy is reduced profits, since the return on short-term investments is normally relatively low. The cost of overconfidence in cash flow estimates—if it means maintaining inadequate liquidity—is frequent cash shortages and the resultant lack of confidence of clients and creditors in the financial acumen of the development bank's management.

A general observation on cash management is that some development banks, while building up excellent capability in managing long-term investments, have paid inadequate attention to deployment of liquid cash resources. Apart from short-term government paper, there may be other profitable and risk-free avenues available for improving the yield on short-term investments (for instance, "bridging finance" against bank guarantees or the interbank "call" market). The management of development banks must be aware of these possibilities.

Conclusion

The discussion of financial policies began with a reference to the growth and survival of development banks. To attain these objectives, development banks have to evolve financial policies that inspire the confidence of their owners and creditors and at the same time allow some flexibility in responding to unforeseen circumstances. As is well known, the World Bank acquires the bulk of its operating funds as borrowings in private capital markets. Its attempts to gauge what ensures market confidence has not led to any clear-cut conclusions. The World Bank's experience, however, is that bondholders (or lenders) tend to form an overall impression of the borrower based not upon any single financial ratio or even a set of ratios, but rather upon the whole package of financial policies and practices that are followed. The principal determinant of confidence appears to be the perception of strong shareholder support for the institution and a sense that the management is prudent. Prudence does not mean avoidance of risk; it implies awareness of risk. In the ultimate analysis, it is the combination of enterprise and a sense of preparedness for adversity that contribute to success in any business endeavor.

Problem of Exchange Risk

It is more or less the standard practice for development banks to insulate themselves from exchange risk in their foreign currency operations by making their borrowers assume the exchange risk or arranging for governments to assume it. The practice varies from country to country and, within the same country, may vary with the category of borrowers. A review of the procedures adopted for seventy loans and credits by the World Bank and its affiliates to development banks in fifty-five countries indicated that as of 1978 the ultimate borrowers carried the full foreign exchange risk in twenty-nine cases, and governments in thirty-three cases. In five cases, the risk was split, the ultimate borrowers carrying the exchange risk between local currency and U.S. dollars and governments carrying the risk between U.S. dollars and the currencies of debt obligation to the World Bank. In one operation, the exchange risk of the ultimate borrower was limited to 3 percent a year, anything in excess being met by a special government fund. In the remaining two cases, medium- and large-scale borrowers carried the exchange risk, while governments absorbed it in the case of loans to small-scale enterprises.

When foreign loans and credits are channeled to a development bank through the government—for instance, credits from the International Development Association or loans from bilateral sources such as Kreditanstalt für Wiederaufbau (KfW) of Germany—the government usually retains the margin between the basic rate, which is payable to the foreign lenders, and the interest rate at which funds are on-lent to development banks. If such margins are sufficient to compensate governments for the exchange risk or if foreign resources are important to the country because of balance of payments considerations, governments are often willing to assume the exchange risk. But if the acquisition of imported plant and equipment confers special benefits on the recipients of loans, it is reasonable to expect them to share the risk; the more so, if there is already an element of subsidy built into the interest rate structure of the development bank. Conversely, the clients of the development bank may be justified in expecting the government or the central bank to carry the risk if there are no severe import restrictions in the country or if the interest rate they are required to pay is not different from that paid by borrowers of domestic currency.

The issue of who should bear the exchange risk is further complicated because several development banks have negotiated foreign loans from more than one source. For development banks associated with the World Bank and its affiliates, this is at least partly a result of the pressures exerted on them by the World Bank to diversify their foreign resources. Thus, it is not unthinkable that a particular bank may have access to several sources such as the World Bank, one of the regional development banks, and one or more of the other multilateral or bilateral agencies such as the European Investment Bank (EIB), KfW of Germany, and Caisse Centrale de Coopération Economique (CCCE) of France. In some cases, the loans are demarcated in specific currencies; for instance, KfW loans are in deutsche marks and CCCE loans in French francs. EIB gives the borrower the option of taking a specific currency or a basket of various currencies, and the rate of interest is adjusted depending on the currencies chosen. But in a World Bank loan, development banks (and their borrowers) know the currency or currencies in which they are obligated to repay only after a withdrawal application has been submitted to the World Bank and disbursement advice has been received, and even then they do not know the order in which the various currencies due will be called up for repayment.

The World Bank, which relied heavily on the private capital market in the United States in the 1950s and 1960s, has diversified its sources of borrowings in recent years, with the result that a substantial part of its borrowings are now from the capital markets of Germany, Switzerland, and Japan, as well as from OPEC countries. Thus, the disbursements on World Bank loans are increasingly denominated in currencies other than U.S. dollars. More than three-fourths of its disbursements in 1978 were in deutsche marks, Swiss francs, and yen, compared with about two-thirds in 1977 and one-half in 1976.

In a major policy change brought about by increasing criticism of its policy, in July 1980 the World Bank adopted a system of currency pooling to deal with the problem of uneven distribution of exchange risk among its borrowers. Under the pooling system, which applies to all borrowers, all currencies are charged to a central disbursement account instead of to individual loan accounts. Each loan account carries a pro rata share of the total exchange adjustment that takes place in the pool. This necessitates a revaluation of the pool almost daily (that is, every time a disbursement or repayment takes place to or from any World Bank client), necessitating a readjustment in the individual loan accounts to reflect the changes in the valuation of the pool. The pooling system does not involve any change in the lending or disbursement procedure; it is merely a change in the accounting procedure.

The World Bank also adopted, as an interim measure applicable to development banks until the general system of currency pooling became operational, a special procedure under which disbursements on loans to development banks were in a basket of currencies consisting of U.S. dollars to the extent of 50 percent and, for the remaining 50 percent, of a mix of deutsche marks, Swiss francs, and yen, as determined by the Bank. The advantage of the special procedure was that it gave some relief to the borrowers both by reducing the exchange risk of hard currencies and by reducing, to some extent, the uncertainty about the currency of repayment.

After the special procedure had been in operation for nearly eighteen months, it was decided to apply to developing banks the new general currency pooling scheme.

While currency pooling will go a long way toward achieving greater equity among the World Bank's borrowers, it will not by itself solve the problem of the development banks, which still have to treat their various borrowers with equity, unless they, in turn, initiate some pooling arrangements for all their foreign currency loans. Most development banks offer loans in both local and foreign currency; this does not mean that local currency loans are always used to finance local costs or that foreign currency loans are used for expenditures incurred abroad. Sometimes foreign currency loans are used to finance a part of the local costs related to indirect imports, imposing the unnecessary burden of exchange risk on the client. Similarly, local currency loans are quite often used to buy foreign exchange from the central bank to import goods or services from abroad, thus relieving the importer of an exchange risk which is legitimately his.

As noted earlier, development banks have started contracting foreign exchange loans from more than one source. Unless a particular loan is tied to procurement from a particular country (which is characteristic of most bilateral credits—KfW loans to development banks being perhaps the only exception), the development bank would have a choice of lines of credit to which it may allocate a particular loan. Since the development bank's interest rates usually do not vary according to the origin of funds, realities of business would induce it to use cheaper sources of funds earlier, or to allocate out of tied bilateral credit whenever there is a project with procurement from that particular country. The development bank's decision may also be conditioned by such factors as the need for a pro rata utilization from several sources and the extent of the free limit or the closing date in a particular line of credit. Each foreign lender may have a stated preference or an unstated prejudice, and a clever development bank manager will always be on the lookout for the line of least resistance in getting his projects approved. Thus, for the clients of the development bank, the line of credit to which their projects are allocated, and hence the currency in which they carry the risk, may very much depend on luck.

There is another dimension to this problem. Since a country's capacity to import is increased by foreign loans negotiated by the development bank, the burden of the foreign loans ought to be shared by all sectors that import goods and services and not merely by clients of the development bank, unless these loans are used for financing imports of only marginal importance.

The discussion so far relates to the risk of higher costs of repaying loans on account of the revaluation of hard currencies in which the loans are expressed. Because of high rates of inflation in most developing countries, the risk of devaluation of domestic currencies is equally important, with precisely the same effect on the liability to repay foreign currency loans. There is, however, one difference: devaluation of local currency usually leads to a corresponding increase in the value of the assets of the borrower, whereas there would be no such increase in the case of revaluation of third-country currencies. It therefore would not be unreasonable to expect the borrower to assume the exchange risk arising from devaluation of the local currency, unless the interest rate on the loans is indexed in one form or another for inflation.

These arguments all point to the need for initiating changes in the procedures followed by some development banks in handling foreign exchange risk. One obvious solution is to adopt a system of currency pooling such as the one referred to earlier. The administrative complexity of such an arrangement, however, would make it impractical for all but the largest and most sophisticated development banks; even then, the pooling system will not be understood by any but the largest and the most sophisticated of their clients. A simpler arrangement would be for government to take or share the risk in one form or another.

As mentioned earlier, there is ample justification for making the borrowers carry the exchange risk if acquisition of imported machinery confers special benefits on them or if the interest rate on loans contains an element of subsidy. The risk to the borrowers, if the arrangement is to be equitable, should, however, be limited to the currency of the country from which they import. Any remaining foreign exchange risk in the foreign borrowings of a development bank should be assumed by the government. It should be feasible, when circumstances so warrant, to charge a fee for this service, either as a levy on all imports, or on a certain category of imports, or as a premium on all term loans granted by the development bank. In any case, the procedures should ensure that the burden is shared fairly by all beneficiaries of the foreign currency borrowings of the development bank.

A final matter of minor detail: even if the ultimate borrower agrees to carry the exchange risk, there could be brief periods during which someone else may have to bear the risk, since it would be impossible to match precisely the timing of repayments of each subloan with the repayment schedule for the entire foreign loan. Governments or central banks usually cover this risk. Some development banks that take this risk on their own account have learned that short-term exchange fluctuations are quite different from the risk of revaluation of a strong currency over ten to fifteen years, and, happily, need not always result in a loss.

Notes to Chapter 12

1. For a comprehensive treatment of these questions, see Douglas Gustafson, "Financial Policy Problems of Development Finance Companies," in *Development Finance Companies: Aspects of Policy and Operation*, ed. William Diamond (Baltimore, Md.: Johns Hopkins Press, 1968), pp. 59–80.

2. Gary L. Hyde, "Development Banking in Asia and the Pacific: Current Issues," working paper presented at the First General Assembly of the Association of Development Financing Institutions in Asia and the Pacific, Bangkok, Thailand, April 1978; processed.

3. For a discussion on the World Bank's attitude on interest rates generally and on the relending terms of its loans to development banks, see World Bank, "Development Finance Companies," Sector Policy Paper (Washington, D.C., April 1976), pp. 28–33.

Chapter 13

Development Banks and the Mobilization of Financial Resources

DAVID B. GILL

IN MANY COUNTRIES, development banks are giving increased attention to finding new ways of mobilizing financial resources. The reasons vary from country to country. In some cases, especially among the more advanced countries, both governments and international financial institutions are reassessing their past practice of providing relatively unlimited amounts of subsidized funds. As a result, they now require development banks to stand on their own feet financially, as a matter of business discipline in a market-oriented economy. In other instances, possibly toward the other end of both the developmental and political spectrums, various pressures are reducing or cutting off governmental and international funds and related interest rate subsidies.

Paradoxically, it is in this latter group of countries that the problems can be most acute for development banks; for market-oriented economies with an emerging industrial sector there is apt to be a volume of domestic and foreign funds at market rates, which can be tapped by those development banks that organize themselves to do so. Nevertheless, it is becoming increasingly important that top management in all development banks think ahead to the time when, for whatever reasons, they must fend for themselves financially, more than hitherto, both because of the possibility of reduced official support and because of the business need to improve the profitability and creditworthiness of their institutions.

In most countries, development banks represent perhaps 2 to 15 percent of the total assets of all domestic financial institutions. In general, the larger and more sophisticated the economy, the smaller the role of development banks in the total financial system; but even in the smaller and least developed economies, development banks represent a relatively small proportion of the total assets of financial institutions compared with that of commercial banks. Nevertheless, development banks may represent 100 percent of the available supply of long-term loan funds in the smaller and least developed countries, and as much as 25 percent in the more advanced economies (such as Greece and Korea). This substantial difference in the importance of development banks in the financial sector of different countries is largely due to the existence, or absence, of a functioning capital market.[1]

The capital market comprises essentially three sectors: (1) long-term lending institutions, such as development banks, agricultural banks, and housing banks; (2) contractual savings institutions, such as insurance companies, social security and pension funds, and investment trusts; and (3) securities markets.

While virtually every country has at least one long-term lending bank,[2] regardless of the state of the economy or the prevailing political philosophy, contractual savings institutions and securities markets are much more likely to exist in advanced market economies. But even in such economies, there are significant differences in the relative size of these two components of the financial system. For example, they are large and important in Korea, relatively insignificant in Spain, and at present, almost nonexistent in Argentina.

The relative size of these subsectors and the factors underlying the differences are important to development banks in considering resource mobilization strategies. The factors and their trends indicate when development banks may find it vital to obtain new sources of funds and how difficult or easy that may prove to be. The presence of large and efficient contractual savings institutions and of a securities market indicates the existence of a broad group of savers already educated in the concept of long-term instruments and in the rational assessment of alternative financial risks and rewards. In countries where political or economic considerations cause savings to flow only into nonrisk, short-term instruments, development banks are especially vulnerable to cutoffs of their normal sources of governmental funds.

Basic Considerations

The following section summarizes some of the important variables affecting approaches to maximizing the availability of financial resources. This will put into proper context the more detailed issues of how to mobilize financial resources.

Debt versus Equity

Usually, development banks that are wholly owned by governments are not overly concerned about the adequacy of their equity base, for their borrowings come either directly from the government or are guaranteed by the government. By contrast, privately controlled development banks—especially in countries where governments do not guarantee their debts or may not in the future—are particularly conscious of their equity base. Nevertheless, one could say that, regardless of the ownership of the development bank or of the stage of development of the country, the long-term interests of the institution would be best served if it were to have what is conventionally considered a strong equity base. There are essentially two reasons for this.

First, especially when borrowings from private sources without government guarantee are needed, a strong equity base is essential to provide an appropriate cushion against possible defaults and a base for some earnings unencumbered by borrowing costs. On this latter point, leaders look to the earnings available to meet borrowing costs (interest revenues less administrative expenses) and measure them as a ratio of interest expense. All other things being equal, the lower the equity base in relation to borrowings, the lower the interest coverage ratio can be. An interest coverage ratio of 1.1:1 might be acceptable when combined with a conservative capital structure and a good management record, but in most instances a ratio of 1.3:1 would be necessary for a prime credit rating. A bank operating with a low spread between its borrowing and lending rates, arrearage problems, and high administrative costs can have a low interest coverage ratio for these reasons alone, even if it has a large equity base.

Second, in most cases development banks should be in a position to make equity investments themselves and, in line with prudent investment policies, their equity investments should not exceed their net worth. Moreover, development banks, while aiming at a reasonably diversified portfolio, should at the same time be able to make equity commitments of a worthwhile size in the individual enterprises they decide to finance. Prudent policy suggests that individual equity investments should be limited to not more than 10 percent of the net worth of the bank. Under such a policy, each equity investment would represent something like 5 to 15 percent of the equity of a project being financed. Thus the equity base of a development bank should be related to the size of equity needed for new enterprises in the particular economy. According to the same rationale, and notwithstanding the fact that many development banks appear to be prepared to lend 50 to 100 percent of debt resources needed by a new enterprise, it would be prudent to link the maximum size of a loan, too, to the institution's net worth—for example, to no more than, say, 25 percent of the bank's net worth.

Another issue relating to equity concerns diversifying the ownership of the development bank. A broad base of domestic institutional and individual ownership should provide significant support for the bank itself, since all its shareholders would be concerned about its success. Conversely, control by one group, whether the government or a small group of individuals or enterprises, can lead to a less than balanced approach to its investment policies. This may not be in its best interest and may make it vulnerable to sudden shifts in either the policies or the financial condition of its controlling shareholders.

Thus the equity base should be as large as feasible, and ownership should be diversified. A reasonable leveraging of debt is, of course, important to maximize profits, but this also depends on the spread between borrowing costs and lending rates as well as the degree of risk in the loan portfolio and the administrative costs of handling it. These, however, are issues related more to financial management than to resource mobilization.

Short-term verses Long-term Debt

Issues discussed in this section are also more appropriately related to financial management than to resource mobilization. It is necessary, however, to raise here the question of matching the maturities of liabilities with those of assets, a matter that is as important to the credit rating of an institution as are its interest rate and its debt-equity ratio.

There have been proposals that development banks should become multibanks or universal banks and, thus, short-term lenders as well as long-term lenders, thereby justifying a debt structure with some short-term liabilities. This may be a reasonable proposition, although it raises the question of the extent to which diversification of functions within such banks will lead to their eventually losing the original sense of dedication to long-term project financing. This has been the case in some countries, such as Colombia, where the monetary and fiscal climate has made short-term financing easier and more profitable than long-term financing.

The more important issue is the extent to which development banks should engage in term transformation (borrowing short and lending long). It has been argued that this is a desirable practice in countries with a shortage of long-term savings. The risks involved are downplayed by the proponents of this practice, who argue that demand and savings deposits tend to be reasonably stable even in periods of severe uncertainty and, thus, that a certain proportion of short-term resources can always be prudently used for long-term lending. This is a plausible argument. In several countries such as Brazil and Mexico, however, internal or external crises of confidence have caused major runs on banks that emphasized borrowing at short term to lend at long term. Such runs have forced governmental refinancing at substantial cost both financially and, indirectly, in their effects on foreign exchange rates and domestic inflation. This problem is not restricted to developing countries, however. The United Kingdom, for instance, experienced problems of this nature in the early 1970s when some smaller banks, heavily engaged in real estate, lost deposits in the course of a severe tightening of domestic credit. Also, in mid-1979 the Bank of England expressed concern about the exposure of the foreign business of British banks: whereas only 15 percent of their resources had a term of more than six months, more than 40 percent of their loans had a term of more than two years.

Direct versus Indirect Financing

Development banks, like most other financial institutions, tend to concentrate on mobilizing resources directly through the sale of their own financial instruments. This means of financing is the cleanest and easiest and frequently costs the least. It also maximizes the size of the institution's own total assets and thus improves its image in domestic and foreign markets. Nevertheless, this direct method of financing depends, among other things, on other institutions (or individuals) having funds to invest in such banks. It also depends on the bank's creditworthiness and on governmental policies, which can limit the volume of resources that can be mobilized and possibly also make the terms of obtaining them more onerous than otherwise.

There are, however, possibilities of indirect financing. These include revolving the portfolio of the bank more quickly, seeking financial participants in new projects to reduce its own commitment to the project, and helping open up other sources of finance for the companies it assists. This third possibility is, in a sense, an extension of the second. The difference between them is that the third calls for a continuous effort by established enterprises to seek funds from the money and capital markets, while the second involves a one-shot effort to find partners, either lenders or investors, in financing a particular project.

Successful endeavors to obtain indirect financing are not only advantageous to the development bank; they also contribute to strengthening the domestic money and capital markets. They influence others to participate in these markets, and, through the physical offering of new instruments, they are practical steps to educate savers in their merits. Success in such an endeavor is particularly important in promoting the establishment of new types of financial services or new financial institutions that will specialize in such functions.

Domestic versus Foreign Financial Resources

Many development banks have tended to become conduits for official foreign exchange loans and, thus, to concentrate on the asset side of their portfolios on foreign exchange lending. Others have been in a position to finance domestic capital requirements as well. The latter, however, appear to be in the minority, except in some of the larger, semi-industrialized countries, such as Brazil and Mexico.

Two principal issues arise from concentration on foreign sources of finance. On the one hand, such finance may not be available to clients for domestic currency requirements. On the other hand, the development bank must find ways of protecting itself directly or indirectly against the foreign exchange risk incurred when borrowing abroad.

It is desirable for any development bank to limit its dependence on foreign exchange borrowings to the foreign exchange portion of projects that will generate sufficient foreign currency income to service the foreign debt. If such an objective is achieved, judicious additional foreign borrowings or acceptance of foreign equity investment can be sought when the financial terms are especially attractive in relation to the terms of obtaining additional domestic resources. The institutions that have demonstrated a high degree of efficiency in managing their total financial exposure (and especially thin exposure in foreign currencies) are, in fact, those that have found it possible to enter foreign bond markets and to obtain long-term capital at a fixed interest and at a relatively attractive price. In the broader market of internationally syndicated bank loans, these institutions are currently obtaining floating rate funds at one-half to three-quarters of 1 percent more than the London Interbank Offered Rate (LIBOR) for periods of eight to ten years when others are paying from 1 to 2 percent more than LIBOR for four to six years, or have not been able to obtain such funds at all.

Put another way, development banks that themselves take, or allow their own borrowers to take, substantial foreign exchange risks are jeopardizing their credit rating and thus reducing their capacity to mobilize both foreign and domestic resources. Nevertheless, a limited degree of foreign exchange risk can be justified when there is an interest rate saving over domestic rates of sufficient magnitude to outweigh the potential cost of a reasonable foreign exchange risk.

More will be said later about some of the characteristics of the various sources of foreign funds and about infrastructural policy issues that can help or impede improved access to foreign funds.

Strategies for Mobilization of Financial Resources

A strategy to diversify a development bank's sources of capital should consist of two parts. First, an effort should be made to influence the government to improve the overall financial infrastructure of the country to increase the size of the capital market and to improve its efficiency. This would tend to make available more, and different types of, finance through a broader array of instruments designed for a wider variety of savers. Second, the strategy should relate to what can be done in an existing environment. The first step therefore calls for leadership in assisting the government to strengthen the capital market as a whole for the national benefit, with, of course, the expectation that the development bank will be a beneficiary in the future. The second involves exploring specific practical steps to take greater advantage of what can be done in existing circumstances.

Long-term Financial Development Policy

Infrastructural improvements that can speed the development of a larger and more efficient financial market are outlined below. All the difficulties in the way of such improvements are unlikely to exist at any one time in any one country, but experience suggests that most occur in various forms at one stage of development or another.

INTEREST RATE POLICY. In many countries the interest rate structure is fixed by government, but in countries with no foreign exchange controls, interest rates (to the extent that they are independent of taxation policies as discussed below) tend to move in line with rates in the major international markets.

The major problems in countries with controlled (that is, fixed) interest rate regimes are that such regimes frequently channel funds to what are deemed priority sectors of the economy at specific points in time (subsidized lending rates). Moreover, they are combined with controlled interest rates on deposits and other savings instruments that favor certain financial intermediaries deemed worthy of special support. Usually, the interest rate structures are not changed promptly to reflect new economic conditions and changing priorities.

At the same time, to keep the cost of finance as low as possible, deposit rates are often kept very low in nominal terms and negative in real terms. When this occurs, the effects tend to be self-defeating, for savers ultimately see the merits of consumption rather than saving, or they prefer exporting their savings or hoarding goods to purchasing financial instruments.

A constructive approach is to encourage governments to establish interest rate policies that provide positive real interest rates to savers to the extent needed to encourage saving in the form of domestic financial instruments. If market forces are permitted to a reasonable degree, interest rates on long-term instruments would tend to provide additional rewards for savers who are prepared to extend the term of their savings beyond conventional demand or savings deposit instruments.

TAXATION POLICY. Next to the current and the perceived future rates of inflation, the rate of taxation applied to income earned from financial instruments exercises the most important influence on the pattern of savings flows. It is also the most important policy instrument within the control of the government for influencing the flow of savings. As a general principle, income from all financial instruments should be treated equally. In practice, however, interest on government paper and bank deposits is often exempt from taxation, whereas interest on private sector instruments and on capital gains from the sale of equities is often taxed at rates higher than on earned income. Such action discourages rather than encourages savings in long-term instruments. Tax policies of this kind can negate the beneficial effects of policies encouraging real levels of interest rates before taxation. In Egypt recently, at the maximum income levels, the effective rate of taxation, even on interest from bank deposits, was about 94 percent, while the maximum personal income tax rate was about 70 percent. Withholding tax on interest was 30 percent even for those whose earned income was too low to be taxed.

In such countries, governments might be shown the merits of a neutral tax policy, under which income from all instruments is treated the same and the maximum rate in no case exceeds the rate from earned income. In more market-oriented countries with strong economic expansion policies, a case could also be made for an income tax policy that would reward savers who committed their funds to long-term instruments and especially to equities. Such a policy would encourage development of the capital market and would make more funds available for long-term investment projects. Korea and Brazil have developed such policies. In Korea, savings from the lower income groups are especially encouraged through an interest rate subsidy on savings accounts. In both countries, investments in equities are encouraged by preferential tax rates on both dividends and capital gains and by lower corporation tax rates from companies that have a significant degree of ownership by investors outside the controlling shareholder group.

INVESTOR PROTECTION. Interest and tax policies presuppose that savers who invest in long-term instruments and stocks of enterprises will benefit both from the economic growth and from the profits of that growth, which will flow equitably from the enterprises to the savers. Economic growth is, of course, beyond the control of development banks. Investor protection, however, is an objective that can be pressed by development banks on their governments.

Among the matters involved in investor protection are company legislation, standards of financial disclosure required by corporations, and reasonable accounting and auditing standards. This necessitates the establishment of regulatory agencies, such as bank superintendencies, securities commissions, and similar entities with appropriate authority to ensure that savers are fairly treated by both financial institutions and business enterprises in general, and that financial disclosure is full, timely, and comprehensible.

In many countries there is opposition to new legislation that requires greater financial disclosure by enterprises as well as by banks. There is also resistance to establishing mechanisms for policing the activities of enterprises that offer their own financial instruments to the public and of institutions that act as intermediaries or agents in the placement of such paper. Although businessmen's fear of overregulation is understandable, it is a fact that in countries without a reasonable degree of investor protection, there are often serious abuses. One consequence is a much lower level of financial savings than would otherwise be the case, especially savings invested in the instruments of the capital market. Moreover, the cost of intermediation is greater in countries with low standards of financial disclosure. By encouraging investor protection development banks can thus benefit their countries generally and can also improve the possibilities for a greater flow of long-term resources in due course into the instruments of the development banks themselves.

INSTITUTIONAL DEVELOPMENT. In many developing countries the level of savings is lower than might be expected in light of their gross national product (GNP) per capita, in part because of the inadequacy of financial institutions. This applies particularly to the smaller and poorer countries where the rates of interest and taxation and the absence of investor protection, combined with a lack of domestic managerial talent, make any form of institutional development particularly difficult. It also applies, however, to some fairly advanced economies because of broad political and economic problems. For instance, the difficulties may be compounded by a legislative structure that impedes the growth of existing financial institutions and limits the establishment of new ones. Some command economies fall into this category; so do several market-oriented countries.

In a broad sense, a satisfactory diversification of financial institutions may be described roughly as a situation in which the central bank or its equivalent holds about 25 percent of the total financial assets of financial institutions; commercial banks, about 30 percent; term banks and other specialized lending institutions (such as finance companies and lending companies), about 25 percent; and contractual savings institutions, about 20 percent. Separately, but in the same context, equities outstanding should be about 20 percent of GNP, and total securities (government and corporate long-term bonds plus equities) should be about 40 percent of GNP.[3] Of course, some of these securities will be held by financial institutions and thus there will be some double counting. There will also be some double counting among institutional assets because some institutions will from time to time be both borrowers from and lenders to other institutions simultaneously.[4] In any event, there is a wide divergence in these ratios from one country to another; many countries that would be considered quite advanced in terms of GNP per capita have remarkably shallow financial systems. In Mexico, where GNP per capita is about US$1,100, total financial assets represent only about 60 percent of GNP, but of this less than 5 percent is held by contractual savings institutions, and securities represent only about 15 percent of GNP.

To achieve an appropriate degree of diversification, legislative and institutional restraints should be relaxed. In some countries development banks have influenced government policy to broaden the institutional framework by permitting new types of financial institutions to come into existence. The Industrial and Mining Development Bank of Iran was an early promoter of domestic securities markets, encouraging appropriate government legislation to strengthen the primary and secondary securities markets and helping establish specialized securities firms. The Korea Development Finance Corporation promoted the establishment of specialized firms to deal in short-term instruments of private enterprises (commercial paper) and also a specialized leasing company to provide more flexible medium-term finance for smaller enterprises. The Industrial Finance Corporation of Thailand has played a similar role by promoting both the first Thai mutual fund management company to encourage investment in equities and the country's first leasing company. The Private Development Corporation of the Philippines (PDCP) played an active role in developing the local money market by participating in policy dialogues with government and by establishing in the early 1960s a specialized money market department within PDCP. Since then, PDCP has worked with government and the securities industry to revitalize the local mutual fund industry and is now in the process of establishing a new mutual fund management company. The Industrial Development Bank of Turkey and the Corporación Venezolana de Desarrollo (CAVENDES), starting in the 1960s, played a role in their capital markets by organizing underwritings of securities issues. The Nigerian Industrial Development Bank and the Corporación Financiera Colombiana have taken similar steps in their respective countries.

In most of the foregoing examples, development banks played an important role, first, in promoting new policies and laws and then, once the laws or regulations were in place, in taking advantage of them. In the interest of both the development of the national economy and the improvement of their own access to additional domestic resources, other development banks can act similarly. Their action is especially important in countries where the necessary infrastructural steps have not yet been taken to develop contractual savings institutions and securities markets, or where the steps taken to date have met with little success.

REGULATORY FRAMEWORK FOR DEVELOPMENT BANKS. One reason development banks have had difficulty either in mobilizing domestic resources or in expanding their operations beyond that of lenders of long-term foreign exchange resources is that often local legislation has narrowly restricted the activities of the development banks themselves. The examples of what some institutions have done, as well as the broad responsibilities given to others when they were established (such as the National Bank for Industrial Development of Brazil, the Korea Development Bank, and the Development Bank of Singapore), suggest that legislation limiting flexibility of a development bank can be changed if a good case for such action is made to the government.

Most development banks have the legal power to make long-term loans, as well as equity investments, from long-term funds from domestic sources. It is difficult to imagine any reason a development bank should be prevented from playing this constructive role. Nevertheless, some are still restricted from attempting to borrow long-term domestic resources and thus are inhibited from making long-term domestic loans (except from their limited equity). Others have no such restriction but have no source of long-term domestic funds because of such problems as interest rate and taxation policies.

Initiatives in Existing Circumstances

Even within the existing legal and institutional infrastructure, development banks can take certain measures to improve resource mobilization.

EQUITY FINANCING. If a development bank is entirely or largely government-owned, there is often merit in dividing such holdings among several government entities, rather than concentrating them in a single governmental shareholder. The advantage of such a division is that different governmental entities with different managements are likely to have different points of view on policies, priorities, and operations. With several such shareholders, even if they are all controlled by the same government, there is a reasonable likelihood of a more balanced approach to policy formulation in the development bank.

The same is true with respect to ownership by private institutional investors and by foreign investors. There is always a risk of conflict of interest if a private individual or a group holds an inordinately large share—especially if the affiliated shareholders form a major financial holding company or industrial group that is tempted to channel resources principally to their own group. Nevertheless, participation by private institutions will bring with it a greater concern for the profitability of the institution in general and, hence, a more businesslike approach to investment policies and to the development of a healthy capital structure.

Private investment can also take place via a public offering of securities. It can be argued that offering shares to individual investors has no merit in the case of a relatively new or small development bank, especially in a country without an organized securities market, because of the risk the investor must take. There can be, however, certain advantages. First, business discipline will be greater if private ownership is broader. The responsibility of the institution will be greater because of the need to disclose financial information and pay a reasonable dividend. Second, a public offering sets a good example for a development bank's client enterprises in cases where the bank wishes to encourage broader equity ownership both to avoid criticism of financing only narrowly based entrepreneurial groups and to reduce the amount of its own financing needs. Third, such a policy broadens the available sources of equity finance for the development bank itself.

Steps can be taken with respect to equity finance when neither the market nor the institution is yet ready for issues of common shares. Among such steps are issuance of convertible debt or preferred stock instruments, whereby investors have the option of conversion and thus participation in the direct benefits of an equity investment later on, but in the meantime have the protection of a more secure instrument paying a fixed rate of interest or a fixed preferred dividend.

LONG-TERM LOANS AND BOND ISSUES. Nothing need be added about long-term loans as a means of direct finance, for loans have long been the principal source of capital for development banks. As for bond issues, the possibility of issuing them depends on the state of the domestic securities market. From a practical point of view, the only difference between a bond and a loan is that the former is a readily transferrable, and thus marketable, instrument of indebtedness, whereas the latter is hardly marketable at all. That is, bonds are certificates of indebtedness representing specific amounts of a given bond issue, whereas loans are direct contracts between a lender and a borrower and thus transferrable only if a new loan agreement is written or if the original lender prepares a separate contract to sell a participation in part of the loan. A certificate of participation is, for practical purposes, a form of bond.

In many instances a development bank could, if it wished, raise debt through an issue of bonds that would otherwise have the same terms (interest rate, maturity, and so on) as that of a domestic loan. Similarly, there would be nothing to prevent a foreign loan from being set up in the form of a bond issue. For example, CAVENDES has recently issued a form of floating rate loan in the Eurodollar market by selling certificates of participation.

The merit of issuing bonds in addition to, or in place of, arranging loans is that their marketability makes it possible for a broader range of savers to be tapped than is the case in the loan market. Of course, in an emerging financial market, the practical value of this marketability may be somewhat limited for there would be few additional sources of long-term loans. But if a capital market is in the process of formation, initiatives in issuing bonds can be quite fruitful if the general economic climate and the level of real interest rates are satisfactory. This is especially the case if contractual savings institutions have been developed, particularly insurance companies and pension funds, which normally welcome the added liquidity that marketable bonds provide. Nevertheless, banking institutions have a historic preference for direct loans even in sophisticated markets where the concept of syndicated bank loans among a large number of banks is well understood. This preference is in part based on the ease of continuing past procedures as against the inconvenience of changing existing procedures. Nevertheless, in periods of illiquidity even this bias can be overcome as the banks themselves discover the merit of being able to revolve their own portfolios.

In pioneering the issuance of bonds, development banks will find it helpful to have the professional assistance of securities market institutions. In most countries, even without organized stock exchanges, there are usually brokers who deal in stocks as well as other assets. Frequently, they can be encouraged to act as advisers and as distributors of bonds. In any event, in a practical sense, there is rarely anything to prevent the development bank itself from preparing and marketing its own issues, with the assistance of its board of directors and shareholders.

Development banks that make such an effort should design instruments that will afford effective protection to investors. This requires an appropriate trust indenture that describes the business terms of the issue, including physical collateral if any, the terms of senior debt, and the conditions under which the institution may issue additional debt ranking equal to the proposed issue. Those conditions might include a minimum ratio of net tangible assets to debt outstanding, a minimum ratio of earnings available to meet all interest payments for the preceding twelve-month period, and such other covenants as not paying dividends or redeeming stock if the effect would be to reduce net worth or working capital below certain amounts. Such a trust indenture would normally be administered on behalf of the bondholders by a trustee, an independent fiduciary institution. In many countries there are already requirements of this nature under company law or a special trust indenture act.

SHORT-TERM DEBT. The issuance of negotiable certificates of deposit (CD) is useful in extending the deposit-taking function in much the same way that bond issues are an extension of the long-term borrowing function. That is, CD are marketable deposits, and since they have more liquidity than other deposits, they are, like bonds, more acceptable to a wider range of savers. The issuance of commercial paper can have the same benefits as issuing CD. The principal distinction between these two instruments is that the former is unsecured, whereas the latter is, in the banking sense, a senior credit. While local law may limit the rights of development banks to issue CD, it is unlikely that it would prevent the issuance of commercial paper, at least to other institutions. To a limited extent it is also possible for development banks to consider the leasing of their own equipment and the factoring of their own receivables.

In considering these various short-term instruments, including demand and savings deposits, development banks should concern themselves with the administrative costs involved. Especially in the case of demand and savings deposits and the factoring of receivables, the average amounts will be relatively small compared with the units of sale of long-term loans or bond issues. Combined with the short-term nature of the transactions, this will make the unit administrative costs high and could well result in an unattractive cost structure. By contrast, the marketing of CD and commercial paper is more a wholesale operation and thus frequently more viable. Conventionally, the minimum size of a CD or commercial paper transaction is likely to be at least ten times that of a demand or savings deposit, and the minimum term might be fixed at, say, a minimum of 30 or 180 days.

INDIRECT FINANCING. Opportunities are readily available in almost all countries for selling participations in outstanding loans and marketing stocks from the equity portfolios of development banks.

A variation of this procedure is to put together unit trusts or investment funds made up of the paper of several different enterprises in the development bank's portfolio to give the purchaser diversification and to deal with the problem of administrative cost. The ability to take such a step may depend on the approval of a government regulatory agency. In many countries, however, there are no relevant regulations. An initiative of this sort would not only be to the short-term financial advantage of the development bank; it would also provide a constructive example for the development of a proper infrastructure for capital market mechanisms.

INSTITUTION BUILDING. Still another example of working within the existing framework is the promotion of new financial institutions to market various types of financial paper. This has been mentioned in the preceding section on policy issues, and some specific examples were given of such activities by development banks. In countries where the infrastructural issues have been dealt with, development banks can proceed directly to promote appropriate institutions. Further, as suggested in the previous paragraph, this type of initiative can also demonstrate the desirability of setting up a more suitable structural environment as part of a long-term government strategy. The development of the regulatory and tax framework for leasing in the Philippines is emerging now as a consequence of the recent establishment by the Philippine Investment Systems Organization of a leasing affiliate with developmental objectives. Previously, leasing in the Philippines had been done on an ad hoc basis by many institutions as a side function, and thus the authorities had not focused directly on the implications.

Additional Thoughts on External Resource Mobilization

The section on basic considerations referred to the merit of attracting external resources and the importance of establishing favorable credit ratings in foreign markets. This section deals with some characteristics of foreign and international markets.

In the syndicated loan market in dollars or other hard currencies, the international banks usually make loans only at a floating rate, and borrowers are thus subject to the fluctuations of short-term interest rates. Borrowing development banks must risk these vagaries if they onlend on the conventional basis of a fixed term at a fixed interest rate. A case can be made that, over any ten-year period, the average rate paid in a floating rate market would probably be less than that in the market for a fixed-interest-rate long-term loan or bond issue; but this is no consolation in periods of high short-term rates, when the spread on the development bank's lending rate may be substantially reduced or become negative. This is especially the case for development banks that have to meet interest-coverage tests for the issuance of new debt.

Somewhat downplayed by lenders when negotiating floating rate issues is that floating rate loans always contain escape clauses for the lenders in the event that they cannot raise matching deposit funds in the currency loaned at each interest rate renegotiation date (usually every six months). The implication is that in the event of a major international financial crisis the lender has the right not only to increase the interest rate but also to change the currency. Consequently, the borrower, unless his own onlending contracts have identical clauses, is in a sense in double jeopardy, since he may have to carry an unexpected foreign exchange risk as well as the better-known interest rate risk. Although there are no known cases of this clause having been used, the possibility that it might happen still exists.[5]

Many development banks have tended to emphasize tapping international floating rate loan markets because of the relative ease of obtaining such funds. This is at least partly because bond financings for developing countries, let alone for individual financial institutions in them, are much more difficult to arrange in foreign international financial markets. (In total, developing country bond issues, mainly for government credits, probably amount to only about 10 percent of the volume of syndicated loans.) This is because the principal lenders in bond markets are insurance companies, pension funds, and trust accounts, which have a greater concern for liquidity than do the international banks. Also, insofar as these institutions are essentially domestic in orientation, they are less willing to purchase (and are frequently legally prohibited from purchasing) more than a minimal amount of foreign securities.

In light of the above, it is worth exploring the merits of attempting to obtain long-term, fixed-interest foreign funds from the bond market instead of remaining dependent on shorter-term, floating rate funds. The problems, however, are considerable and are summarized below.

First, the foreign and international bond markets usually demand a greater degree of financial disclosure and stricter terms in trust indentures than do the syndicated loan markets. Second, in most major foreign markets laws governing the investment of funds by insurance companies and other trustee-type pools of funds usually permit the purchase only of securities that meet specific credit criteria. These may include a first mortgage as collateral and, in conjunction with the higher financial disclosure requirement, frequently also a formal credit rating by an acceptable independent credit-rating agency. The latter applies only to the U.S. markets in the strictly legal sense. This would, however, represent probably 50 percent of the total foreign and international markets. Moreover, most professional buyers are aware of the U.S. credit-rating system, and, even if they do not restrict their purchases to issues with acceptable credit ratings or the equivalent, they tend to extract an interest rate penalty on purchasing bonds that do not meet these requirements.

Third, the costs of organizing bond issues, especially in the U.S. public market, are higher than the costs of syndicated loans. The legal and printing expenses of a prospectus and a trust indenture, as well as the fees paid to the trustee and the registrar (an independent institution that polices the physical issuance of bond certificates), can be considerable. For example, a public bond issue in the United States, registered with the U.S. Securities and Exchange Commission (SEC), would probably cost about US$150,000 in legal, printing, and registration fees over and above the underwriters' commission, the annual cost of trustee services, and so on. Underwritings for a

U.S. private placement (a bond issue sold only to a limited number of institutions that are not required to be registered) and for Euro-dollars or Asian dollars would probably cost only about half as much. Nevertheless, frequently the total cost of a bond issue in excess of US$25 million, even as a publicly registered U.S. issue, when taken as an annualized percentage rate over the ten- to twenty-year term that such an issue might have, can often be less than the cost of a syndicated bank loan under current market conditions. This, of course, depends on the relation between short-term and long-term interest rates at a point in time and on the market of issuance since the underwriting fees may vary from less than 1 percent to more than 3 percent, depending on the amount of the issue, the quality of the credit, and the market of issuance.

Notwithstanding the above, some foreign markets are less strin-gent than others, and it is therefore often possible, for example, for a development bank that could not market a bond issue in the United States to do so in the Asian-dollar market, especially if it is located in the region itself.

Nevertheless, development banks interested in diversifying their sources of foreign financing and in improving the financial terms on which they can borrow should, over time, adjust their capital struc-tures and improve their standards of accounting and disclosure to obtain favorable credit ratings and meet U.S. sec registration re-quirements for public issuance purposes. These standards may, at first sight, be considered unduly complex. In practice, however, countries that have become used to them are convinced that they are worth the trouble and the expense. Not only is the market for offerings broadened and the financial terms improved, but also the financial reporting required has proven useful to the management of such institutions in controlling their own businesses. The fact that probably at least half the available long-term funds comes from U.S. institutions is also important, as is the fact that U.S. insurance companies and pension funds, at least at present, will consider maturities in the fifteen- to thirty-year range as compared with five to fifteen years in the Eurodollar and Asian-dollar markets.

Concluding Remarks

Although this chapter encourages development banks to devote more managerial time to the conscious planning of the liability side of their balance sheets, it is recognized that this takes time, which is itself money. But the time and money will be well spent if the development banks expand their own economic and financial opportunities in the short run and fulfill their broader and longer-term responsibilities to their national economies.

Another point of view is that development banks would be well advised to be opportunistic in their outlook and to conduct business in terms of the immediate, short-run advantage. It is suggested that this approach has worked better in the past than it is likely to do in the future. Even for the short-run goals of maximizing current business and profits, the judicious long-term planning for resource mobilization as well as a more progressive and innovative approach to tapping savings can pay off in due course. In this connection, the record of the Korea Development Finance Corporation (KDFC) is particularly impressive. For example, as a result of initiating the establishment of the Korea Investment Finance Company (KIFC) to develop the newly opened commercial paper market in Korea, KDFC's equity investment in that company is now producing a dividend return of more than 27 percent annually on original cost.

A final thought on this subject is that possibly a major benefit of accepting the discipline of a competitive marketplace for finance is a more professional approach to the financial management of the development bank. This benefit will flow from the need to adopt more sophisticated internal accounting and control techniques. These, in turn, can be applied to the assessment of the risks and rewards of alternative investment opportunities. When the demand for funds exceeds the supply, selectivity can be a key to financial success which, in its own turn, improves the availability of those limited funds.

Notes to Chapter 13

1. Except in countries with command economies, which favor more direct allocation of resources.

2. With the same exception as in note 1 above.

3. Of course, these are only approximations. Holdings of contractual savings institutions in developed countries would probably average 25 percent of the total and in developing countries, 5 to 10 percent. Total securities would range from 50 to 100 percent and from 5 to 40 percent of GNP in developed and developing countries respectively.

4. For example, a commercial bank might have, simultaneously, interbank deposits from other commercial banks and loans in its asset portfolio to, say, housing banks.

5. See the reference on p. 217 to the reported concern of the Bank of England on this point.

Part VII

Organization and Staff Development

THE QUALITY AND EFFECT of management's decisions depend on the mechanisms by which decisions are reached, the information on which they are based, the judgment of the decisionmakers, and the communication between those who make the decisions and those who are responsible for carrying them out. The flow of information, the decisionmaking process, and the quality of communication among all levels are thus intimately intertwined.

The sponsors of a development bank often involve themselves in this process while the institution is still being formed. It is up to the chief executive, however, to establish an organizational structure and operational procedures conducive to sound and timely decisionmaking. He confronts this problem from the moment he is appointed and must consider many questions: How should the functions of the staff be organized and interrelated so as to ensure cooperative and coordinated action? To what degree can authority be delegated among the various levels of decisionmaking? What procedures are required so that management receives the information it needs for decisionmaking and control? How can an unimpeded flow of information be established from the chief executive to all levels of the staff? How can management keep in touch with the institution's operational programs so as to make modifications when needed and to ensure their success? What role does the board of directors have in decisionmaking? What can be done to ensure productive relations with government and with other providers of finance, a sympathetic general public, cooperation with other relevant institutions, and relations with clients that encourage both effective use of the bank's resources and a continuing flow of new business?

The chief executive's responses to many of these questions will ultimately be reflected in the assignment of staff responsibilities and in an organization chart. That scheme of organization will not ensure sound and timely decisionmaking. It can, however, impede or facilitate it.

Although the questions are common to all development banks, the answers are not. For one thing, they are affected by the environment and are to a significant extent culture-bound. The functions of boards, the ways in which authority is distributed, the mechanisms for achieving cooperation among the individuals in an organization, the manner in which communication takes place in a hierarchy, the relations a development bank needs to establish with other institutions in the community—these are functions of tradition, as well as of law. Responses to the questions differ with the age and experience of the development bank itself and with the evolving professionalism of the staff. Responses also reflect the working style of the chief executive and his professional background. It follows that it is not possible to generalize about the organizational structure appropriate for a development bank and its information and communications systems, and that there are no once-and-for-all formulas for smooth, sound, and timely decisionmaking. Indeed, the far-sighted chief executive will want to build mechanisms into his systems and organization to ensure continuing review and appropriate revision from time to time to take account of growth and changes of function.

The chapter by R. K. Hazari, "Organizational Structure and Communications Systems," is neither a systematic ncr a comprehensive review of the organizational setup or management's information requirements in a development bank. It is, rather, a reflection on a wide range of organizational issues such as the need to establish and develop sympathetic understanding between the development bank and the external institutions and persons on whose support it depends, and the need for clarity of communication between top management and staff on whose information decisions are based and whose understanding is required to carry them out. Some of these same subjects were dealt with in chapter 2.

An effective organizational structure and sound operational policies and procedures require a program of staff development in general and of staff training in particular. Training has long claimed the attention of the chief executives of development banks. Yet, as chapter 15 suggests, chief executives may not have fully appreciated the implications of staff development or its intimate links with the task of management. Several points might be made in this connection.

The first is that the objectives and strategies of the institution determine not only the nature and size of the staff but also the kind of training that must be provided. It is in the articulation of objectives and strategies that management is first and most decisively involved in staff development. The second point is that training cannot be isolated from the general personnel policy and administration of a development bank. Recruiting qualified staff, motivating them, honing their technical expertise, preparing and grooming them for management, and holding on to them are interrelated. Third, a broad range of activities falls under the head of training: orienting new staff in the objectives, policies, and practices of the institution, guiding them in applying to their daily work in the bank the skills they learned in formal courses, expanding and refining their technical skills, sharpening their perceptions of their jobs, and preparing them for more responsibilities. Training in this broad sense takes place not only in the classroom but also at work, indeed, primarily at work. Fourth, the decisionmaking process is itself an instrument of training. If it involves staff at many levels and makes evident use of the skills in which staff have been trained, it not only reinforces training but also induces staff to take training as a means of advancing their careers.

In "Training Starts at Home" William Diamond develops some of these points. He focuses in particular, however, on the need for each development bank to develop its own training programs. Training outside the institution and outside the country is likely to be required in some countries, for some purposes and at some levels, for some time to come. But overdependence on outside training runs the risk of divorcing it from the realities that confront the institution and thus of diminishing its effectiveness.

Chapter 14

Organizational Structure and Communications Systems

R. K. HAZARI

BY WAY OF INTRODUCTION, three comments must be made: one concerns the function and role of development banks; a second, the institutional environment in which they operate; and the third, the people who staff development banks. All three have a bearing on the system of information and communication required to ensure smooth, sound, and timely decisionmaking.

As for the first, development banks have become part of the delivery system for economic and social development in developing countries. They may once have been thought of simply as financial institutions. Today, however, they have become far more complex entities. They have assumed (or have had forced upon them) responsibilities for the promotion of enterprises, for the development of capital markets, for ensuring the sound execution and operation of the enterprises they finance, for advising governments on measures and programs to reduce regional disparities within a country, and—in recent years—for helping alleviate poverty and remove social inequalities. Some have been set up to deal with particular sectors, and others have acquired sectoral specialization. In short, they have become a widely diverse group of institutions with sometimes complex patterns of ownership and a variety of functions, and they have evolved highly professional staffs trained in several disciplines.

What specific function or range of functions a particular development bank adopts within the broad spectrum of possibilities depends on the national goals deemed relevant to the bank, and on the corporate goals and strategies accepted or adopted by the bank in the light of those national objectives. Also relevant is the national policy on the structure of development banking. A country may have only one development bank for a defined group of purposes or, if the country is large enough, more than one bank for the same purpose or for various purposes. In a large country there may be a regional structuring of development banks in addition to, or in place of, a functional structuring.

Themselves part of a drive for institution building, development banks are responsible not only for encouraging entrepreneurial growth, but also for building up the corporate strength of their clients. The relation of a development bank to its clients is not limited to the tenure of a particular equity investment or of a single loan facility. As a result of the successive expansions of their clients, the continuation of large equity holdings as a matter of national policy, market compulsions, or their involvement with enterprises in trouble, development banks are permanently concerned in the affairs of many, if not most, of their clients.

The second point is that, perhaps fortunately for themselves, development banks are not the only parties with a stake in their clients. Commercial banks, which provide a bulk of the working capital and allied facilities and, quite often, part of the term capital as well, are also deeply interested in the enterprise and are at times tied into the same loan security. Moreover, commercial banks, insurance companies, unit trusts, and mutual funds mobilize resources from the public (part of which goes to development banks through subscriptions to their share capital or bonds), while development banks, by and large, raise funds from or through governments. The stake of these other institutions can represent a more broadly based public interest than that of the development bank itself.

Third, the development bank is something more than a collection of individuals working in and for it. In time, much more quickly than is generally expected, the staff reaches a size that makes it no longer feasible to maintain the relatively free-and-easy relation possible when the bank was new. Structure and organization become essential, and so does a degree of layering. At the same time, the staff becomes specialized, divided into professional groups often talking different languages. There inevitably emerge problems of corporate structuring, personnel policy, premises, and internal communication gaps.

Clearly the prospects of a development bank and its ability to perform the tasks for which it was created depend critically on the relations that management is able to establish with the external forces on which it depends for support, with the productive community which is the recipient of its resources, with other institutions in the community with related interests, and with the staff which must be molded into a team to carry out the development bank's programs. The establishment of such relations rests on mutual understanding of objectives and roles. And that understanding requires the existence of close and fruitful communications among the many parties concerned.

A management information system is meant to be used by and to be useful to the management. Information itself provides the background data and knowledge that can help in making or implementing decisions; in a large organization or complex society, it is the only known substitute for personal observation or hearing. Decisions can be and often are made without information or in disregard of it. The human mind, especially the top management mind, is gifted with the capacity for insight and daring, but that faculty need not disregard the five basic senses. An information system does not, however, constitute a communications system unless it allows some feedback to the starting point and produces understanding at all links of the chain of what all the pother is about. And an information system has little meaning or usefulness unless it is suitably intermeshed with the objectives and structure of the organization.

Organizational Structure

There is no unique or ideal organizational structure valid for all times and places. The structure is not determined by "management science"; it is, rather, largely a matter of convenience, historical forces, and the interplay of persons—a mixture to which judgment is applied. It may be helpful to contemplate organizational structure in three functional dimensions:

Operational	Planning	Housekeeping
Project appraisal and approval	Long-term corporate planning	Accounts and financial control
Disbursement	Resource mobilization	Internal audit
Follow-up	Promotion and business development	Legal
		Personnel
Economic evaluation of project performance	Economic research, including sector studies	Premises
Investment management	Environmental information (technical, financial, economic, and legal)	Office equipment
Specialized activities (such as merchant banking, export finance, and commercial banking)	Management information	
	Corporate evaluation	

This grouping of functions is to some extent arbitrary. While much of it is standard and will be generally accepted, some of it is open to debate. Some might argue, for instance, that the legal staff is more appropriately tied to the chief executive's central staff than to housekeeping activities.

Most of the operational grouping is fairly conventional. Economic evaluation of project performance is meant to assess the impact of assisted projects on the economy or on particular sectors, for example, their effect on output, employment, income, forward and backward linkages, and regional balance. Keeping performance evaluation under operations should ensure more effective feedback into better appraisal and monitoring of projects. The investment management function is important not only for market reasons, but also for exercising financial and managerial control over enterprises in which development banks have acquired a permanent or quasi-permanent interest or for handling the liquidation of enterprises that are beyond hope. When a country has more than one development bank or when several financial institutions desire a common course of action in relation to the enterprises in which they have a large interest, it might be desirable to establish a suitable common forum for servicing investments or for providing management advisory services to clients.

Merchant banking and term credit for export are useful areas of diversification for development banks and provide, in addition, much needed support to the business development of present and potential clients. Locating these functions within a development bank can safeguard against the excessive multiplication of specialized institutions attending to the same clients and can also economize on skilled manpower. In a small country it may even be worthwhile for a development bank to take up commercial banking, preferably wholesale rather than retail.

Planning is essentially a staff function, oriented toward assisting the top management in decisionmaking from an overall corporate viewpoint, as distinct from the project or investment viewpoint required of the operations group. More specifically, the functions of corporate planning are to:

- Articulate the corporate goals in the light of national goals
- Continually review objectives and strategies with a view to their revision at appropriate intervals, say, every three to five years
- Formulate multiyear and annual plans with suitable phasing on the basis of a systems approach that takes account of resources, profitability, and personnel implications

- Periodically review performance against the plans, looking not only at the quantitative aspects but also at the goals for geographical areas, special programs, technical assistance, and so on
- Assist top management in the formulation of views on such special topics as "bunched" projects,[1] terms to be set for normal financing and for special programs (for example, those that expect a higher economic return than financial return or that involve national policy considerations), cover to be maintained on security, foreseeable cases of variances from the norms, and interest rate spreads

A few specific dimensions of promotion and business development and of economic research may be mentioned. When the reduction of regional imbalance is an important objective, one must decide how much emphasis to place on area development (which involves agriculture and infrastructure in addition to industry), building up of growth centers in suitable phases, and individual projects. In identifying gaps in the industrial structure, account must be taken of such matters as viability, linkages, and government policies from the center down to local levels. Similarly, the promotion of small enterprises requires action in concert with other agencies. A main consideration that should weigh with a development bank entering this field is how far it should enter with direct finance and whether and to what degree it is feasible to offer support for refinancing and staff training to local agencies. Overall, the cost and foreseeable earnings of promotional activities have to be kept under close and continuous scrutiny.

Promotion is closely related to environmental scanning, that is, scouting for information about relevant developments in the country (and, indeed, in the world). Scanning funnels into the bank data on technical processes and innovations, trends in financial markets, or patterns of financing important sectors of the economy, together with economic policy announcements and administrative decisions pursuant to these announcements, important court rulings, and possible ways to ease legal problems. Such information must, of course, be reinforced by close liaison with the institutions concerned and with the publicity media. When the development bank is in export finance also, it is necessary to build up economic and business profiles of the countries in which contracts are likely to be secured by clients. Country exposure limits, which can be fixed in consultation with government, the central bank, and large commercial banks, are indispensable for safeguarding against excessive risk.

Management information (of which more later) is a summary of information collected from a variety of sources, and it must be formally designed and issued regularly. While the design and content of management information cannot be fixed indefinitely, it is unwise to alter it frequently in or for fire-fighting operations. Moreover, notwithstanding the wonders that mechanization and computerization can achieve, it has to be remembered that the basic data required by the machines are essentially the product of manual effort; even the finest impersonal system rests upon human beings with finite capacities for motivation, patience, and useful output. As far as possible, new forms for data collection should be introduced only along with deletion or merger of some others. In short, there is an acute—and chronic—need for management information.

Corporate evaluation of a development bank's activities as a whole is useful for assessing their effect on the economy. This exercise is useful for internal assessment and for revision of future objectives, policies, and methods. It is also handy for reporting to the government, legislative bodies, and international institutions to which the bank is accountable. Indeed, objective self-evaluation often becomes an essential first line of defense against external pressures. Where accountability has become an important issue, it may be necessary to place the self-evaluation function at some distance from the top management to ensure objectivity or, at least, to convey the impression of objectivity.

Resource mobilization is of particular importance. So far development banks generally have done little to mobilize resources for development, other than to build up fairly impressive reservoirs of financial and technical skills. They have tended to rely too much on government and on international institutions for financial resources. This is, perhaps, one reason development banks have not been as effective as they could have been in influencing government economic policies. In the future, a more determined effort is required to raise funds on the financial and operational strength of the development banks themselves.

In the realm of housekeeping, a development bank cannot afford to be less than exemplary if its advice is to carry conviction with the government and with its own clients. For financial control, apart from the usual and basic accounting requirements, it is necessary to have a clear idea of the cost of overhead and of promotional outlays.

Although many developmental expenses are likely to be unremunerative, they have to be covered without undermining the viability of the development bank itself, especially when a significant part of lending is on concessional terms or, though originally on "normal" terms, has turned concessional because of clients' problems. One way to exercise control over such expenses is to debit them to a special fund earmarked annually out of undistributed profits. The existence and utilization of such a fund are, among other things, good for the development bank's public image.

Internal audit of accounts, not in replacement of external audit but in addition to it, is a prudent and constructive safeguard. It is more continuous and generally more thorough and comprehensive than an external audit. As with other instruments of self-evaluation, the feedback from internal audit is timely and effective, even though its financial cost may be high.

Legal work may appear, at first sight, to be a routine function. Its purpose, however, is not simply to keep the institution within the law but also to seek innovative interpretation of the law to further the objectives of the development bank. For instance, this is particularly necessary in questions relating to stipulations about mortgage and security cover. Does mortgage necessarily mean completion of mortgage with all its complications and delays, or would an agreement to mortgage suffice for a disbursement? What is a bank to do, consistent with the laws, when security cover is not adequate? As time passes, what constructions should be placed on the general or ambiguous clauses of the development bank's charter? The scope for innovational understanding in legal matters is, perhaps greater than is generally recognized in financial institutions, perhaps because lawyers are too often kept in a separate compartment rather than made part of the management team.

Personnel, premises, and office equipment form an important, though standard, part of the housekeeping function. Their quality and maintenance have to be good not merely for the bank's image or presentations but also for staff effectiveness in dealing with clients and working internally.

Of course, none of the three categories of functions is watertight. The members of each category are bound to change from time to time for any number of reasons, the most important of which is, generally, the exercise by top management of an option considered more conducive to effective operation. More important, every function affects others, in other categories. As essential as a sensible organization chart, therefore, are a free flow, among all parties, of information relevant to the efficient execution of the responsibilities of each function, and mechanisms for reaching prompt decisions on matters that require the participation of several parties.

Board of Directors

Except in a few countries (such as those with a German or Dutch corporate tradition), development banks do not have a formal separation between a supervisory board (which represents various constituencies of the community or various stockholders) and a management board (of full-time executive directors). Nevertheless, informal practice is perhaps not very different. That is, although a board's role is very important, management has responsibility for operational decisions.

There are broadly four variations on the composition of a board of directors: (1) all part-time directors with a nondirector as general manager and chief executive; (2) a full-time chairman who serves as managing director, with all other directors part-time; (3) a full-time chairman plus a full-time managing director, with all other directors part-time; and (4) a part-time chairman plus a full-time managing director, with one or more full-time directors and the rest part-time. The exact pattern and even the statutory requirements for board composition are less material than the board's style of functioning. The principal functions of the board, which ought not to be delegated—especially by a board in which part-time members constitute the majority—are to lay down the corporate objectives, policies, and programs, review progress and difficulties at periodic intervals, provide guidance on difficult issues, appoint the chief executive, and make (or at least consult on) senior appointments. Except in cases involving an abnormally large number of exceptionally unusual features, it is not advisable to involve the board in routine investment decisions; it would simply either ratify the decisions already made by top management or, in effect, preclude top management from making decisions. True, the board has to take responsibility for the decisions of top management, and the system of reporting to the board must keep this in mind, but its own involvement is most productive in laying down the parameters for programs and the mechanisms for their implementation and in reviewing performance in order to confirm or modify parameters and mechanisms.

Even when the board has to be involved in comparatively routine matters, an attempt can be made to focus its time and attention on broader issues. One way of doing so is to present the agenda so that it provides the most time for important matters and the least time for the routine; for instance, the latter could be discussed at the end of a meeting rather than at the beginning. The following format might be followed:

1. Items on programs and methods of implementing them, including the criteria for variances from the normal terms of assistance
2. Items on reviews of performance in sectors or regions or special programs
3. Items relating to the development bank's own financial performance and housekeeping
4. Items involving cases that require the board's approval because the requisite powers have not been delegated, there are unusual features, or, since the solution to the problem would be novel, the management feels the board's protective umbrella is desirable for abundant caution or for handling similar cases in the future.

Appointment of a committee of the board to approve investments on behalf of the full board is a frequent practice. Unless the committee is constituted entirely of full-time members (in which case it is a top management committee), this practice divides the board into tiers, however, clothing some members with more authority than others. Moreover, given the exigencies of politics, administration, and transportation, some members of the board qualify almost automatically for committee membership while others do not, particularly if they reside at some distance from headquarters. Although it is true that some members tend to have more clout than others because of their rank, age, constituency, or even competence, the benefit derived from "tiering" the board is doubtful.

The role of the government directors, that is, those who are appointed by virtue of the posts they hold in government, is delicate and crucial. Whether or not it is a shareholder or creditor, the government represents the community as a whole, and the main function of its directors is to maintain close liaison between the government and the development bank to promote the work of the bank. The question that arises sometimes is whether government directors are privileged and whether their views are more or less binding on the board. When this question arises, presumably there is either some inconsistency between government or national objectives and the development bank's corporate objectives or there are conflicting views on individual transactions or proposals. If, as suggested earlier, the institution's corporate objectives have already been intermeshed with national objectives, that is, if corporate goals have been determined in the light of national requirements, any conflict between them should not normally arise at the board level. It should, rather, be resolved by discussion between the bank and the government authorities concerned. Environment and personalities are undeniably important elements in such a discussion, but the point is that this issue is between the government and the development bank, not to be resolved within the board. In the event of fundamental disagreement, the development bank must bow to the government, with or without a change of management.

In the case of conflicting views on specific items, the government directors are on a par with other directors; they can persuade but should not expect to exert more than their proportionate strength. They have to realize that the other directors also represent the community or an important segment of it. Moreover, some other directors, including the chairman or managing director, are often nominated by the government or appointed with its implicit approval and therefore partake of some of the character of government directors. Nevertheless, government directors are expected to perform a dual role. They represent the most important single constituency in the board, and they seek the active help and involvement of various government departments to advance the bank's programs, projects, and public image. A development bank's autonomy would not be diluted or the equality of board members disturbed by frequent informal encounters of top management with government directors to mobilize their backing for such matters as dealing with various official agencies or disciplining recalcitrant clients.

Top Management

The substance of decisionmaking lies more with the full-time top management than with the board. At that level, and at the senior and middle management levels, there is need, particularly in large institutions, for executive teams and team leaders, drawn from both line and staff, to provide both horizontal liaison and vertical communication from one level to another. The routine flow of information and circulars to staff members is not a substitute for face-to-face discussion and frequent work and travel together. Team orientation helps evolve a systems approach that sees a proposition through to fruition rather than let it fall or be delayed between interfunctional boundaries. There is some truth in the saying that in committees minutes are kept but hours are wasted and that responsibility becomes obscured. At the same time, the various disciplines—technical, financial, legal, and economic—that have to be brought to bear on most problems require the joint attention of many minds. Cooperative effort cannot be replaced by the free play of individual personalities or the vertical movement of papers within a division from one desk to another or attempts at high-level coordination at some selected points near the top of the hierarchy.

Genuine coordination is a combined consultative and executive function. It implies pooling information from various sources, applying analytical insight, and accepting the coordinator, with a view to achieving predetermined ends that transcend the status in the hierarchy of the participants. Such coordination must be effected among various disciplines and divisions at all levels. Confining it to the top tends to replace information and knowledge with insights and experience that are not always relevant; it clutters top management with individual transactions at the expense of overall perspective; moreover, views that are softened by mutual understanding at middle levels tend to harden and become compartmentalized in the upper echelons of the hierarchy. Every effort must be made to prevent top management from becoming so involved in the activities of day-to-day management that it neglects its primary role of leadership.

The authority, inspiration, and vision of personalities are material to framing objectives, setting style, effecting major innovations, and setting differences of approach or view. There must be elbow room for the development of such personalities, a concept quite different from making the entire decisionmaking process hang on a single peg. When Carlyle characterized history as being the history of Great Men, he left out the environment and the institutional structure that help produce the Great Men, along with other forces that shape events. Even Great Men, important as they are at the turning points of history, need staff support to elaborate and sustain their perceptions and to help in the pursuit of opportunities. Eventually, the Great Men have to be succeeded by others, who may not be equally great, partly because the gap between the top and the average might by that time be shortened. It would be unrealistic, nonetheless, to suggest that the design and mechanism of the decisionmaking apparatus should be independent of the personalities at the top; that is a mechanistic idea, consistent more with administrative routine than with a sustained sense of direction and innovation.

When situations are less than ideal, which in fact all situations are, an informal management structure generally supplements (but does not necessarily, indeed should not, supplant) the formal structure. No organization or work flow chart plots the level jumping or closed circuits that usually embellish the working of all institutions. Some persons carry more weight in decisionmaking than their formal functions or status in the hierarchy would signify. Sometimes the key persons belong to the same ethnic group or to the same social class. The phenomenon is not unique to development banks, but its existence has wider implications than in other business organizations because of the nature and ramifications of the development banks' business. Rather than sweep the phenomenon under the carpet or dust it in public, the relevant questions to ask in this context are:

- Are the making and implementation of decisions (which, one hopes, remain consistent with the development bank's objectives) improved or speeded by this informal "confidence" system?
- Is this system conducive to executive development in the long run?
- Does it clog the information and communications system, or does it make it more achievement-oriented?
- Is entry into the top rungs of management open to merit?

Communications System for Top Management

As noted earlier, an information system can facilitate effective communication only when there is feedback—when it provides a stream of information in both directions. Conveyance of information upward or sideways inspires confidence—and encourages regularity—when one sees prompt use (or at least some use) of the data supplied and some benefit to oneself from the exercise. Subject to this consideration, a development bank's system comprises four channels of information: reporting to government and creditors and informing the general public; receiving from clients information structured to the nature of their relations with the bank; maintaining relations with other institutions whose activities infringe, directly or indirectly, on the activities of the development bank; and reporting internally in a form structured for various levels of management and various functions and designed both to stimulate staff and to control operations.

Reporting to Government and the General Public

Reporting to government must convey information, first, to fulfill the need for institutional propriety and safety, second, to provide control data and, third, to permit policy formulation and monitoring. No matter how prestigious a development bank and its management might be, they need government support, protection, encouragement, and confidence, all of which depend ultimately on performance consistent with objectives. But this record needs to be consistently bolstered with information, written and oral, on corporate programs that contribute to national economic achievement. Since few governments are monolithic economic entities, this means an exchange of information not only with the specific ministry that has administrative oversight of the development bank but also with other parts of the national and local government concerned with planning, industrial regulation, and development.

The supply of control data must, however, be restricted to the ministry to which the development bank is directly accountable. Its design and content require political awareness, acquaintance with administrative routine, and professional competence. For instance, a quarterly report on performance in relation to the budget for the quarter and to the corresponding quarter of the previous year may cover new proposals brought forward, approved, and carried out; disbursements by purpose and region; cash flows; promotional work undertaken; and highlights of reports from capital and commodity markets, clients, and regional offices. A six-monthly report may contain, in addition, highlights of investment management, the results of corporate planning exercises, assessment of environmental information, financial performance of the development bank itself, and changes in personnel including the upgrading of its quality. The annual report is generally preoccupied with statutory accounting and publicity requirements and need not, perhaps, be encumbered further. It would be a useful innovation to prepare (say, every three years) a perspective and review report covering objectives, programs, resources, management structure, personnel development, and corporate evaluation—in short, the development bank's place in the economy. Although the bulk of this corporate review should be done within the institution, it may be useful to associate outside experts or consultants with it. This would prove helpful not only to the development bank but also to such external agencies as a legislative committee or an international mission. This species of accountability has much to commend it and is preferable by far to accountability (formal or informal) for individual transactions.

With the depth of its involvement in industry, and with the skills, experience, and detachment that it may be presumed to possess, a development bank is in an ideal position—certainly in a better position than chambers of commerce, industry associations, or labor organizations—to assess the effect of incentives or taxes or other policy devices on investment trends and to advise government on the basis of this assessment. There is a feeling that development finance institutions have played a rather passive role in this respect. The making and transmittal of such an assessment, it should be remembered, can be effective only when it is regular, factual, and systematic, not when it is casual, impressionistic, personal, or ad hoc.

Reporting to creditors need not be substantially different from that described above, except for the specific framework that might have been laid down by the creditors (including those required in their loan contracts).

Informing the general public is largely determined by the national environment. Subject to that overwhelming consideration, it is useful to remember that, although publicity is not a substitute for performance, it is an indispensable accompaniment of institution building. Neglect of publicity can be bothersome for the institution just as excessive familiarity of the management with the publicity media can be irksome to politicians and administrators. Apart from periodic handouts to news agencies and financial journals, it is useful to keep in touch with the journalists and academic writers who mold public opinion.

Receiving Information from Clients

Obtaining information from clients is sometimes confined to documentation on the project itself and the monitoring of capital expenditure. This is, however, far from adequate, especially in the case of a project in an already operating company. In such a case, there must be a reporting system that covers the actual operation of the company in sufficient detail and with sufficient frequency to permit the development bank to keep its finger on the pulse of the enterprise. Reporting from clients will continue for many years after a project is completed, until the loan has been repaid. Moreover, keeping a finger on the pulse of the company will help the development bank establish and maintain a relationship with its clients that will stimulate new business from them in the future.

When such a reporting system works to mutual satisfaction it may be a more effective device for keeping a finger on a client's pulse than putting a nominee on the client's board of directors. The objective of the system is to devise a comprehensive discipline for client managements, which cannot be accomplished by an additional director who fires salvos of impromptu wisdom at periodic intervals.[2] The information can help spot a client's incipient difficulties and ensure smooth movement from one expansion to the next, quite apart from keeping the development bank regularly in the know of things. The investment management staff of the development bank can process this information and maintain a dialogue with the clients.

In reciprocity, a development bank can keep its clients informed of industrial, financial, and market trends. In a sense, some of this information seeps through in the course of appraisal and follow-up, but this seepage has the rather limited perspective of the transaction immediately at hand. What needs to be developed is the bank's overview of events and trends as gathered from the collective experience of its clients, and this overview must be conveyed to the individual clients.

Among the institutions with which a development bank needs to maintain relations, banks—especially other development banks if the country has more than one—now loom very large. In most countries financial institutions are multiplying, and many of them are doing business with some of the clients of the development bank. At least informal discussion on common affairs is then important. Beyond this, however, there are a growing number of formal consortium arrangements to provide joint financing for a particular project or for an enterprise at a particularly important point in its history. Where there is a consortium, somewhat greater formality in the exchange of mutually valuable information is usually needed. In either case, financial institutions may well have somewhat different outlooks and objectives, and one purpose of the formal or informal exchange of views is precisely to iron out differences and to ensure a common approach in dealing with the client.

Internal Reporting

Internal reporting must seek, first, to collect, assimilate, process, and present information originating from outside and, second, to generate and present information from within the institution for various levels and functions of management. Correspondingly, there must be a structured flow back of information from the top to lower levels.

Starting with general background information, it is useful for management to have a brief daily roundup of urgent news items; a weekly analytical digest of political and economic comments at somewhat greater length; a monthly digest of environmental information on financial and economic matters; and, at less frequent intervals, a digest of information on technical processes, case law, licenses issued by government, other financial and development institutions, and highlights of information from clients including, to the extent possible, an analysis of investment targets and forecasts. This may seem to be a tall order, but there is no other way top management can have access to a broad range of information of critical value.

Aside from reports on individual transactions and conventional quantitative data, it is useful for top management to receive at regular intervals information on the interesting features (as distinct from the numbers involved) and problems in new proposals noticed at the stage of preliminary contacts, in the course of appraisal, and during the formalities required for disbursement. Once these features and problems are spotted and brought to the notice of top management, it should be easier to initiate corrective action on groups of cases rather than go through the tedious routine of handling each case separately. Regular scrutiny of delays and the reasons for them is an invaluable device for maintaining efficiency and integrity; in this matter particularly, top management should be known to be personally accessible to staff and clients alike. Depending on the volume of business, there can be a quarterly, half-yearly, or annual reporting on projects completed to the commissioning stage, followed by studies on the financial and economic evaluation of project performance when a suitable interval has elapsed after commissioning. Since performance evaluation is a delicate task, such studies should be completed, preferably, only after the senior management has seen and discussed drafts. At the board and top management level, the studies should come up for consideration along with recommendations for corrective action.

Reporting on investment management for operational action may be divided in two parts: one for market or interinstitutional operations (normally, the sale of investments, sometimes the sale of participations in term loans) and the other for exercising the financial and management control that goes with permanent or quasi-permanent interest in clients. When investments are held as a result of underwriting or subscription commitments with a view to selling them in due course, the timing and quantum of their sale are a matter of informed judgment. Apart from an assessment of the clients' prospects, account must be taken of capital market trends, the effect of a sale on the market price of the scrip, and the development bank's prospective realization of capital gains or losses if a block of scrip is disposed of. If a capital market is not developed or cannot absorb a large transaction, or if national policy requires continued holdings of large blocks of equity by institutions, the development bank may, in some countries, consider sale to another institution that can afford to have a longer stake at the ruling market official price or at a negotiated price—always on the assumption, of course, that such a sale does not run contrary to the interests of the client whose shares are involved. Such an operation requires skills and staff work that are not significantly different from those well established in investment banking.

In the second area of reporting on investment management, that for financial and management control, one encounters uncertain ground, confusing jurisdictions, and ambiguous objectives. Development banks were not designed to be holding companies but have reluctantly become so as a result of market imperfections, national policies, or the difficulties confronting their clients. The current reporting system from clients can form the core of information for financial and management control. It has to be supported with an inventory of available talent that can be mobilized for full-time, part-time or consultancy work, preferably at the expense of the client; if that is not feasible, at the expense of the development bank itself. For purposes of internal control, the clients in which the bank has a large permanent or long-term stake can be segregated from those in the "orthodox" category. A committee of senior executives can receive, say, quarterly reports on the general run of clients and monthly reports on selected problem cases. Such reports should contain an analysis of their operations, their annual plans, and their capital expenditure programs and should be phased over the year to reduce the workload of the staff. In many cases, the development bank may have to call for assistance from commercial banks, government authorities, suppliers or buyers, and courts to put the enterprise back on its feet. In some cases, of course, the decision may be to write off the client and wind up the enterprise.

Finance and personnel are the two principal resources of a development bank. Internal control must, therefore, concentrate on getting the best return out of each of them. Cash is to a bank what materials inventory is to a manufacturing concern, and cash management is the key to financial control. The familiar dilemma of liquidity versus profitability is more acute for a development bank than for a commercial bank. A development bank deals in less liquid assets, which will be profitable only in the distant future, even though its cash outflows are more predictable and, to some extent, more controllable than those of a commercial bank. For management control, it is necessary to have monthly and quarterly cash flow budgets within the framework of the annual performance budget, and an annual cash flow budget for a three- or five-year forecast, which lays down the procedures for watching for and remedying variances and provides guidelines for the investment of cash balances.

Inflows are normally influenced by the seasonality of amortization and interest receipts, as well as of budgetary releases by government and of market bond flotations. Outflows in the shape of investments, loan installments, interest, dividends, and tax payments also are seasonal but with a timing different from that of inflows. The result is wide variations in cash balances. Depending upon banking conventions and regulations, the ideal arrangement is either (1) to have facilities for temporary advances from the central bank and for automatic investment in treasury bills and government securities of excess balances with the central bank or (2), if these are not permissible or attractive enough, to have similar facilities with commercial banks. In the second alternative, it may also be worthwhile to explore taking limited short-term participations in working capital loans extended by commercial banks. It should not be difficult to lay down a target rate of return on cash balance investments for each quarter and for the whole year. Then, for purposes of operational control, there is a framework to go by on a weekly and daily basis. Appropriate sophistication in cash management can be a useful addition to corporate profits. But it must be remembered that politicians and administrators tend not to view it with sympathy, for it is alleged to be a distraction from development activity. Conveying its usefulness and consistency with national objectives is a matter of communications skill.

The integrated use of financial control and personnel comes about in drawing up programs, assessing their benefits and costs, and implementing them at the budgeted pace. Once the activity centers are identified, it is possible to assign responsibility for various segments or aspects of the program. For public industrial undertakings, a reporting system along the following lines has been suggested:[3]

Management control	*Operational control*
1. Setting commercial (project) objectives	1. Setting up short-term targets for production, sales, and inventory
2. Setting noncommercial objectives and determining standard cost-benefit ratios for them in lieu of usual operating ratios	2. Controlling expenses within budgeted levels and attaining revenue targets
3. Manpower planning	3. Designing marketing programs
4. Determining working capital needs	4. Controlling employment within targets
5. Determining marketing strategies, sales volume, and product-mix within constraints of pricing policy	5. Measuring and evaluating departmental efficiency
6. Training and development of managers	
7. Measuring and evaluating managerial performance	

When this pattern is adapted to a development bank's requirements (so that it practices what is preached to clients), it is clear that, first, management control has to be separate from operational control; second, programming, finance, staffing, marketing, costing, and evaluation have to be treated as an integral whole; and, third, upgrading the quality and input of personnel requires the sustained attention of top management.

Informal Information

No manager relies entirely on formal, systematized reporting, from inside or outside the development bank, for the information he needs to lead, manage, and control. Indeed, it is doubtful that he would want to do so even if he could. He is constantly bombarded by a flow of information which may be as valuable to him as the data he receives through the formal arrangements he has set up. The flows come on the golf course, at dinner, by telephone from friends and colleagues in other institutions, from visitors—from the entire range of connections the top manager has developed in his professional career over the years. Indeed these useful connections constitute one of the principal assets he brings to his task, and he is always on the lookout for new ones.

There are advantages to such informal information. It is fresh. It often is firsthand, carrying or stimulating insights that cannot be captured by statistical data or systematized in-house information. But it may also have a heavy component of gossip, and it may be affected by self-interest.

The same is true of informal information from inside the development bank. Most chief executives will call on particular members of their management teams or other senior staff to provide them, out of channels, with qualitative information quite independent of the formal information and communications systems. These have some of the advantages as well as disadvantages of informal outside information. There is the added danger that consultation outside the hierarchy and formal channels of information may be perceived as playing favorites and may result in some staff disaffection.

The risk of misuse of informal information is substantial. Nevertheless, no chief executive can rely entirely on the predigested data his formal information system spews forth. Both are needed and both are used, but the informal must be used with more than the usual care applied to other sources of information.

Finally, informal internal information raises the question of participatory management. In a large, growing, and therefore increasingly impersonal organization, it is indeed necessary to identify who should participate in everything. Quite aside from participation, even consultation is not open-ended: there must be definite points and target segments for consultation, which in turn requires a semi-finished product that invites expressions of opinion. The finishing touches should incorporate at least some of the opinions expressed, but not all, if clarity and consistency are to be respected; alternatively, the product can be scrapped and the exercise repeated. In essence, consultation and participation are mechanisms for securing involvement in and commitment to certain objectives, strategies, or tactics, and for encouraging innovation and initiative; they are meant to improve the quality and effectiveness of decisions more than to make decisions.

It is important to guard against affirmative opinions expressed too readily; in some quarters opinions rise instantly to expectations, while in others they remain congealed in silence till the benefit of hindsight is available. Genuine participatory consultation comes by habit and style, not by order or demand; abundance of prescriptions notwithstanding, it is largely a matter of personalities and modes of teamwork. Certain personalities can get on and achieve their objectives without genuine participatory consultation, at least for some time, until spectacular error or sheer discontent breaks through to the surface. As in civilization, so, perhaps, in institutions, poetry is useful inspiration for prose but highly inflammable as a substitute. Participatory management is one means of internal communication; it is useful, perhaps necessary, but rarely sufficient.

Notes to Chapter 14

1. Quite often several proposals from the same industry or for making the same product come within a short period.

2. This view should not be interpreted as an argument against appointing nominees to the boards of directors of client companies or against giving specific guidelines to the nominees.

3. S. K. Bhattacharyya, "Management Reporting System in Public Undertakings," *Economic and Political Weekly, Review of Management*, vol. 4, no. 22 (May 31, 1969).

Chapter 15

Training Starts at Home

WILLIAM DIAMOND

THIS CHAPTER discusses the ways development banks can foster an environment in which staff training is encouraged and in which full advantage is taken of the benefits of training. Too often training is dealt with as though it took place in another city or another country and as though it were quite separate from other aspects of the administration of a development bank. Neither of these is the case. Most training inevitably takes place at home, and it is most effective if fully integrated with the administration and the day-to-day activities of the development bank. The chief executive of a development bank, concerned about the effective use of the resources at his disposal and about the development of his company, is directly or indirectly involved in training at all times—for training is an indispensable tool for enabling his staff to do a better job today and to prepare for higher responsibilities tomorrow. What can and should a chief executive do at home, in his own institution, to further these purposes? Answers to that question, put into practice, will do much to foster and to strengthen the effect of training—and will, incidentally, encourage external agencies to do more than they otherwise might in this critical area.

The Mounting Demand for Training

The central role of training for the effective achievement of the objectives of development finance institutions is no longer a subject of debate—if, indeed, it ever was.

Reprinted (with minor revisions) from "Development Bank Training Starts at Home," *Malaysian Management Review*, the journal of the Malaysian Institute of Management, vol. 13, no. 3 (December 1978), pp. 60–73. It was prepared as a working

Not so long ago, when development banks were still unfamiliar institutions in most countries, new staff and managers found little firsthand experience on which to draw.[1] At that time, it was often the external friends of such institutions (foreign sponsors and financiers) that had to try to convey to government, local sponsors, board, and management an idea of the objectives and potentials of a development finance institution. They often had to enlighten others involved in the development bank of the technical skills they would need to have at their disposal to do their jobs effectively. They needed to urge them to seek experienced (which often meant external) advice and assistance until indigenous staff could be found and trained and until indigenous management could develop its own experience. These external agencies often provided the main impetus for training, and they offered some of the few available training facilities.

With increasing appreciation of the creative role development banks can play, and with the growth in the number and experience of development banks, internal pressures for professional improvement have become far more important. Staff and management have become aware of their banks' pioneering role in their countries. Self-consciousness of role has grown as staff trained in a variety of disciplines have found their once distinct professional identities subordinated to a new sense of purpose that calls for multidisciplinary outlook and techniques. Self-consciousness has been further heightened by frequent meetings of staff and managers from similar institutions in other countries, at which common problems are discussed and experiences exchanged. Such exchanges among development banks go back at least to 1958, when the World Bank convened a group of chief executives to discuss common problems. Since then the United Nations Industrial Development Organization (UNIDO), the regional development banks, national agencies, and the regional associations have sponsored one such meeting after another. If he liked to travel and to attend meetings, it would be possible for a development bank manager to spend almost all his time on the road.

Inevitably, the spread of knowledge of development banks, the expectations they have engendered, and the sense of professional identity their staff has developed have generated a demand for training. The problem is no longer to persuade development banks

paper for the workshop on training at the general assembly of the Association of African Development Finance Institutions, Libreville, Gabon, April 28–29, 1978.

of the need for training to improve technical and management skills; their demand for it increases steadily. The problem now is to provide adequate training appropriate to the current state of the art of development banking and to the diverse environments from which the demand comes.

The establishment of regional associations of development banks (in Latin America in 1968, in Africa in 1975, and in Asia and the Pacific in 1976) was a response to the professionalization of development banking and to the banks' growing sense of identity. Their insistent demand for training and exchange of experience is reflected in the constitutions and the work programs of the associations. One function of the Association of African Development Finance Institutions, for instance, is "to organize symposia, seminars, courses and other training programmes for personnel of development finance institutions in the African region." In its first biennial report (April 1977), the executive committee of the association gave the highest priority to "activities to improve the technical briefing of members, or to provide for their training," or both. The promotion of training programs and facilities evidently has a high priority in this association's work plans, as it also does in those of the other associations. These objectives and programs are evidence of the fact that development banks themselves—with capabilities now firmly based on extensive experience of their own—are able to take, or at least to share with other institutions, the responsibility for planning and participating in the training programs they require.

Against this background, it is unnecessary to labor the need for training or the priority to be attributed to it.

Risks of Reliance on External Aid in Training

The high priority assigned to training is reflected in the pressures on the international and national agencies involved in development bank training to provide more courses for, and to take more trainees from, African development banks. The pressures are particularly great on such institutions as the Centre d'Etudes Financières, Economiques, et Bancaires (CEFEB) of the Caisse Centrale, the German Foundation for International Development, and the Economic Development Institute of the World Bank, which are among the principal providers of useful courses and seminars. It is also reflected in the numerous approaches to those agencies and to such others as UNIDO for assistance, not only in financing training programs but also in designing and in providing staff for courses to be given in Africa, generally at the regional or subregional level and sometimes at the level of the individual development bank. Those agencies often find it extremely difficult to cope with the demand. For this reason alone, the stress on external assistance in training needs to be reexamined. But there are other reasons as well for concern about the heavy reliance on external assistance and for considering what development banks themselves can and should do to provide training and to make it effective.

External institutions have made an invaluable contribution to the development banking profession in Africa. When African development banks and their associations plan for in-house, national, or regional training programs, it is natural for them to look to experienced financial and training institutions and to aid agencies outside Africa for advice and assistance in preparing programs, designing courses, and carrying them out. External assistance will no doubt be needed for some time to come. However, courses given abroad—and courses in Africa planned and carried out by external agencies—run the risk, no matter how carefully they are laid out and executed, of being somewhat divorced from the real needs of African development banks. It is no disparagement of their contribution in the past nor of the contribution they can make in the future to suggest that external perceptions of training requirements may not be exactly the same as African perceptions. External perceptions may be useful, but they should not govern. Home-planned, home-grown, and home-staffed programs will be much closer to the problems that face a specific development bank than are programs of an international or foreign national institution, and they are likely to be more sensitively alert to the need to adapt techniques to different environments. Closeness to the field of operations is the more important because of the institutional dimension of development bank training; a development bank, like other institutions, is deeply influenced and constrained by the environment in which it operates.

Heavy reliance on external assistance may also result in underutilizing indigenous training capacity. It is often forgotten that some African development banks are as much as twenty-five years old, and some staff and even managers have been with them for many years. Many staff members have had substantial training, both at home and abroad, as well as a wealth of practical experience. For instance, 410 fellows of the Economic Development Institute from

Africa have taken the development banking (50), agroindustrial projects (49), general projects (160), and industrial projects (151) courses. Some of these fellows have the experience as well as the training needed to be excellent trainers. A much larger number have trained in CEFEB and have worked in French financial institutions. And still others have taken courses in other countries. Thus, there now exist cadres of professional staff and management who are qualified to train new and less experienced staff and to devise training programs for their companies and for national and regional institutions. Their participation in planning and teaching will help ensure the practical orientation of development bank training. There are also in many African countries institutions (universities, institutes, and professional associations) with experienced staff who can make significant contributions to training for development banks. In designing and carrying out training programs, to ignore or to neglect the indigenous expertise and experience that already exist would waste resources and time.

External training institutions or sponsors of training should be considered as valuable partners of, or advisors to, development banks and national and regional institutions in formulating and carrying out the latter's training programs. They need to act not as principals but as guides, and even that on a temporary basis only.

Another reason for concern about the stress on external agencies to sponsor courses in Africa is that such approaches tend to focus on regional and subregional training programs, rather than on in-house programs in individual development banks or even on national programs. There are, of course, situations and environments in which local training is difficult or impossible to arrange. Moreover, some subjects and levels of training can most advantageously be dealt with on a regional or an international basis. Indeed, the higher the level of personnel being trained, the more important is exposure to a variety of experiences and ideas and interaction with comparable personnel in similar institutions in the same or other countries. Thus, there is a very important role for regional training and for training outside Africa. Yet there is a danger that excessive reliance on such programs will lead to neglect of training at home, which in the long run will be the most important. There is also the danger of forgetting that—until the level of senior management is reached—the farther from home that training takes place, the greater the likelihood of its being divorced from day-to-day realities. Perhaps the temptation to focus on foreign training is the greater because it seems to be someone else's responsibility, and because foreign training offers elements of glamour which domestic training does not.

Still another factor is that the concentration of attention on training outside the development bank, especially in regional or international courses, emphasizes the tendency to deal with training as an autonomous subject, separate from other aspects of administering a development bank and independent of its operational policies and day-to-day activities. Three aspects of this segregation are worth noting.

First, it is hard to visualize training without a clear concept of the objectives, policies, and expected operations of a development bank. Unless one is clear about these, there is no basis for deciding what the training is for and what its content ought to be. Nor is there a basis for ensuring that training planned and offered actually serves the objectives of the company. For instance, project analysis, which generally makes up the bulk of development bank training, is not different from the analysis needed by a conventional commercial bank unless it is explicitly directed toward designing an economically as well as a financially sound project. Also, a development bank whose purpose is to foster small-scale enterprise cannot avoid training staff in its promotion.

A second risk implicit in the separation of training from the day-to-day life of the development bank is that the training may not be entirely relevant to the bank's operational procedures and decisionmaking process. They, more than the development bank's charter and organization chart, determine its effectiveness. There must always be an organic relation between the content of training and how things are organized and done in the particular bank. The acquisition of a technically qualified staff may call for changes in how things are being done and decided upon; not making those changes can frustrate the effect of training and discredit it.

Third, it is hard to visualize training except in relation to general personnel policy. After all, the first step toward development of an effective staff is not training but the determination of the technical and management skills the development bank requires. The second step is still not training, but recruitment. Then, perhaps, comes training—but the first part of training a new recruit consists of instilling in him a sense of corporate objectives, appreciation of the tasks the corporation faces, and an awareness of his part in carrying them out. After that, more formal training might be appropriate. But at all times management has the task of making the working environment attractive for potential recruits and congenial to the retention of staff—a task that involves not simply physical and monetary rewards but psychological satisfaction as well.

Many development bank managers have faced the problem of losing trained and experienced personnel to other jobs. They may seek solace in the fact that such staff are lost to the company but not to the country. A certain amount of this is inevitable and acceptable. But there may come a point at which this erosion threatens the survival of the development bank and is damaging to the country as well as to the bank and the clients it is supposed to serve.

These observations (and the suggestions that flow from them) are by no means original. They reflect recent literature on training. In their application to development banking, they may be found, at least implicitly, among the papers presented at the meeting on "Training for Development Bank Personnel" sponsored in Berlin in May 1977 by the German Foundation for International Development. Attention is drawn in particular to one paper by a chief executive (Vicente R. Jayme, "Training in a Development Finance Institution—the PDCP Experience") and two papers by teachers and organizers of courses (Majur C. Shetty, "Role and Function of Training for Development Bank Personnel," and Heinz-Gunter Geis, "Bases of a Concept on Personnel Training in Development Banks of Asia and Africa").

If these observations are at all valid, it is difficult to avoid the impression that, however strong the statements of development bank managers about the vital role of training and however insistent their requests for assistance in developing training facilities, the full implications of a training program are not always realized, and that training does not adequately engage their attention and is not fully integrated into their managerial task. That is, a question arises as to whether training in Africa is in fact receiving the high priority generally accorded to it in principle by the development banks of the region. Chief executives ought to examine critically their own policies and practices in this regard to see whether they contribute to the effectiveness of the training their institutions are receiving or are seeking. They need to ask themselves what they can do to ensure and improve the effectiveness of training. Each manager will have his own responses to this critical question.

Training Should Start at the Top

One set of responses is likely to center on the principle that training should start at the top of the development bank. This does not mean that chief executives need training even before staff. Of course, executive training is desirable. A chief executive who does not adequately understand and appreciate the skills that need to be at the disposal of his institution may be prepared to accept someone else's prescription for the kinds of training his staff should have; but he is not likely to be able to take full advantage of the training his staff does acquire. Such a situation has often been a source of frustration for newly trained staff. A manager does not need to become an expert technician. But he should know what kind of technicians he needs and how to make effective use of their knowledge, and this no doubt means some minimal exposure to analytical techniques.

Much more important, however, and lying behind the suggestion that training should start at the top, is the observation already made that training is random and may be pointless unless it is directed toward attaining specific objectives. It is a principal function of management to articulate the objectives of a development bank (or of any institution, for that matter) and to convey a sense of how those objectives are to be met, not only in today's environment but, more important, in tomorrow's. Ideally, management should have a specific strategy in mind. There are many reasons such an articulation of objectives is needed by the development bank. One of the more important is that the objectives determine the kinds of skills required and hence the content of the training to be provided. Management may have specialists available to lay out a training program, design courses, and work out their content. But those specialists will have to base their work on the objectives management has articulated. It is not enough to express the objectives of the institution; a full understanding of them is needed. Without such an understanding, there is likely to be frustration for those who teach, to say nothing of frustration for those who have undergone training to further their careers, and of course frustration in the end for the development bank itself.

Achieving such an understanding of objectives is not as easy as it sounds, especially in a relatively new institution. Moreover, it is not something that is done once and for all. Objectives need continuing review, as do the strategies for achieving them; they will need to be redefined from time to time in the light of the changing economic environment, changing perceptions of the development process, and the evolving experience of the development bank itself. That understanding of purpose must be conveyed to all new staff members as they arrive, for they need from the start a clear picture of the institution's mission and of their role in it; and the entire staff needs to be kept abreast of changes in objectives and strategies as they take place.

It has become commonplace that, if training is to be effective, it requires the unwavering commitment of the chief executive. The importance of that commitment cannot be overestimated. It is not enough, however, to issue a public statement at an international conference or even an internal administrative circular affirming the importance of training. The statement needs to be backed up by specific actions and procedures to encourage training and to ensure that the institution benefits from it.

The first action a chief executive might well take is to place a staff member in charge of training, or to appoint someone to head a training unit if the institution is large enough to justify one. It should not be just any staff member and not necessarily the director of personnel or of administration. Rather, it should be a person of standing in the development bank, who has the confidence of his associates, who has (and is known to have) the confidence of the chief executive, and to whom the training assignment is not a secondary or interim job (although it might be combined with other duties). He should have, or be able to establish readily, close relations with senior operational staff. Above all, he needs to be personally interested in training, to appreciate its role in the achievement of the corporate objectives, and to understand that his own future depends on the effectiveness with which he does his job. Such an appointment will ensure that the training effort receives the day-to-day attention of a senior person and will provide concrete evidence of management commitment. The chief executive will no doubt want to keep in close touch with the emerging training program and to monitor its progress with reasonable frequency.

Training as an Aspect of General Administration

A second set of responses to the question, What should the development bank do for itself? is likely to concentrate on the principle that a training program is only one aspect of the overall administration of the company.

A training officer, even with the confidence and backing of management, will not go far in the absence of a training policy and a manpower program. One of his first tasks, therefore, might well be to work with others in the institution to translate the institution's objectives and strategies into specific skill requirements. Another task, of equal importance, is to formulate a training policy for the institution, if one does not already exist—a policy that will attract, develop, and hold on to the staff the development bank needs to achieve its objectives. These matters call for management attention no less than does its financial policy, for only the chief executive can decide on some of the elements.

Management's statement of objectives and the strategies to achieve them determine the company's decision criteria. They also provide the foundation for a definition of the development bank's skill requirements. A comparison of those skill requirements with the inventory of skills already available in the institution is the basis for both a recruitment program and a training program. In preparing such a comparison, and the consequent statement of recruitment and training needs, obviously it is not so much today's requirements that need examination as tomorrow's. Nor can the recruitment and training programs be considered fixed, unchangeable. To the contrary, they need reexamination annually and revision as appropriate to conform to new objectives and strategies. Training programs so established will result in training directly linked to corporate objectives.

The company's operational procedures and its decisionmaking process also affect training needs. Staff members' skills, whether technical or supervisory, come into play within that framework. While certain technical skills are necessary no matter what the decisionmaking criteria and process, some types of training are relevant only in a given environment of investment criteria and management. These must be taken into account in laying out both recruitment and training programs.

As for a training policy, each institution must develop its own. But all training policies are likely to have some common elements. In the first place, the objective is to increase the effectiveness with which the development bank pursues its objectives and to help ensure, not simply its survival, but its capacity to adapt to changing conditions. The individual's training is intended both to improve the quality and effectiveness of his work and to prepare him for greater responsibility. Thus training is closely related to recruitment and to general personnel policy. A training policy will be wasteful and expensive in the absence of an environment that will attract and keep competent staff and that motivates them to make full use of their potential. Such an environment includes the ability of the development bank to compete with other institutions in the country and in the region for staff with the skills and experience it requires. It is important to identify those competitors, so as to be able to match or to better them. If the development bank competes for staff with the private sector, one set of conditions must be met; if the competitor is the civil service, other conditions must be faced. Beyond a certain minimum, satisfaction, challenge, and a sense of participation can be as important as, if not more important than, monetary rewards.

A training program will include arrangements to introduce staff members to the bank, later to sharpen their professional tools, then to prepare and groom them for supervisory and management responsibilities. In a dynamic institution, provision will need to be made for continuous updating of skills. The training program must encompass a variety of methods: on-the-job training, formal seminars and courses (whether in-house or elsewhere), and outside ad hoc assignments. The mixture will depend on the experience of the company, the prior training and experience of the individuals, and their level of responsibility. A new or young development finance institution may at first have to rely primarily on training outside the institution. But on-the-job training will inevitably become the primary method, and senior and supervisory staff should be made conscious of the role they must personally play in training their staff—and should be judged by the results. Although formal and external training becomes relatively less important, it nonetheless remains significant, especially when new skills are called for (for instance, by new corporate objectives, policies, and practices) and when broader experience is needed than can be obtained within the institution (for instance, grooming for top management).

A training policy will gain much if it calls for the participation of the entire staff. Each staff member should have the primary responsibility for the training required to further his own career; each supervisor has a responsibility to help every member of his staff decide on the training needed to make the fullest use of his talents and the greatest contribution to the institution. Obviously, fulfillment of these responsibilities calls for a shared understanding of what the development bank is supposed to do and what each staff member can contribute. Making each staff member appraise his own training needs and making each supervisor review and discuss his staff's self-appraisals will help promote a common outlook and understanding of objectives. Such a policy also helps ensure the relevance of training to the day-to-day work of the development bank. And it helps each staff member consider consciously the relation of his own work to that of the whole company. Such involvement increases the commitment of the entire staff to training. Thus the chief executive's effectiveness in conveying an understanding of the bank's objectives and strategies, his commitment to the importance of training, the active involvement of each staff member and of his supervisor in planning the individual's training all converge to make training an instrument for helping each staff member achieve a fulfilling career, for ensuring greater effectiveness of the institution, and for guaranteeing its growth.

The Private Development Corporation of the Philippines (PDCP) provides an example of how this process can work. Since 1974 the PDCP's training department, the Development Finance Institute, has conducted an annual survey of training needs. The first step is to ask each staff member—professional, nonprofessional, and managerial—to complete a questionnaire on his needs for training in the light of his personal plans and his views of his department's work. This is followed by interviews with supervisors and managers in order to reconcile training needs as perceived by the staff with needs as perceived by management and to establish training priorities. Only after this does the institute devise appropriate training programs and implement them. Incidentally, the program includes not only in-house training but external training as well. (A staff member can take an external training course only with the specific consent of the senior vice president and on the advice of the head of the Development Finance Institute.) The training program that thus emerges represents a reconciliation of the views of the many parties who have had a role in devising it. The process of its formulation is as important as the program itself, for it is visibly related to each individual's expected performance and prospects as well as to the institution's development.

The dialogue between staff, supervisors, and managers is reviewed year by year and forms the basis of a continuously evolving training program. Vicente R. Jayme, the president of the PDCP, has commented (in the paper mentioned before) that "we cannot delude ourselves and presume that a training course is effective because we have received favorable feedback and that we would be content in running the same courses over and over. We do not proceed with the assumption that a particular training activity can last a lifetime. In other words, we must guard against obsolescence . . . In today's rapidly changing world, no organization can be guaranteed a permanent place unless training efforts are anticipatory and innovative."

PDCP's president suggests that the value of an analysis of training needs rests "not only in the planning of the various training activities but also in the establishment of organizational support and involvement." Obtaining this support and involvement is "the key ingredient of success and effectiveness." This does not come about automatically; "planned and concerted efforts must be undertaken" to achieve it. He stresses particularly the active involvement of the operating groups in his bank which are in close touch with its "organizational needs and familiar with . . . knowledge or skill deficiencies." They can best assure training content specifically tailored to staff needs and a satisfactory balance of theory and practice.

The exact procedure followed by PDCP may not be replicable everywhere. But the principles on which it is based are sound and are adaptable.

Training Starts at Home

Thus training starts and takes place mostly at home—in the development bank itself. Contrary to common belief, planning training and the training itself need not be carried out by advisors and consultants or take place in another city or country. The formulation and implementation of a training program cannot be fully delegated to parties outside the development bank or take place entirely outside it. External advice and assistance may always be desirable and are sometimes essential. Development banks will want to draw heavily on experienced external agencies and individuals for advice and assistance, but that advice and assistance may be largely academic unless it is directly related to the bank's specific objectives and strategies and translated into specific skill requirements. These are matters on which advice can be sought, but the last word must be said at home. Moreover, training cannot be segregated from general personnel policy, which must also be a home product. Each institution must provide its own orientation for new staff. In-house training will always be the principal method. When an institution is large enough, it may provide some of its own formal training courses before outside training is sought. Finally, the decisionmaking process in a development bank is itself a tool for in-house training that can, moreover, be structured to encourage team effort and to involve each individual in day-to-day decisionmaking at some level. It can be a training device far more potent than a formal curriculum.

At some point, and in some development banks that point may come early, training outside the institution (in the country or abroad) is essential. But even if training takes place abroad, actions taken at home can maximize its benefits. For instance, a manager will want to assure himself that a staff member who has taken a course uses in his day-to-day work what he has learned. That, after all, is the object of training. Moreover, the potential benefit of training outside the company is often lost because the returned trainee does not take, or is not given, the opportunity to transmit to his colleagues some of the lessons he has learned. A trainee returns home with many kilograms of course handouts, textbooks, case studies, and other teaching materials. Sometimes they remain in his home; sometimes they find their way into his bank's library. Rarely is he asked by his supervisor to organize what he has learned into a series of discussions with his colleagues. The urgency of the task of the training is so great that no such opportunity should be lost to obtain the benefit of multiplication.

There is still another aspect of beginning at home. Discussions of training programs almost always stress the preparation of teaching materials for export, and some training institutions are devoting substantial resources to packaging materials for use by others. Certain teaching materials can be used anywhere, as long as a good teacher is available. Others are not so universally usable and effective. Among the latter are case studies, which play a significant role in training. The institutional dimension of development banking requires that a case study be recognizable and credible in the environment in which the development bank operates. Of course, any trained person can prepare an effective case study. But case studies are best done by those who will use them in teaching. Moreover, the development bank itself is in the best position to establish the sympathetic rapport needed to persuade a client to allow its experience to be used as the basis for a case to be studied by others. Home-produced training materials can help increase the effectiveness of training programs.

A final suggestion is that training programs, whether in-house, national, or regional, should make the fullest possible use of the teaching capacity that already has been developed. In Africa, for example, this is not negligible either in size or quality. African staff should be drawn on to contribute to such courses to the greatest extent possible. Programs sponsored or carried out by non-African agencies should make explicit provision for an increasing level of African participation by very perceptible stages. External training institutions or sponsors of training may play a key role in establishing national and regional courses, but a part of their contribution must be the grooming of African staff to take over the running of those courses as quickly as possible.

Training should not be expected to produce rapid results, especially not external training. The new analytical techniques a trainee has "learned" need to be "domesticated"; that is, they will have been learned only when they have been effectively applied to the concrete problems he faces in his own institution. This will take some time, for such application depends not only on the trainee but on others as well. Many staff members returning from courses abroad find themselves unable to communicate with many of their colleagues and supervisors. They have acquired techniques that are unfamiliar to those they work with. A certain critical mass of trained staff has to be achieved before the full effects of the training begin to be felt. The need to achieve a critical mass as quickly as possible is a powerful argument for stressing training at home and for ensuring that returning trainees act quickly to use and to pass on what they have acquired abroad.

Managers will know from their own experience what actions they can take at home to promote training and to benefit from it. The few suggestions summarized below are put forward to stimulate thinking on the subject by chief executives and to provide a basis for their discussion.

- The chief executive should clearly articulate the objectives of the development bank and his strategies for dealing with them.
- He should have a strong and visible commitment to training, and he should closely monitor the training program.
- He should have a personal appreciation of the technical skills his bank needs to have at its disposal.
- The decisionmaking process should itself be a tool for training. Training that results from everyday work is particularly effective.
- A first-rate individual who has the confidence of the chief executive should be put in charge of training.
- The bank's objectives and strategies should be translated into specific skill requirements.
- A training policy must be part of a personnel policy designed to recruit, train, and hold persons with the required technical and

managerial skills and to motivate them to make fullest use of their talents and potential. There needs to be a climate conducive to each individual's professional growth.

- A training program should include orientation, the sharpening of technical skills, and preparation for supervisory and management responsibilities. It may also have to include some preparatory work in basic skills.
- In-house training sooner or later must dominate a training program, and all senior and supervisory staff have a part to play in it.
- The entire staff needs to be involved in training, beginning with the individual staff member who should have primary responsibility for devising his own training program.
- Managers should make sure that a staff member who has had a training program will put it to use in his daily work.
- Staff members trained outside the bank should be required to pass on to their colleagues the benefits of the training they have received.
- Efforts should be made to develop local teaching materials, especially case studies.
- Indigenous staff (from universities, institutes, professional associations, and, above all, development banks) should be drawn into training to the greatest extent possible.

The at-home grounding and the self-help implicit in these suggestions should make training far more effective than it sometimes is. They will also have an important corollary benefit. External training institutions engaged in financing, planning, and implementing training programs are under increasing pressure to provide assistance to development banks. They cannot do all that is being asked of them. The top management of development banks must recognize their own indispensable role in planning training, have a clear and active commitment to training, and be willing to make full use of their own emerging teaching capacity and resources. These evidences of self-help will do more than mere appeals to encourage external institutions to step up their assistance. Requests for such assistance from development banks or from national or regional training institutions should, if they are to produce the desired results, include explicit reference to their own actions in developing and carrying out a training program.

Note to Chapter 15

1. This and the following several paragraphs draw heavily on the author's address at the inauguration of the Development Banking Centre of the Management Development Institute, New Delhi, November 23, 1977. See *MDI Bulletin*, vol. 1 (1977), pp. 8–13.

Part VIII

Government and Development Bank Relations

IN VIRTUALLY ALL DEVELOPING COUNTRIES, the government stands in the position of father, mother, midwife, or godfather to development banks—or has several of these roles at the same time. To say that the relationship between them is close is an understatement.

The reason is that development banks are institutions "affected by the public interest." That is, whatever their ownership, they have generally been established in pursuit of national development objectives. Governments are therefore deeply interested in the efficiency and effectiveness of the institutions, and the institutions depend heavily on a broad range of information, services, and finance from government, to say nothing of the government policies that help form the economic environment in which the institutions operate.

Government policies deeply affect the ability of a development bank (whatever the structure of its ownership) to mobilize resources, and they influence the ways in which it can allocate them. Aside from the government's role in setting the parameters within which the institution operates, there is at one extreme the case in which the government holds the share capital of a development bank, provides much or all of its financial resources, appoints some or all of the members of its board of directors, including the managing director, lays down the rules of staff recruitment and service, determines operational policies, and is involved in individual investment decisionmaking. At the other extreme, the government provides or guarantees much of the development bank's capital resources (even though it may hold no equity), appoints at least one member of the board, seeks to influence operational policy, and finds ways of making itself felt in the selection of the chief executive. While the provision of government finance (even dependence on it) might lie at the heart of the relationship between the government and a development bank, the links between them are in fact many, complex, and close.

As a result, it is difficult to discuss any aspect of the management of a development bank without touching on government activities and relations. Top management must deal with government, and the development of communications between them emerges as a priority matter. Careful scanning of government policies and intimate knowledge of its plans are called for in devising strategies and objectives. Development banks have an important potential role in influencing government policy. In the area of resource mobilization, development banks depend directly or indirectly on various aspects of government policy and finance.

In chapter 16, P. M. Mathew has brought together these many aspects of government—development bank relations in a single, wide-ranging survey. He stresses, of course, that the situation calls for delicacy and understanding on both sides and the gradual development of mutual confidence. But Mathew does not suggest a set of conditions that will ensure a continuously smooth relationship. To the contrary, he takes the quite sensible tack of suggesting that there is no escaping continuing stress on a wide range of issues. He discusses those issues and indicates the range in which both government and development banks can maneuver without forcing the confrontation that would frustrate the objectives of both.

Chapter 16

Government and Development Bank Relations

P. M. MATHEW

DEVELOPMENT BANKS are an outgrowth of the yearning for economic development after World War II that caused governments to turn to less traditional banking structures. The 1950s saw the creation of two distinct types of development banks—some fully government-owned with broad planning as well as financing functions, especially in Latin America and in the Far East; and others, often the result of World Bank initiatives, owned entirely by private (including foreign) shareholders but heavily supported by governments and concerned mainly with appraisal and financing. The exceptions were a few institutions (such as the Industrial Finance Corporation of India) with a minority private shareholding joined to a predominantly public ownership. The 1950s were obviously a period of experimentation, with few existing models on which to build.

The 1960s witnessed a rapid acceptance of the concept of private development finance companies, but with an important modification. Although faith in the private sector as the vanguard of development was still riding high, the government was often invited to take a minority participation.

The late 1960s and the early 1970s were an era of rapid growth in the number of government-owned development banks. The main factors responsible appear to have been the emergence in the late 1950s and early 1960s of many new sovereign countries with an undeveloped private sector, the political popularity (for this reason or for ideological reasons) of governmental agencies as the means of promoting rapid growth, and a decline of faith in foreign and private initiatives as pacemakers of economic development. Several of the more recently created development banks in this category,

however, have some private ownership or are open to such ownership as it becomes available.

In the late 1970s a new type of development bank was created,
mainly in the oil-exporting countries or in other countries supported by them. (The reference is not to the external aid agencies of
these countries.) Typically, these development banks are domestic
public institutions charged with promoting rapid industrialization
in their country, using low-cost funds as a powerful tool. They are
somewhat similar to the planning agency type of development bank
because of their importance as an allocator of subsidized funds;
they seek to combine this role with the traditional functions of
project development and appraisal.

As institutions have evolved, the term "development bank" has
come to mean a wide variety of institutional types. In the discussion
that follows, this term (and "development finance companies,"
which is used as a synonym) excludes at one end funds and financial
institutions that are mainly planning agencies. At the other end, it
also excludes companies that, while financing investment in the
business sector or performing service functions relating to investment, generally do so with market funds, exist almost entirely to
make profits for their shareholders, and have only a minimal and
clearly incidental concern with development, if at all.

Links with Government

The above capsule history should show that, irrespective of how
they might have evolved, development banks were created with
important links to governments. A great many are fully owned by
governments. Several others are predominantly government-
owned. Many of the private development banks have an important
government minority ownership. In a few, the governments have
become significant shareholders through subsequent movement
toward domestic or public ownership in shareholder-owned institutions. The proportion of banks that are fully private in ownership and yet perform the functions customarily associated with
development banks is now much smaller than in the mid–1960s.

In addition to ownership links, many banks have developed other
ties to governments. Several received at their inception government
loans that have long terms, long grace periods, and a low cost. Many
have continued to borrow from governments or government agencies. Almost all have received government guarantees for loans

from bilateral or international sources. Indeed, the funds they have raised from market sources and without public guarantees are small in relation to their total resources. Some have received favorable tax treatment. A few have access to public subsidies or grant funds for specific purposes. Many have been entrusted with the execution of specific public programs. These obligations have become so common and pervasive that the distinction between public and private development banks has become largely blurred.

Public Interest versus Business Orientation

Despite the emphasis the development finance companies and their well-wishers like to place on their character as business enterprises, they are undoubtedly public-interest institutions, irrespective of whether they are privately or publicly owned. Fortunately, there need not be an irreconcilable conflict between a development bank's business orientation and its public interest. It is precisely this reconciliation, and the constructive efforts of governments and development banks to achieve it, that provides the outstanding success stories in the annals of development banking.

By any definition, development finance companies are favored institutions within the financial setup of any country. The reason is that they are pioneering agencies designed to serve the public interest in the difficult areas of investment promotion and financing. The degree of stress at the policy level that typically arises between governments and development banks, whether private or public, depends on their respective perceptions, often differing, of two issues: Given the particular circumstances in which the development finance company operates, what are legitimate expectations as to its contribution to the public interest? Given the same circumstances, to what extent should the unlimited opportunity to prosper financially be subordinated to a pursuit of the public interest?

An immediate question concerns the definition of the public interest, especially since differing perceptions of it are a cause of stress. The public interest ought to consist of what is good for the general public. Who decides what this should be? Depending on the freedom of discussion within a country, various groups claim to speak for the public at large: political parties, special interest groups (including the academic community), and, most prominent of all, the government. What is in the public interest in one political climate and one economic system may be the opposite in others and with the passage of time.

The freedom with which development banks can interpret the public interest and undertake actions in support of their own interpretation varies with the political and economic regime. Governments that have adopted central planning or direction generally take it upon themselves to be guardians of the public interest to the exclusion of other guardians or spokesmen. The predominance of this type of economic management in a less developed country limits the room for maneuver available to development banks in supporting or protecting the good of the general public. Much of their independent action is confined to seeking to change the government's perception as best as they can.

As an institution operating within the local economic and policy environment, the development bank is naturally affected by that environment. If the economy is centrally controlled, the bank comes under some kind of central control. If the economy is deficient in foreign exchange, the bank and its clients typically operate under a system of resource allocation. If the economy is open, the development finance company comes into competition with other local and foreign sources of finance for better business opportunities. If the country has an interest rate regime that favors low rates for investment capital, the company comes under pressure to seek sources of scarce low-cost capital or to shave closely its spread on borrowed funds. If the government's commitment to economic criteria in the choice of projects is weak and its political orientation is toward prestige projects with poor economic content, the company comes under pressure to finance such projects. If the government or senior officials are generally in the habit of throwing their weight around, much of the weight gets thrown on the development bank.

If the government assumes the position of guardian of the public interest, it perceives itself as having a legitimate right to pressure the development bank to conform to public goals. If the government attaches priority to the development of backward areas, it becomes entitled to press the institution to exert itself in this direction. Similar pressure becomes legitimate in regard to sectoral priorities, the development of small-scale or employment-oriented enterprises, project development, support of export-oriented enterprises, local processing of raw materials, and the like. Given an economic regime in which the government prescribes goals and given a predominance of government-derived funds among the development bank's resources, the government's right to exert pressure on the bank to support government goals is not in dispute—only the extent to which and the manner in which the pressure may be applied.

Stress and the Development Bank's Effectiveness

A financial institution can significantly serve the public interest (however defined) only to the extent that it is effective and is recognized as a success in the financial field. It may be stated in the abstract that government pressure on a development finance company is legitimate if it does not go beyond the point at which the latter's effectiveness begins to be diminished. To pressure it beyond this point would obviously be self-defeating. And pressure is legitimate if applied in a manner that is open and not clandestine. When does effectiveness begin to diminish? What kinds of pressure are counterproductive?

Effectiveness is to be measured against set goals and guidelines. These are laid down by the development bank's board, which takes account of the public interest as best interpreted by the board. The capacity of a development finance company to be effective and, equally important, to maintain an image of effectiveness is diminished if the ability of its board and management to manage is threatened. When the right to manage is under attack, whether deliberately or otherwise, the ability to manage is automatically curtailed. The bank's capacity to be effective is also undermined if its financial strength is drained by pressure to incur costs, reduce earnings, or take risks beyond limits that are prudent in relation to its special situation and needs. The limits for development banks whose private shareholders seek a return on their investment would be different from those whose owner, the government, has agreed in advance to forgo such a return or has permitted the banks to use the return for public-interest purposes.

If governments press development banks to undertake operations or services that are too costly or risky, the latter have a right to expect that governments will provide them with resources of a kind and at a cost (including subsidies where appropriate) that will enable them to cope with those costs and risks and still maintain their financial viability. Continued growth and financial strength are essential to any development bank to attract new resources that will broaden its services and impact. They are also essential to attract and retain competent staff and management. Development finance companies that have to maintain access to the market in order to increase their share capital cannot do so except on the basis of a history of steady growth in dividends paid to shareholders and resulting growth in the price of the stock. Thus, to them, viability is much more than the mere avoidance of loss.

The effectiveness of development banks can also be impaired if the government criticizes them in public forums or does not adequately defend them against criticism by others. The banks cannot be expected to defend themselves adequately in such situations. Disclosure of information provided by their clients in confidence, to which the government may obtain access through the government director or through fiat, is also destructive. In countries with a strong private sector, clients often prefer commercial bank financing, even though not appropriate to their needs, for fear that information given to a development bank may end up with the tax collector or a political opponent.

Legitimate pressure becomes interference when it runs counter to autonomy, professionalism, and objectivity in decisionmaking. Bringing pressure to bear on development bank boards and management in regard to individual investment matters (other than those of national consequence), the choice and promotion of individual staff, and favors to individuals are actions that destroy professionalism. Such interference typically does not stem from governments in the abstract but from particular persons in positions of power. Although this is an ever present problem, common sense has generally curbed it. Many top managers have learned to get around the problems by being flexible without giving in on principle.

The Government Director

Conflicts between public interest and institutional effectiveness give rise to stress at several points of contact between the development bank and the government. A few of these stresses are examined below.

A normal point of contact between the government and a development finance company arises from government ownership, whether the ownership is total, predominant, or in a minority. At the minimum, government ownership results in the appointment of a government representative as a director on the board. Sometimes a creditor relation is sufficient for the government to have the right to appoint a director. The director is the government's spokesman and watchdog. If there is only one, he is usually a senior government

official. If there are more than one, they may all be government
officials or some may be nominated from financial or business
circles. The government director is a vital link between the government and the development bank and hence the manner in which he
carries out his task of representation and monitoring becomes crucial to both parties.

The laws of most countries imply that a member of the board of a
company cannot abdicate his duty to it on the pretext that he
merely represents the interest of a particular shareholder or shareholding group. He has necessarily to do his best to reconcile the
interests of the company with that of the shareholder or group he
represents, or else resign. Often excessive zeal in carrying out the
representational function causes stress.

The development bank is entitled to look upon the government
director as the spokesman of the government in its entirety and not
merely of the ministry that he represents. This often casts a heavy
burden on the director. The compartmentalization of modern-day
governments is so great that it takes painstaking effort on the part of
one individual to represent the points of view of several arms of the
government. The development bank would find it hard to deal with
all those other government agencies on its own.

Just as the government director has the important role of holding
the bank to the government's priority interests, he has an equally
important role in reverse: to act as the development bank's lobbyist
to his ministry and the government. This is a very difficult role to
perform in countries where governments are more used to giving
orders than to listening.

In predominantly private institutions, stresses arise when the
government director serves as a watchdog to prevent private shareholders from playing favorites or feathering their nests at the expense of the public with funds derived from the government. Pre-
dictably, stresses also arise when the government director becomes
the source or channel of pressure from individuals seeking narrow
personal or political favors.

When a development bank is predominantly or fully owned by the
government, some of the problems mentioned above are compounded. For example, several officials representing different government agencies might act out in the bank's board meetings their
internecine battles, leaving the management and other board members confused about the government's real interest. Or officials
might use their collective voting strength to stifle the exploration of
alternatives and to rubber-stamp decisions made outside the board

room. Government pressure tends to become less intense and more dispersed when the government chooses one or more nonofficials from the business and financial circles to represent it.

For several of the matters mentioned below, the government representative on the board is the point through which stress is transmitted to the development bank. Since some of these matters are important in themselves, however, they will be examined separately.

Management

In some development banks, the management function rests with the chairman or president. In others it is vested in an executive vice president, managing director, or general manager. The choice of the top manager is an occasion for controversies and stress.

If the government is the sole or the majority owner, the government naturally chooses the top manager. Although this rarely involves stress, the decision can be made without sufficient regard for its effect on the true public interest. The history of development banks bears ample testimony to the difference that an imaginative and aggressive chief executive, who can handle the stresses of external relations, has made to the course of his institution and to the significance of its contribution to the country. Some governments tend to think of the top manager's position in a development bank as a way station for officials on the move, with the result that the position is allotted to people with little preparation, short tenures, and little serious interest in the success of the institution. The position can also be given deliberately to someone who will toe the party line regardless of the ultimate destruction of the development bank's reputation, which is immensely valuable to preserve for the bank's effectiveness, professionalism, and objectivity. Good sense and an eye for long-term benefits have to be the guiding factors in these decisions, and often they have prevailed.

Stress sometimes makes its appearance in the need to reconcile government and private interests when choosing the chief executive of a private development bank. Although the choice is the prerogative of the board, which is entirely or predominantly private, it has become customary in many countries to involve the government in some way. Here again, discretion and good sense should be the keynotes. Sensible private shareholders recognize that, given the public interest in the company as a result of government support, a choice that does not have at least the implicit approval of the government—even though the government is not a shareholder—would become an embarrassment in relations between the government and the institution. Sensible governments recognize that imposing their choice on unwilling shareholders deprives development banks of initiative and harmony and reduces their potential contribution to minimal levels. Thus, informal consultations often precede formal action; such consultations defuse potential tension and crisis.

Reference was made earlier to letting the manager manage. In the case of private development finance companies, this rule is seldom broken by government interference, but it has been known to happen. It is in the case of the government-owned companies that the danger is ever present. Ownership can become the pretext under which interference creeps in and quickly becomes the pattern, destroying commitment, initiative, and a sense of responsibility. That it does not invariably happen is a tribute to the wisdom of governments and to the strength of individual managers who stand their ground when they have been given the right to decide. (Interference by private shareholders is equally bad; however, that does not happen to be the topic under discussion here.)

With significant exceptions, the managements of public institutions are comparatively more at ease raising resouces than are their private counterparts but less confident of their ability to pursue long-term strategies and flexible initiatives. Many governments try to apply political remedies to economic problems, and the managements of public development banks often have less ability to resist the current than do private ones. Because their public ownership automatically brings them into close contact with the government, personality clashes with government officials are a more frequent danger to them than to private bank managements.

Salaries

Given government ownership or, at a minimum, government assistance in resource mobilization, development finance companies, both public and private, come under pressure from governments to conform to government salary scales. In most countries, government salaries are low in comparison with business. The problem is often more acute in the case of the senior staff of the companies.

The kind of training and experience that development bank staff acquire make them valuable professionals who command active markets in countries undergoing rapid growth in the business sector. Also, when a development bank becomes mature and the rapid growth that prevailed in its early years slows down, professional growth slows down too. Without vertical movement and new challenges in their jobs, the more active staff become restless and seek careers elsewhere. Managers of development banks thus have the constant problem of minimizing staff losses and competing with the market in attracting new staff. In this situation, salaries and benefits become a critically important factor.

In some countries, central banks as well as business enterprises operated by governments are permitted salary levels higher than for government workers. This concession often applies to development banks too. While those that can afford to pay market salaries should push for market salary levels, it is prudent to expect government resistance beyond a point and to devise alternative methods to attract and retain staff. For want of better alternatives, some banks have accepted rapid turnover as inevitable and rely on extensive recruitment, internship, and outside training programs to minimize the effects. Others resort to the creation of second-generation institutions that provide opportunities in related fields and provide growth opportunities for some of their mature staff. Still others fight and win the battle for reasonable salary levels and attractive fringe benefits.

Dividends

There are few government-owned development banks that the governments expect to become sources of public revenue. Governments are usually content if the banks are prudently managed, earn a profit, and use those profits to support useful but risky or costly activities that the private sector cannot be expected to finance. Stress can occur between the managements of public development banks and their governments concerning the types and extent of such activities.

Reconciling private shareholders' dividend expectations with the government's ideas is, by definition, a problem only for companies with substantially or predominantly private ownership. Most private shareholders are financial institutions and business houses which, because of the developmental tasks the banks are performing, are often content voluntarily to limit direct returns to modest levels. As already mentioned, however, banks that wish to attract the general public to their shareholding, and especially those listed on stock exchanges, are under market pressure to maintain dividend levels compatible with the normal expectations of local investors. Governments are apt to believe that much of the dividend-paying capacity of development finance companies is derived from the use of funds provided or facilitated by the governments and that, in consequence, returns to private shareholders should be limited.

Imaginative boards have sought to deal with this problem in a variety of ways. Many retain, whether by statute or by voluntary shareholder action, portions of their surpluses in general reserves and pay out only the rest. These reserves or unallocated surpluses increase the net worth of the banks and the book value of their shares. Where a bank stock has a market and is listed, the higher book values result in higher quotations, which enable the institutions to raise the price of stock issued to new shareholders. Often there is less objection to stock dividends than to cash dividends, and the former are resorted to as a substitute or a sweetener. The underlying strategy in all these cases is to postpone present returns in favor of higher but less visible future returns, balanced by the need to maintain access to the market.

Resource Raising

It has already been noted that the predominance of government finance in their resource mix is the main reason development banks come under pressure from governments. Excessive dependence on governments and on government-guaranteed bilateral and multilateral sources provides a wide-open door for interference and creates uncertainties for the banks themselves. When rapid industrialization was perceived as the main key to economic salvation and the availability of term funds (and especially foreign exchange) was seen as the major limiting factor, development finance companies had little difficulty in attracting local funds at less than market rates from governments and foreign exchange from external public sources. But economic winds have shifted, strategies for social fulfillment have justifiably changed, and the banks are beginning to find that, although their financial strength and creditworthiness have greatly grown and their reputation for effective service remains high, credit allocations to them from both budgetary and external credit sources are becoming increasingly uncertain. Private institutions are not alone in this difficulty, although their problem is more serious.

Although not entirely through their own fault, few banks have reached or even approached the takeoff stage in resource raising. Part of the reason, however, is the false sense of security nurtured by an era of overprotection. It is a truism that the availability of favors tends to direct effort toward maintaining or increasing the favors rather than toward winding them down and seeking innovation. The answer to the problem of government dominance lies precisely in the extent of the banks' efforts and their eventual success in raising funds without the underpinning of governments.

Some of the more mature development finance companies in countries that have recently entered international markets have begun tapping those markets on their own credit and with reasonable success. These efforts need to be intensified. The resultant lower margins will probably be offset by revenues from growing business volume and by greater productivity through economies of scale. Bold initiatives are yet to be taken to reconcile the type of foreign funds available (variable interest rate, medium term) with the needs and preferences of the bank's clients (fixed interest, long term) and to meet the draw-down requirements of market funds.

In contrast to the shortage of foreign currency resources that characterized the early years of many companies, the present problem is more the shortage of domestic resources, and innovative approaches to raise them are yet to take root. Cost considerations inhibit many banks from placing their debt instruments in the domestic market, and most domestic markets for term resources are rather thin. It is gratifying, however, that some governments are beginning to realize that regulatory actions might be needed to alter the extreme preference of domestic savers for liquid investments. In addition, development banks need to ease their excessively conservative attitudes to money management in favor of initiatives to transform the terms of resources, whether local or foreign. As a partial solution to this problem, some African banks have begun to perform certain limited banking functions for their own clients and for certain classes of depositors. Providing banking services for regular clients would enable a bank to monitor clients more intensely at less overall cost, as well as to retain some of the clients' liquidity at no cost. Attracting certain kinds of deposits would probably help the banks obtain additional resources at margins that, though perhaps not equal to those of commercial banks, might approach them in the medium term. The liquidity needs of these deposits are something less than 100 percent, and the balance could be used (on the basis of experience) as a float that is available for the development banks' regular needs, probably protected by stand-by lines of credit from other financial institutions. Also, new sources of revenue need to be established by initiating and rapidly increasing profitable service activities. The examples of the Development Bank of Singapore and several Latin American financieras that have considerable experience in these fields are worth studying in this context.

Interest Rates

Partly because they are heavily dependent on government funds and partly because of government policies that (often unjustifiably) subsidize long-term capital, development banks find themselves charging lower rates than commercial banks while borrowing at considerably higher cost. The pressure to keep interest rates on their loans low is incompatible with the general expectation that their dependence on governments will soon diminish and that they can be floated on the market. If history can be a guide, unfortunately it is not be expected that many governments will permit domestic long-term interest rates to be based on opportunity cost or be positive in relation to the rate of inflation. The significance of attractive money rates in promoting savings is often forgotten by public authorities in their eagerness to promote investment through subsidized credit that has often to be derived from those same savings. Thus the initiatives to improve their modus vivendi have to come from the development banks themselves. Meanwhile, pressure on governments to change their perceptions of lending rates needs to continue.

Support of National Priorities

Although the banks generally undertake activities that are supportive of national goals and priorities, they are seldom in the forefront of such activities. They are often perceived by governments as reluctant participants who have to be goaded. It is only occasionally that they have themselves suggested activities to the government or taken initiatives; often they conform under pressure. Several development banks have needed to be pressed to spread their operations beyond the industrial metropolis in which they are typically located to clients beyond the gilt-edged variety, to projects in unfamiliar subsectors, to small-scale enterprises, and to projects of national priority that require heavy and costly promotional effort. Some have achieved considerably more than others in these areas. The recurrent question, however, is whether they are doing enough, and there is no consensus as to what is enough.

Largely because of the availability of public funds, many development banks have built themselves up into some of the more solid institutions in their countries, both in terms of their asset size and the competence of their staffs. Their ability to innovate and take risks should therefore be high; if public expectations of them are high, those expectations are apparently justifiable.

From their standpoint, when they innovate or take risks, development banks are skating on thin ice because risks are not always matched by rewards, and their margins are thin. A few losses here and there can quickly destroy creditworthiness. Development banks have therefore necessarily to be prudent. New initiatives involve staff and management time as well as risks. Both cost money.

In many countries the battle on this subject was stalemated for a long time but now appears to have ended in a truce. Many development banks are now involved in activities related to their countries' economic goals on which they are probably not making any money. Government criticism is in general less severe than some years ago. The situation varies from country to country, however.

Some institutions have accepted a degree of expense in time and money on such activities that does not greatly affect their financial performance. Some have earmarked portions of their earnings either for capital or current expenses associated with economic priorities. Others have gone further. They have identified other sources of grants or cheap loan funds, to which their own resources can be added or to which some of their costs can be debited, and thus expanded substantially the scope and volume of those activities. In some cases, they have themselves provided ideas as well as nucleus funds for new institutional arrangements to carry out or facilitate the preferred activities. Governments have often backed those initiatives with public funds. In the best of circumstances, the banks have come to learn that activities in support of the countries' economic priorities are essential both for the political stability of their countries and for their own survival; and governments have learned to recognize that the financial viability of the institutions, whether public or private, is vital to their ability to serve the public good.

One way in which the more mature institutions have discharged their responsibility to promote economic development is by sponsoring other institutions in the financial sector. Here the record is mixed. Some companies have perceived this opportunity and promoted such institutions as soon as they themselves became reasonably well established. Others waited for many years, and some have not yet started. The initiatives that have been taken are typically in the areas of venture capital companies, leasing companies, money market institutions, merchant banks, investment banks, housing finance companies, and investment trust management. If such initiatives can become widespread without exposing the development banks to charges of monopoly, they would constitute a visible repayment to their countries for the preferential government support they received in the past.

Competition and Cooperation

Several countries are large or developed enough to support more than one development bank. In many such countries, especially those in which private business has been allowed a dominant role, public and private development banks or several public banks coexist. They have evolved ways of constructive cooperation alongside competition.

They cooperate mostly in the joint financing of projects too large for any one of them to handle alone or when, for a variety of other reasons, the sponsoring development bank needs partners. Exchange of information for the purpose of appraisal is common in such cases. Joint appraisal by the interested institutions is also common but perhaps less so. Joint financing is often necessary and certainly very appropriate in the case of projects promoted by a bank that is the main sponsor. In such cases appraisal by another financial institution with a view to commitment of funds provides much needed objectivity. Seeking such external funds primarily for the sake of this objective evaluation, even in cases in which the sponsoring institution can provide all the needed financing, would be a good practice.

Development banks also often cooperate in training programs, studies that relate to specific industrial subsectors, and conferences or seminars of one kind or another. More can be done in this area.

The existence of several development finance companies (and other financial institutions) provides a healthy choice for project sponsors. But when good projects are scarce and project promotion is not a regular function of the institutions, competition can be stiff and becomes a factor in a client's choices. Longer terms and grace periods, larger participation in equity if desired by the client, and ability to meet the client's entire financial needs are some avenues of competition. Efficiency of services, including the ability to reach decisions quickly and to respond constructively to changes in the project's needs, is another competitive factor.

Competition becomes destructive when, under the pretext of quick decisionmaking, the standards for appraisal and supervision are lowered beyond the needs of the case. This erosion takes the form of an insufficient check on the process and the know-how, poor monitoring of cost, acceptance of weak management, willingness to live with risky debt-equity ratios and debt-service capability, and disbursements without adequate scrutiny of needs and progress. Although there is no monopoly on these questionable practices, public development banks, since they are able to take greater risk, may succumb more to the temptation than do private ones. Fortunately, the practices seem to be on the decline, as experience has begun to show that they are destructive in the long run.

Influencing Public Policy

Since development banks regularly allocate investment funds and determine the worth of investment projects, it is in their own interest to be in close touch with government policy toward investment, the financial sector, and the various sectors of business they finance. Close knowledge of policy is also of immense use to their clients, who are entitled to turn to development banks for expert advice on these matters. This is especially true of foreign investors seeking a first entry into a country and partners of the banks in promoting new projects. Understanding of policy and closeness to policymakers enable development banks to foresee new policy directions and to consider consequent adjustments in their own strategies. The essence of good management consists of the ability to anticipate and deal effectively with change.

The clientele of mature development banks covers a wide spectrum of business enterprises in their countries. The information and judgment that development banks accumulate as a result of this coverage, which is both intensive and extensive, are important assets to their economies, and they deserve to be put to proper use. In some countries this material is analyzed and presented in forms that are useful to businessmen, both financial and industrial, and to policymakers; the practice deserves to be adopted elsewhere.

Development banks are in the unique position of being deeply knowledgeable about policy on the one hand and about the practical effects of policy on the business sector on the other. Senior development bank staff thus deserve to be close to the government's policymaking apparatus and to be consulted on policy changes. This, too, is becoming an established practice in some countries and needs to be taken more seriously in others. As already noted, in countries where the government is the prime spokesman for the public interest, a development finance company has few options to promote its own interpretation except to sell it to the government.

Some observers believe that closeness to government through membership in public councils, participation in governmental bodies relating to investment incentives and regulation, and other frequent contacts can pose a danger to development banks. They contend that closeness might diminish objectivity, trap their companies into unsound commitments, and invite interference on a personal level. These risks are genuine, but nevertheless the benefits of participation in government thinking seem to outweigh the risks.

General Summary

Because of their role in economic development and the government's role in resource raising, development finance companies and governments are necessarily linked. The intensity of their relationship is only partly affected by government ownership and is not amenable to codification.

The government sets direction and has oversight. If the demoralization and ineffectiveness that inevitably result from external domination are to be avoided, governments have to perform these functions in a statesmanlike manner, allowing the managers to manage. They have also to recognize the limits of financial prudence for development banks and refrain from too heavily taxing the companies' strength. While following policies that will increase the ability of the institutions to raise resources without government backing, governments and international agencies have to lower their expectations in this regard on the basis of the lessons of history. To the extent possible, governments should reduce competition for borrowed resources between themselves and other (potential) users of capital such as development banks. Governments also have to do more to orient and progressively pressure domestic savers toward longer-term savings so that, as the banks (and other borrowers) become more aggressive in the search for market resources, they begin to be available. Government interest rate policies that poorly reward financial savings and discriminate against term lending should be constantly reviewed.

Development finance companies themselves need to have active programs for priority development activity: one based on their own resources and a supplementary program based on special inputs for which they wish to canvass public bodies. The natural tendency for mature institutions to continue doing what they have been doing well, rather than to innovate, needs to be curbed. Innovative sponsorship of other institutions in the financial sector should become more widespread. More aggressive and imaginative actions to tap resources that are not dependent on government concessions are needed. Limited movement into commercial banking might be one option, together with portfolio sales and a revamping of present liquidity concepts to take into account the capability of development finance companies to transform the terms of funds.

Development banks also need to make greater efforts to analyze the data available to them for their own use and to share the information with the business community and the government. They need to join with each other more in undertaking such studies, whether nationally or within a region. While accepting every reasonable opportunity to influence government thinking on matters relating to business, they should not entertain any exaggerated notions about their monopoly of wisdom in this field, nor become so closely involved that they lose objectivity toward their banking functions.

The Contributors

V. V. Bhatt, an Indian national, is an adviser in the Economic Development Institute. From 1975 to 1980 he was the chief of the Public Finance Division, Development Economics Department, World Bank. He holds an M.A. in economics from Bombay University and a Ph.D. from Harvard University, where he was a teaching fellow. He taught economics at Bombay University before he joined the Research Department of the Reserve Bank of India in 1953.

In the Reserve Bank, Bhatt held a variety of positions including that of economic adviser. During 1970–72 he was general manager of the Industrial Development Bank of India. He was also a member of the board of directors of the State Trading Corporation of India, the Industrial Finance Corporation of India, the Unit Trust of India, and the Syndicate Bank. In 1964 and 1965 he was on the teaching staff of the United Nations Asian Institute of Economic Development and Planning, and he was a senior lecturer in the Economic Development Institute from 1972 to 1975.

He is the author of several books and articles dealing with various aspects of economic development.

Jayarajan Chanmugam, from Sri Lanka, has been on the staff of the World Bank since December 1960. He was senior engineer and then deputy director of investments for Latin America in the International Finance Corporation and in 1972 was appointed engineering adviser in the Development Finance Companies Department of the World Bank. Currently, he is the senior operations adviser of the Industrial Development and Finance Department.

He holds a doctorate from the University of Cambridge, England, was a member of the faculty of the School of Engineering at Princeton University, and worked in industry before joining the World Bank. He is a fellow of the Institute of Chemical Engineering in England and a member of the American Institute of Chemical Engineering.

295

William Diamond, a U.S. national, is a former staff member of the World Bank and now a consultant. Since 1947 he has held a variety of posts in the World Bank, including that of director of the Development Finance Companies Department in the International Finance Corporation and the World Bank from 1962 to 1972. During 1972–75 he was director of the South Asia Department of the World Bank, responsible for the Bank's lending programs in that region. After two years as special assistant to the vice president for finance, he completed his World Bank career as senior fellow (1977–78) of the Economic Development Institute, of which he had been a staff member from 1955 to 1958.

Diamond holds a Ph.D. from The Johns Hopkins University. He is the author of several books and numerous articles, most of them, in recent years, on the policies and operations of development finance institutions. He is a member of the boards of FRIDA Investments and Consultancy, Ltd. in London and of Sociedade Portuguesa de Investimentos (SARL) in Oporto.

David B. Gill, a Canadian national, has been since 1971 director of the Capital Markets Department of the International Finance Corporation. He is also director of the Bank of the Near East (Lebanon) and director of Sociedad Española de Financiación de la Innovación, S. A. (Sefinnova), Madrid.

Before joining the World Bank, he held senior positions in Nesbitt Thomson Securities Ltd. of Canada and affiliated companies in which he was employed from 1952. His last appointments in Nesbitt Thomson were as director (1959–70) and senior vice president (1968–70) and, concurrently, as president of its New York affiliate; director and vice president of Schroder Capital Corporation, New York; and director of a few associated companies.

R. K. Hazari, an Indian national, is an economic consultant and director of several industrial companies in India. He was visiting lecturer in the Economic Development Institute from November 1978 to May 1979.

From 1969 to 1977 Hazari was deputy governor of the Reserve Bank of India. He was in charge of the banking operations and development and the agricultural credit departments for most of the period. He was ex-officio chairman of the Agricultural Refinance and Development Corporation (1973–77), chairman of the Credit Guarantee Corporation of India (1971–77), and vice chairman of the Industrial Development Bank of India (1970).

Before joining the Reserve Bank, Hazari taught economics in St. Xavier's College, Bombay (1951–64) and was professor of industrial economics at the University of Bombay (1964–67) and editor of the *Economic and Political Weekly* (1967–69). He is the author of several books, dealing mainly with various aspects of industrial development in India.

F. Leslie C. H. Helmers, a Dutch national, is chief of the National Economic Management, Industry and Development Banking Courses Division of the Economic Development Institute. He has a Drs.Ec. from the University of Amsterdam and a Dr.Sc. (cum laude) from the University of Wageningen.

Before joining the World Bank in 1964, Helmers held various positions with the Union Financière Belge des Tabacs—Tabacofina S. A. and was treasurer of FAROKA in Indonesia, director of Canadian Tabacofina in Canada, and director and administrateur délégué of Tabacongo, Zaïre. He was also economic adviser to Carton en Papierfabriek W. A. Scholten, the Netherlands.

While with the World Bank, he spent 1967–69 in Abidjan, where he was involved in preparing projects in West Africa. Subsequently, he was chief of the Agro-Industries Division (1969–72) and division chief (1973–77) in the Country Programs Department of the East Asia and Pacific Region.

He is the author of *Project Planning and Income Distribution*, published by the University of Wageningen in 1977; the second edition was published in 1979 in the Development and Planning Series of Erasmus University, Rotterdam.

A. H. M. Kamaluddin, a citizen of Bangladesh, is the chairman and managing director of the Bangladesh Shilpa Bank (BSB).

Kamaluddin, who obtained his M.A. from the University of Dacca, spent eleven years with the National Bank of Pakistan. In 1961 he joined the Industrial Development Bank of Pakistan, the predecessor of BSB, in which he held a variety of positions. He became the chief executive of BSB when it was established in 1972. He is a member of the board of a number of corporations and business institutions in Bangladesh.

P. M. Mathew, an Indian national, has been a staff member of the World Bank and the International Finance Corporation since 1962.

He has been associated with development finance institutions throughout his career in the World Bank and International Finance Corporation, including the deputy directorship of the Development Finance Companies Department from 1967 to 1971. Thereafter, for five years he was adviser to the executive vice president of the International Finance Corporation on development banks, and from 1977 to 1979 deputy director of its Capital Markets Department. During 1966–67 he was adviser to the Nigerian Industrial Development Bank, and from 1979 to 1981 was senior adviser to the National Development Bank of Sri Lanka.

Before joining the World Bank, Mathew was a senior official of the Indian Administrative Service specializing in economic administration and held a variety of posts in his native state of Kerala.

V. S. Raghavan, an Indian national, is the International Finance Corporation's representative in East Africa. Prior to joining the staff of the Corporation, he was a senior lecturer in the Economic Development Institute, responsible for training programs for development bank staff.

Raghavan has held positions of deputy secretary, Export Credit and Guarantee Corporation (India); general manager, Industrial Development Bank of India; and managing director, Development Bank of Mauritius. He has a B.Sc. and M.A. in economics, mathematics, and statistics from the University of Mysore and the University of Bombay, and a diploma in economic administration from the University of Delhi.

Raghavan has contributed articles on Indian industry, industrial finance, and export guarantees to various Indian newspapers and journals.

Thomas A. Timberg, a U.S. national, has a Ph.D. from Harvard University in political economy and government. He has been a consultant at the World Bank since 1977, working on small-scale enterprises and informal credit markets. From September 1972 to June 1978 he was assistant professor at American University, College of Public Affairs. He has been a consultant for Kramer Associates International on a variety of management problems. In 1977–78 he was chairman of the course on South Asia at the Foreign Service Institute. Among numerous other publications, he has written a book, *The Marwaris: From Traders to Industrialists*, about a group of industrial entrepreneurs in India.

The full range of World Bank publications, both free and for sale, is described in the *Catalog of World Bank Publications*; the continuing research program is outlined in *World Bank Research Program: Abstracts of Current Studies*. Both booklets are updated annually; the most recent edition of each is available without charge from the Publications Distribution Unit; World Bank, 1818 H Street, N.W., Washington, D.C. 20433, U.S.A.